Legacies of Nineteenth-Century American Women Writers

The Hermaphrodite

Julia Ward Howe

Edited and with an introduction
by Gary Williams

UNIVERSITY OF NEBRASKA PRESS
LINCOLN AND LONDON

Publication of the manuscript (*51M-
283 [320], box 4) is by permission of the
Houghton Library, Harvard Library.

Library of Congress Cataloging-in-
Publication Data
Howe, Julia Ward, 1819–1910.
The hermaphrodite / Julia Ward Howe ; edited
and with an introduction by Gary Williams.
p. cm.—(Legacies of nineteenth-century
American women writers)
Includes bibliographical references.
ISBN 0-8032-2415-X (cloth : alk. paper)
ISBN 978-0-8032-1887-1 (paper : alk. paper)
1. Gender identity—Fiction. 2. Hermaphro-
ditism—Fiction. I. Williams, Gary, 1947
May 6– II. Title. III. Series.
PS2016.H47 2004
813'.4—dc22
2004009187

Contents

Acknowledgments

In preparing Julia Ward Howe's Laurence manuscript for publication, I have been lucky to have a diverse group of interlocutors to respond to my hypotheses about the significance of this narrative. These include Paula Bennett, Christopher Looby, Wendy Dasler Johnson, Valarie Ziegler, Janet Gray, Greg Eiselein, Kenny Marotta, Dave Barber, Walter Hesford, Sarah Nelson, Susan Belasco, Sharon Harris, Karen Dandurand, and the University of Nebraska Press's anonymous reviewers. I have benefited prodigiously from the interest these friends and colleagues have taken in this project. In particular, Valarie Ziegler's familiarity with the Julia Ward Howe collections at Houghton Library has been an important resource for me in checking details large and small, as has been her willingness to share perspectives elaborated in her recently published biography of Howe. Research for the introduction was supported by a research fellowship in 2000 from the Idaho Humanities Council and by grants from the University of Idaho English department's Lillian White Endowment. Sharon Harris and Karen Dandurand's early commitment to the publication of the manuscript, and their hard work in finding the right venue for it and other books to follow in the series, were gifts of great value. Valarie Ziegler, Wendy Johnson, Sharon Harris, and Dave Barber read drafts of this volume's introduction and offered valuable insights. Ralph Kaplan at the University of Massachusetts Press granted permission to use portions of my *Hungry Heart: The Literary Emergence of Julia Ward Howe* (1999) in the introduction to this volume. The manuscript is reproduced by permission of the Houghton Library, Harvard University (Leslie A. Morris, Curator of Manuscripts). Jim Reece's knowledge of Schiller helped me grasp the significance of "Die berümte Frau." Jim Robinson assisted in transcribing the manuscript. Ladette Randolph and Beth Ina at the University of Nebraska Press, with the assistance of copyeditor Daniel Simon, expertly guided the project into publication. My wife, Joy Passanante, has shared my excitement about this manuscript since I first read it in the summer of 1995 and, from her novelist's perspective, has offered splendid perceptions about Howe's characters and Howe herself. Much gratitude to all.

Speaking with the Voices of Others
Julia Ward Howe's Laurence

In 1865 Julia Ward Howe's beloved, versatile brother Sam Ward published a collection of poems, including one dedicated to his sister. The poem, titled "Metempsychosis," is in part an argument for the superiority of poetry to literal image as a way of preserving and transmitting the potent human spirit of past ages. Statues of great dead men give us "but traits"; actions and words "embalmed in song," on the other hand, serve as sparks to new endeavor. The poem's conclusion seems an admonition to Julia to persevere in her singing, even though her current themes may be woe-laden:

> . . . bend every string
> Thy hand can grasp, with zealous care!
> Though from thy lyre but hoarse despair,
> Fate's ruthless sweep at first should wring.
> Strain on! Until thy spirit's Sire
> Awake that chord of happier fate
> Whose jubilance shall modulate
> Thy woe to joy's celestial quire.[1]

Since Howe had by the mid-1860s quite deliberately stepped away from the writing of poetry,[2] we might read Sam's poem as a plea that she not relinquish the genre altogether. Her first two collections, *Passion-Flowers* (1854) and *Words for the Hour* (1857)—both of which bear a heavy cargo of sadness—had brought admiration and notoriety, and she had relished such recognition. But as the country moved toward war, her early literary labors seemed (she wrote later) "almost a period of play," comparable to "the tuning of instruments before some great musical solemnity,"[3] and particularly after experiencing the celebrity arising from publication of "Battle Hymn of the Republic" (1862), Howe had turned to philosophy and ethics as a focus for her intellectual work.

We may also, however, understand Sam's encouragement in a broader sense: as reaffirmation of his belief in her literary talent (a note he alone, among the male Wards, consistently sounded) and perhaps additionally as indication of his belief in the value of her particular voice to struggling singers in future generations—"shadowy" now, but audible later to souls who will quicken to its sound. In light of the manuscript now published here for the first time—a text Sam is unlikely to have read, but one that in certain crucial ways he arguably enabled—his lines to Julia resonate with a prescience beyond their probable intent.

The writing of what is here called *The Hermaphrodite* probably began in the winter of 1846–47, about three years after Julia Ward's marriage to Samuel Gridley Howe and after the births of her first two (of six) children. The approximately 350 pages of manuscript at Harvard's Houghton Library are in fact several distinct pieces, the various sections difficult to date precisely.[4] The first page and key bridge passages are missing, and even when one can deduce how Howe intended various episodes to fit together, ambiguity about chronology remains. Information about the project, apart from what the manuscript itself suggests, is scanty. The earliest unequivocal reference in Howe's letters is from May 1847, in a note to her sister—and confidante—Louisa. She apologized for not having written for months, citing her "studious, meditative, and most uncommunicative frame of mind," and mentioning that, although she had written much poetry during the winter, "it is of a kind wh[ich] I do not readily show." She did, however, enclose four stanzas of a poem entitled "Eva to Rafael" and offered to send more of her characters' "correspondence," should Louisa be interested. "I have made quite a little romance about them," she added.[5]

Eva and Rafael's story, viewed in the context Howe eventually created for it, is not the central narrative, but rather an intact (mostly prose) piece set within a larger primary story, of which the protagonist is variously called Laurence or Laurent. His conspicuous characteristic is that he is a hermaphrodite.[6] Whether this character was part of Howe's earliest conception of the narrative, or whether the two stories arose independently and were later welded, is impossible to determine with certainty, but one undated piece of evidence suggests they were conceived simultaneously. On page 30 of her 1843 diary appears this fragment, evidently a piece of a letter to an unidentified person:

Yet my pen has been unusually busy during the last year—it has brought me some happy inspirations, and though the golden tide is now at its ebb, I live in the hope that it may rise again in time to float off the stranded wreck of a novel, or rather story, in the which I have been deeply engaged for three months past. It is not, understand me, a moral and fashionable work, destined to be published in three volumes, but the history of a strange being, written as truly as I knew how to write it. Whether it will ever be published, I cannot tell, but I should like to have had you read it, and to talk with you about it.

This is almost certainly a reference to the Laurence portion of the work, and although the fragment isn't dated, its location in the diary adjacent to other fragments argues strongly that the characters of Eva, Rafael, and Laurence all date from this period.

Julia was twenty-eight years old in May 1847, living in a small house near the Perkins Institution for the Blind in South Boston, trying to maintain emotional equilibrium while beset by myriad disappointments and deprivations. The narrative, as I suggest below, is solidly rooted in the psychological terrain of that period of Howe's life. However, the ground for its germination was cultivated about ten years earlier—the moment of her brother's return from a four-year sojourn in Europe, during which he acquired and shipped home an extraordinarily rich array of Continental literature. The history of The Hermaphrodite properly begins with Sam's reentry into the life of 2 Bond Street in New York City in 1836, when Julia Ward started to read French novels.

The impact of Sam on his sister's sense of the world can hardly be overestimated. Howe characterized him in Reminiscences as "my ideal and my idol," who, when he returned from four years abroad, "brought into the Puritanic limits of our family circle a flavor of European life and culture which greatly delighted me" (67–68). The title of Louise Tharp's lively 1956 account of the intertwined lives of the Ward siblings—Three Saints and a Sinner—suggests the nature of this impact. While away, Sam had embraced life in Paris, Heidelberg, and Dresden with unambivalent gusto, playing out in actuality the wicked delights hinted at in Edward Bulwer's novel *Pelham* (which he had read on the sly while a young boy). He drastically overspent his expense account and repeatedly delayed his return, meanwhile enjoying the charms of numerous demimondaines. In Paris he became an intimate friend of Jules Janin, critic for the influential *Journal des Débats*; took singing lessons three times a week from a teacher who shared his apartment with Franz Liszt; attended the opera and other cultural events almost nightly; and in these ways came to know—certainly by reputation and possibly in person—George Sand. When Sam returned to the United States, he brought with him several of Sand's early novels.

In their late-life memoirs, both Sam and Julia tended toward the decorous in describing (or often eliding) their youthful verve, but their letters from the 1830s and 1840s uncover the passionate intensity with which they each embraced the possibilities afforded by their station in life and with which they satisfied their hunger for intellectual and aesthetic pleasures. Although Howe's *Reminiscences* notes that after Sam's return she "read such works of George Sand and Balzac as [Sam] would allow [her] to choose from his library"—implying that he exercised an older brother's regulatory prerogative—and although Sam claimed to his European friend Charles Mersch that in New York he always wore an "iron mask," it seems likely that the information-flow between sister and brother was uninhibited. Julia's daughter Maud Howe Elliott, who published Sam's letters, tellingly undercut his dour metaphor: "If Sam wore any mask at all it was the classic serio-comic mask, tragedy on one side, farce on the reverse. The clear eyes of his sisters and brothers saw through his masquerading. They saw him as he was, brilliant, frail, unstable, above all kindly, generous, fascinating."[7]

Sam, far from intervening censoriously in Julia's desire to expand her horizons, provided not only the means for growth but some protection as well. Howe described her father—"with all his noble generosity and overweening affection"—as her "jailer"; Sam was the senior Ward's combatant in his efforts to narrow and control the scope of Julia's life during these years. A July 1838 letter illustrates Sam's typical role: "You always exact too much of her," he complained to his father, "in desiring not only that she obey you but be happier in so doing than in following up certain wishes of her own" (Elliott 176). Julia, for her part, "greatly coveted an enlargement of intercourse with the world"—which she satisfied by availing herself of the books her father built a room to house. "My sphere of thought," she asserted, "was a good deal enlarged by the foreign literatures, German, French, and Italian, with which I became familiar"—by these, and, always, by Sam's presence, which "opened the door a little for me. . . . His wit, social talent, and literary taste opened a new world to me, and enabled me to share some of the best results of his long residence in Europe" (*Reminiscences* 58, 48–49).

Exactly what might Julia Ward have read in the late 1830s, thanks to her brother? Many of the books Sam acquired are a matter of record, since they formed the nucleus of the library that John Jacob Astor (with the help of the Ward family's in-house tutor and close friend, Joseph Cogswell) assembled in the 1840s. Sam commissioned a catalog of the bulk of the books in 1833; this ornately scripted volume was acquired by the New York Public Library in 1880.[8] In a section headed "Belles Lettres" are included works by Chateaubriand, La Motte-Fouqué, Janin, Lafontaine, Lamartine, and others. Novels by Balzac or Sand do not appear in this listing, but their absence is not surprising, since the catalog emphasizes the mathematical and scientific works that formed the heart of Sam's purchases, and since novels, especially recently published ones, would generally have been regarded as occasional or ephemeral reading, not appropriately a part of such a record. Howe's *Reminiscences* identifies four works by Sand that she read soon after her brother's return: *Les Sept Cordes de la Lyre*, *Spiridion*, *Jacques*, and *André* (noting also that it was years after this time that the 1842 novel *Consuelo* "revealed to the world the real George Sand, and thereby made her peace with the society which she had defied and scandalized" [58–59]). This list—supposing we can assume accuracy in Howe's memory of a period more than sixty years past—is notable in two ways: first, for its indication that some of the reading she did of Sand's works could not have been the result of Sam's having acquired the books during his time abroad;[9] and second, for its relative tameness. Of these four works, only *Jacques* might have been thought inappropriate for an unmarried woman.[10] Missing from Howe's list are the early Sand works that had made her notorious—*Indiana*, *Valentine*, the first version of *Lélia*—works of the kind Howe seemed to have in mind when she described Sand in 1861 as "a name of doubt, dread, and enchantment."[11]

Whatever she read, the impact is not in doubt: the novels changed her world. Howe remembered Sand as the touchstone for her youthful thinking about "the world's great struggle between conservative discipline and revolutionary inspiration":

> We knew our parents would not have us read her, *if they knew*. We knew they were right. Yet we read her at stolen hours, with waning and still entreated light; and as we read, in a dreary wintry room, with the flickering candle warning us of late hours and confiding expectations, the atmosphere grew warm and glorious about us,—a true human company, a living sympathy crept near us,—the very world seemed not the same world after as before. She had given us a real gift; no criticism could take it away. The hands might be sinful, but the box they broke contained an exceedingly precious ointment. ("Sand" 514)

It would be years before this "gift" bloomed conspicuously in Howe's own writing, yet one might fairly say that her desire to be a writer, her early conviction that she would "write the novel or play of the age" (*Reminiscences* 57), was due in some measure to the impression Sand made. Very few women of Julia Ward's age, class, and marital status considered writing to be an appropriate activity. For an unmarried woman to be "literary" was to invite opprobrium and to put at risk her desirability in the marriage marketplace. [12] Despite such attitudes—rendered palpable to her by discouragement from her father and her uncle—it is perhaps no coincidence that Julia's first published work, a review of Lamartine's long narrative poem *Jocelyn*, was written in the year of Sam's return from Europe with Sand's novels. If *The Hermaphrodite* is somehow an expression of the mental liberation Howe attributed to her reading of Sand around 1836, it is tempting to draw a further connection between that year and her hermaphrodite narrative. Lamartine's work, although in tone nothing like Sand's fevered novels, does nevertheless bear the impress of a fascination among French writers of the period with the figure of the ambiguously gendered creature.

The best guide to this preoccupation is A. J. L. Busst's comprehensive and detailed study, "The Image of the Androgyne in the Nineteenth Century." [13]

mental liberation [handwritten annotation in margin]

Busst's tracing of the image in the thought of Saint-Simon and Pierre Leroux and in such novels as Latouche's *Fragoletta* (1829), Balzac's *Séraphîta* (1834–35), and Théophile Gautier's *Mademoiselle de Maupin* (1835) uncovers competing interpretive conventions. The phenomenon is allied both with redemption—the androgyne restores original perfect human unity and is therefore the ideal toward which all life strives—and also (in Busst's priggish terms) with "cerebral lechery," "decadence," and "perversion." Later in the century, in particular, but also in this period, the hermaphrodite additionally emblematized homosexuality.

The Balzac and Gautier novels illustrate all these motifs. *Séraphîta* describes an androgynous figure—first called Séraphîtus, later Séraphîta—who offers instruction to two young people on how to move beyond materiality to a sexually undifferentiated plane of spiritual existence. The young people, Minna and Wilfred, are each separately in love with Séraphîta, to whom s/he appears as the opposite gender, either male or female. The work (which reflects Balzac's interest in the theological mysticism of Emanuel Swedenborg) ends with Séraphîta's ascent into heaven through an act of will; this apotheosis inspires a salvific vision in Minna and Wilfred and enables their own psychological escape from the skepticism of their envious minister.

Gautier's novel, in contrast, represents androgyny pruriently from start to finish: the trope conveniently introduces a variety of titillating situations. The work is mainly an epistolary novel, beginning with letters from the Chevalier D'Albert to a (male) friend, Silvio, describing his amatory activity. D'Albert initially settles his affection on Rosette, who, though an energetic lover, does not fulfill some undefined need of D'Albert's. Enter Théodore de Serrano, a young cavalier who immediately speaks to this need: D'Albert notes his grace, his "soft and undulating" walk, and especially his delicate features, and thinks, "Here, then, is at last one of the types of beauty that I dreamed of realised and walking before me! What pity it is that he is a man, or rather that I am not a woman!" [14] Théodore is before long revealed to be female; she is in fact Mademoiselle Madelaine de Maupin, a curious and restless young woman who (as readers learn through her confessional letters to her friend Graciosa) has determined to masquerade as a man in order to spy. "I felt there were many faulty and obscure sides to their lives," she explains, "which were carefully veiled from our gaze, and which it was very important that we should know. . . . It is a frightful thing to think of, and one which is not thought of, how profoundly ignorant we are of the life and conduct of those who appear to love us, and whom we are going to marry" (152, 154). Madelaine's true physical nature eventually dawns on D'Albert through their mutual participation in a production of *As You Like It*, but Gautier contrives to maintain ambiguity for a while longer, and finally confounds the notion of rigid gender identity altogether in Madelaine's statement that "It often happens that the sex of the soul does not at all correspond with that of the body, and this is a contradiction which cannot fail to produce great disorder. . . . Beneath my smooth forehead and silken hair move strong and manly thoughts" (225–26). By the end Madelaine feels distant from the emotions and modes of behavior of both sexes: "I have not the imbecile submission, the timidity or the littleness of women; I have not the vices, the disgusting intemperance, or the brutal propensities of men: I belong to a third, distinct sex, which as yet has no name: higher or lower, more defective or superior; I have the body and soul of a woman, the mind and power of a man, and I have too much or too little of both to be able to pair with either" (282). In the novel's last chapter, Madelaine does, however, "pair" with both D'Albert and Rosette (who, like D'Albert, has fallen in love with "Théodore") in a glorious night of sex, one extravagant hedonistic indulgence, before she leaves them both. This conclusion is triply salacious, offering readers the voyeuristic pleasures of same-sex and opposite-sex couplings, as well as the spectacle of a woman controlling both the evening's agenda and its no-strings aftermath.

Gautier's central plot echoes a seventeenth-century narrative that had appeared in the weekly paper *L'Artiste* in 1830, but he was also moved to write the work, according to P. E. Tennant, by widespread public interest in an ambiguous relationship between George Sand and an actress, Marie Dorval.[15] Indeed, Sand's writings account for only part of the attention she attracted in the early 1830s; she was at least as famous for her cross-dressing and for the gossip arising from her possibly physical friendship with Dorval as for her novels. When Sand—then still Madame Aurore Dudevant—first moved from her husband's country estate to Paris in 1831, she adopted male dress partly because it was less expensive and more convenient (men's boots, in particular, enabled her to negotiate Paris's cobblestones with ease), but also because it rendered her invisible to men and thus free to move among the artists and intellectuals she had come to the city to join. When she began to publish in 1833 under the pseudonym George Sand, both French and English reviewers made sure readers knew she was female, although it seems not to have been until 1837, four years later, that the fact of her crossdressing also entered reviewers' assessments of her work. In the British journal *Atheneum*, Jules Janin wrote: "George Sand, in his own home, is, by turns, a capricious young man, of eighteen, and a very pretty woman of from five-and-twenty to thirty,—a youth of eighteen, who smokes and takes snuff with peculiar grace, and a grande dame whose brilliancy and fancy at once astonish and humble you."[16] Several of Sand's early works, too, blurred the male-female distinction. Isabelle Naginski notes that her fiction "is rife with narrators grammatically defined as male. And when these voices develop into fully embodied characters in the text, they appear in male costume, with the physical traits and the traditional occupations of . . . men."[17] The name itself, George Sand, refuses linguistic association with either gender, since the French version of the English male name "George" requires an *s* at the end.

Much of this information about Sand, I think we can assume, Julia Ward heard from her brother; it is likely part of what she meant in saying that Sam "brought into the Puritanic limits of our family circle a flavor of European life and culture." Like his friend Janin in the sentence quoted above, Sam was deeply struck with Sand's intersexual self-positioning. He wrote in 1839 to Longfellow that he considered Sand superior to Balzac, finding it "inconceivable how the free genius of that woman gives birth to ideas of the highest order of masculine beauty" (Elliott 251). A few years later, when Longfellow asked him to pave the way for a meeting with Sand, Sam wrote:

> As for George Sand, nothing will be easier than for you to know him, should your travels lead you her way. I will furnish you with a warm letter to Janin who will have great pleasure in making you known to him, and I candidly think her worth seeking. Besides his genius for writing she has an impulse toward perfectibilitification, and is intimate with that fiery apostle Lammenais who sympathises in his efforts to elevate people and recognizes in her a kindred spirit. Should it be your fortune to fall in with him do not fall in love with her.

Speaking with the Voices of Others

He will enchant you more in an evening, if the fit of Psychic
inspiration be upon her, than any being you ever knew, & is
a kind of moral hermaphrodite. (Elliott 342–43)

It was presumably in a context in which such issues were in some way "on
the table" that Julia wrote her review of Lamartine's Jocelyn.

The piece appeared in the December 1836 Literary and Theological Review,
a journal edited by one of her father's friends, Leonard Woods. It suggests
remarkable breadth of reading in both French literature and European culture: Julia authoritatively distinguishes Lamartine from his poetic prede-
cessors and draws on differences between styles of pre-Renaissance Italian
painting to illustrate the nature of the distinction. She clearly sets forth the
grounds for the aesthetic judgments she renders and shows herself capable
of severity in the judgments themselves.[18] Unsurprisingly for a girl raised in
a religious household, she finds the chief value of Jocelyn to be in its picture
of the virtuous heroism of the title character: "His enthusiastic piety, the
spirit of devotion and humility in which he sacrifices happiness to duty, his
universal benevolence and philanthropy, diffusing itself alike over all men,
his deep and unchanging love, form one of the fairest modes of excellence
which ever suggested itself to a poet's imagination." This opinion leads
her to conclude that the surest way for a "monument of literary renown"
to resist the encroachments of time is to be built on "the sacred ground
of truth and moral excellence" rather than "the mere force of intellect"—
a sentiment underscored in her own inclination toward religious subject
matter in her early poems.

The review, published of course anonymously, attracted comment from
those who knew it to be her work. It was distinctly not the kind of thing
her culture expected a seventeen-year-old female to produce. John Ward,
Julia's uncle, undoubtedly spoke for many of the males around her when,
after showing her a favorable notice of her essay in a daily newspaper, he
said: "This is my little girl who knows about books, and writes an article
and has it printed, but I wish that she knew more about housekeeping"
(Reminiscences 20). In this review (and in a second, published three years
later, on John S. Dwight's collection of translations of poems by Goethe
and Schiller), Julia speaks without reference to gender, either hers or that
of her supposed readership. It is a tacit assumption that her reflections

and assessments will carry the sort of impersonal authority automatically assumed to be that of the male literary critic. During this historical moment, among American writing women whose efforts are known, only the work of Margaret Fuller, Elizabeth Oakes Smith, Elizabeth Ellet, Lydia Maria Child, and Elizabeth Palmer Peabody (ranging from six to thirteen years older than Julia Ward and all the beneficiaries of strong and extensive male intellectual communities) exhibits comparable confidence and scholarship. Yet the fact of its having been written and printed, and even its display of erudition, are less notable signals of Julia Ward's heterodoxy than its one or two indications that her aesthetic frame of reference might have been wider than her father or Uncle John could have countenanced.

Lamartine's eponymous hero is a young man studying for the priesthood at the time of the French Revolution, forced at the outbreak of the Terror to take refuge in a cave high in the Alps. Two other refugees, father and son, find their way to Jocelyn's hideout, but the father has been wounded and soon dies, leaving his child—a beautiful boy whose name happens to be Laurence—in Jocelyn's care. Love grows between the two—described at first in asexual, quasi-Platonic terms as the attraction of soul for its lost other half—but as intimacy grows, Jocelyn's fascination seems increasingly the product of Laurence's physical appeal.[19] He notes the beauty of his forehead, eyes, hair, voice, way of dressing, et cetera, and ultimately is forced to ask himself whether such powerful feelings aren't somehow tainted:

> I condemn oft in me those sympathies which melt
> Much too sudden in me, much too sensibly felt,
> Those instincts of the first sight, and those first movements,
> Which of my slight impressions soon make sentiments;
> I've said to myself often, perhaps God doth blame
> Those inclinations which may profane the heart's flame,
> But alas! spite of us tow'rds the light our eyes rove,
> Is't a crime O my God! beauty too much to love? (137)

The emotional center of *Jocelyn* is the "Fourth Epoque," essentially a collection of rapturous love-duets exchanged between Jocelyn and Laurence, which continue until one day Laurence injures himself and Jocelyn discovers, in treating him, that Laurence is actually a woman.

Julia's review indirectly addresses the oddness, the potential indecency, of the relationship between Jocelyn and Laurence. She praises Lamartine for not "guiding us through the diversified regions of fancy to mislead us at last." Lamartine is not Byron, she says; we don't worry that he is "casting a robe of noble and majestic imagery around that which in itself is base and polluted; nor that his love for the beautiful, his worship of the sublime is but a mask beneath the shelter of which he may scorn and blaspheme the Being whose image is impressed upon all that is beautiful and sublime. Every word carries with it the conviction that it comes from the abundance of a heart purified and refined by the influences of religion." On the same page of Howe's *Reminiscences* in which she describes her early encounter with Sand's novels, she notes that, although Shelley was forbidden, Byron was "sparingly conceded" to her and her sisters (58), and she quotes two lines from *The Giaour*. The reference in the *Jocelyn* review is general, and yet in this context the allusion inevitably invokes Byron's own ambiguous sexuality—possibly even the specific ambiguity of the "Thyrza" elegies, Byron's love poems to a fellow choirboy at Cambridge, the pronouns of which he changed from male to female to conceal the nature of his affection. It does not require too strained a stretch of credulity to imagine this review—perhaps including the decision to review this particular work—as of a piece with the general "great emancipation" coincident upon Sam's return. Lamartine, Sand, Balzac, possibly even (as I urge in greater detail below) the louche Théophile Gautier brought about a change of perspective that both made imaginable the woman Julia Ward was to become and provided certain specifics—a character's name, a narrative circumstance, a theme—for a story that, in 1836, she certainly could not have foreseen the need to write.

Julia Ward's decision to marry Samuel Gridley Howe in 1843 was the culmination of a process of development that began with her first visits to Boston; he was far from what her family had assumed would be her marital destiny. In 1837 Julia had met Mary Ward of Dorchester, Massachusetts—not a relation, but also the daughter of a banker and, like Julia, intellectually inclined. Through this friendship, Julia was gradually exposed to Unitarian and transcendentalist thinking, and to the Boston intelligentsia, including Fuller, Emerson, Longfellow, and Charles Sumner. Boston, Julia wrote to

Mary, was "an oasis in the desert, a place where the larger proportion of people are loving, rational, and happy." Her growing investment in "its pure intellectual atmosphere and its sunlight of kindness and truth" seemed to reach an apotheosis in Howe.[20]

Samuel Howe was widely regarded as handsome. Late in his life, a woman told Laura Richards, his daughter, that when in his twenties and thirties he would ride down Beacon Street on his black horse, "all the girls ran to their windows to look after him."[21] Julia Ward had just turned twenty-two in the summer of 1841 when Longfellow and Sumner drove her, her sisters, and Mary Ward out to the Perkins Institution in South Boston. Howe—internationally famous war hero in his youth, decorated for his service to Greece, now in midlife equally renowned for his philanthropic work with Laura Bridgman and other blind children—galloped into Julia Ward's young life in just the way to make the strongest possible romantic impression. It is hardly surprising that she would find him attractive. He seemed the very embodiment of two of Boston's most salient characteristics in Julia's mind: high seriousness and passionate commitment to the alleviation of social evils.

The marriage lasted thirty-three years, until Samuel Howe's death in 1876, yet its periods of tranquility were rare. It was from earliest days—before it even took place, in fact—plagued by a sharp misalignment in their expectations of each other and by Howe's reluctance or inability to transfer his deepest emotional commitment from his best friend, Charles Sumner, to his wife. The vague shape of the relationship between Samuel Howe and his nine-years-younger friend rests on hints, scraps, scissored letters, truncated expressions, a sense of a fuller interchange the texts of which have either disappeared or possibly never existed as actual "texts." Its clearest articulation leaps out from a letter to Sumner that Howe wrote in September 1844. He tells his friend: "When my heart is full of joy or sorrow it turns to you & yearns for your sympathy; in fact as Julia often says—Sumner ought to have been a woman & you to have married her: but I should not agree to this in any monygamic land, for Julia is my love as a wife."[22] Suggested in this jocular remark, I believe, is a plausible explanation for at least one of the forces that eventually propelled Julia to the writing of The Hermaphrodite. Sumner, though perhaps not the cause of her husband's distance, grew to be for Julia more or less the focus of it, and her mode of understanding this intense connection between her husband and his younger friend was to recast it as a narrative of guilt, imperfectly understood desire, and sexual ambiguity.

Howe's close friendship with Sumner, which began in 1840, was sufficiently intense by the spring of 1842 to provoke humorous comment from their mutual friends. Two running themes in letters exchanged between the two men, as well as in their friends' letters, are Sumner's inability to find a woman to fall in love with and his inseparability from Howe. As Howe's relationship with Julia Ward began to deepen, Sumner exhibited a series of telling responses to the situation, ranging from various subtle articulations of hostility toward Julia to a scheme to marry Julia's sister Louisa to melodramatic lamentations over Howe's impending desertion. Once the engagement was announced, Sumner wrote to Sam Ward to sing Howe's praises—and, secondarily, to give vent to his own anxieties:

> I feel sometimes that I am about to lose a dear friend; for the intimate confidence of friendship may die away, when love usurps the breast, absorbing the whole nature of a man—as the nourishment that supports a tree gradually retires from the distant branches, absorbed entirely by the trunk. But Howe's nature is too generous, I believe, for such a fate. His heart is large enough for her to whom he has given it, & for his friends besides. Him I shall not lose, then; & have I not gained a friend in Julia? I trust she will let me be the friend to her, that Howe will say I have been to him.

For his part, Howe penned numerous notes and letters to Sumner in a strenuous effort to assure him that his fears were groundless. Excerpts from one written immediately after docking in Liverpool on his wedding trip and another written a month later are illustrative:

> Your forebodings are not realised—the torrent of affection which is continually flowing from my breast toward the new object of my love diminishes not by one drop the tide of feeling which ever swells within my bosom at the thought of thee dear Sumner: I love thee not less because I love her more. . . .

You complain of your lonely lot, & seem to think your friends will lose their sympathy with you as they form new ties of love, but dearest Sumner it is not so with me and in the days of my loneliness & sadness I never longed more for your society than I do now in my joy & in the whirl of London life: hardly a day passes but [I] think of you & long to have you by my side.

Despite such pledges, Sumner's already-fragile stability vanished during the first winter of the Howes' marriage. He fell into a severe depression, which he tried to alleviate through overwork, which in turn brought on tuberculosis. By mid-July 1844, a month before the Howes returned from Europe, he was so weak and ill that his doctors declared him beyond hope of recovery (a false prognosis, of course).

How Julia positioned herself in relation to this vortex of emotion is already suggested in her remark—quoted by her husband later that fall—that Sumner ought to have been a woman, so Howe could have married "her." The portrait of Sumner in Julia's *Reminiscences* is of small use in discerning how she felt about him in the early days of her marriage; the memoir was written twenty-five years after his death and is inevitably colored not only by her own advanced age but by consciousness of the decades of distinguished service Charles Sumner gave to the United States. We learn little from her letters of the time, either: both her sisters were with her for most of the first year of married life, and so Julia had not much occasion to write self-revealingly. Generally, when Sumner's name appears, the tone is wryly affectionate, humorously sarcastic.

What we do have, which seem to bring us near the truth of her feelings, are several poems in a diary Julia began keeping in 1843—sharply personal poems exhibiting a woman in a pit of depression over the departure of her "powers," her "soul," and over a husband whose emotional distance seems to prevent him from offering solace. "We are not born alike," she laments in one of these:

Often I turn away
From thee, to weep and pray;
I cannot rise on high,
My sad soul looks to God, and asks him why.

Speaking with the Voices of Others

He says: "ye are not akin,

Your union was a sin;

Your natures meet and jar,

And thus, the order of Creation mar."

Despite notes of mea culpa and hopes for joyful reconciliation, despite alleged resolutions in which "regret departs, and love is born anew," one can't help reading these teary plaints in light of many similar sentiments (similar but harder-edged, and less likely to eventuate in happy closure) voiced in letters to her sisters through the later 1840s and 1850s. Is such despair a result specifically of her husband's affectional apostasy in Sumner's direction? Viewed in the context of the "Laurence" manuscript, I believe this is the likeliest explanation.

The narrative, as indicated earlier, is disjointed. Yet the handwriting and paper are consistent throughout all sections, and the fictional characters are uniform and reasonably cohesive. In piecing together a more or less continuous story from these fragments, I have been led by indications within each segment of a likely chronology of events. The tale, which Laurence himself narrates, is of his repudiation by his family; his involvement with an attractive widow; his subsequent wanderings and eventual attachment to a sixteen-year-old boy, Ronald, whose tutor and love-object he becomes; his estrangement from Ronald; his own tutelage by a Roman nobleman named Berto (and by Berto's sisters); and his ultimate reunion with Ronald just before death.

Section 1 begins with Laurence's account of his youth—raised as a male, he tells us, to give him freedom "to choose my own terms in associating with the world, and secure to me an independence of position most desirable for one who could never hope to become the half of another." He is sent to a boys boarding school "that I might become robust and manly, and haply learn to seem that which I could never be" (3). Two story lines dominate this section. The first chronicles Laurence's involvement with Emma von P., ending with her discovery that her beloved is no man but a "monster" (19), and her immediate death from grief. The second follows Ronald's increasingly passionate obsession with Laurence, culminating in an explosion of jealousy, lust, and remorse that propels Laurence to flee for his safety. Approached with knowledge of the Howes' marital tribulations, this portion of the manuscript reads plausibly as an interior narrative—a repository for certain of Julia's most deep-seated anxieties and a staging ground for conceptualizing the causes of the situation in which she found herself.

In a letter to Louisa at the end of January 1847, Howe exulted that for the first time since her marriage she had "*waked up*," escaped the sleepwalking state in which her concerns were limited to digestion, sleep, and babies. Though she acknowledged that the causes of her dullness were in part physical, the burdens arising from childbirth and its aftermath, she also wanted Louisa to understand her husband's role in having produced this lethargy: "It is partly, sweet child, the result of an utter want of sympathy in those around me, which has, like a winter's frost, benumbed my whole nature. Do not chide me, my blessing, for thus faintly explaining to you what has so long been cold and heavy at my heart. You cannot, cannot know the history, the *inner history* of the last four years."[23] Despite the fact that she was ill with a light case of scarlet fever in March, the period was full of energy and confidence, seeming to climax in the May letter to Louisa that included the Eva-Rafael poem. She was "thin & languid" but clearer of mind than since before her marriage, feeling both the difficulty and the necessity of holding on to her sense of self against the world's efforts to strip her of it.

The trope of the hermaphrodite seems to have offered a scaffold for trying to understand in corporeal terms why a man (or an apparent man) might wish to deflect the attentions of a beautiful and devoted woman. Samuel Howe's indifference to her (and responsiveness to Sumner) is then a function of his very constitution rather than the result of shortcomings on her part. It is not coincidental, I think, that Emma von P. is precisely Julia Howe's age. Discovering the "truth" about Laurence drives Emma into mental instability and early death, a melodramatic but still recognizable version of the state of mind Julia describes as hers beginning just weeks after her marriage. The outcome, of course, is disastrous in both fiction and fact, but to attribute the rejection to a *physical* cause (the logic would go) renders her husband in some measure less blameworthy. This remarkable empathy is compounded by the fact that the first-person narrative necessarily foregrounds the torment Laurence lives with and his readiness to sacrifice his own prospect of happiness in order not to inflict his debased self on another person.

The character of Ronald, and Laurence's ambivalent response to him, became another means by which Julia Howe limned for herself the "inner history" of her marriage. The younger man whose beautiful face draws Laurence back from the abyss of a religious trance replaces Emma in his emotional life; she vanishes from the narrative. Although at first Ronald believes Laurence to be a woman in male attire, Laurence's insistence on his behavioral maleness ensures that the affection that grows on both sides will be understood as happening between two men. Ronald's adoration of Laurence is clear from his first appearance, but Laurence's reciprocal emotion is presented as something of which he is imperfectly conscious or inclined to deny to himself. Although he calls Ronald "my pretty young Baron" (60), and although he can't decide whether it is the setting sun or "a pair of starry eyes" that warms his soul (60), Laurence professes to be uneasy when Ronald wants to kiss him or to declare his love. The seeds Laurence says he never intended to sow, the impulses with which he says he can't sympathize, do seem to have found fertile soil in his own constitution as well as in Ronald's.

To posit similarities between the Ronald-Laurence and Sumner–Samuel Howe relationships may seem overstatement, and a crude one at that, given the equivocal quality of the "evidence." It may even strike some as perverse, in light of the fact that Julia Howe's husband (unlike the Whitman self-described in his infamous letter to John Addington Symonds) did indeed father six children and later upset Julia by expressing a desire to marry a younger woman. I make no argument for a physical relationship between Sumner and Samuel Howe. Yet the eroticism in the attachment between Laurence and Ronald inevitably seems predicated, in some degree, by Julia's feeling that Sumner "ought to have been" a woman, and thereby a legitimate love-object for her husband. In Julia's thinking, her spouse was himself in some sense a "woman" in the intensity of his feelings for Sumner. Since he was married, however, and therefore culturally male, the female element in the conjunction would have to be supplied by Sumner, though it resided in both. At any rate, although other readings of the manuscript's ambiguously gendered protagonist are equally plausible, there is sufficient reason to feel that Laurence is at least in part an embodiment of the "beautiful monster" Julia Howe discovered she had married.[24]

But suppose, now, a different sense in which the manuscript inscribes Julia Howe's newly waked-up state four years into her marriage. Although Emma's plight seems to reflect Julia's grief in marriage, the idea of the hermaphrodite was arguably also useful as a screen on which to project certain other aspects of her situation. Laurence may be Samuel Howe, yes, but "he" is also Julia, a being fusing culturally ascribed impulses of both genders and thereby consigned, according to the logic of American domestic ideology, to a loveless and sexless existence. Julia's intellectual ambitions—her determination to engage in the unwomanly activity of publication or advanced study generally—had caused male anxiety about whether she would be adequately prepared as a wife and housekeeper. Some of this anxiety Julia clearly internalized. Both her *Reminiscences* and the letters from her early married life testify to the difficulties she encountered in trying joyfully to embrace conventional expectations of domesticity. Her pregnancies coincided with the periods of deepest estrangement between the Howes and became, for Julia, both an occasion for self-doubt and a grim emblem of the way marriage impeded her intellectual and aesthetic development. At such moments the hermaphroditic existence of a George Sand must have exerted great, if guilt-laden, appeal.

Laurence's function as a site for Julia Howe's contemplation of her own psychological androgyny becomes clearer in section 2. The spirit of this section is conveyed in Berto's explanation of his plan to educate Laurence, not with books, but with experience: "Know that I abhor onesidedness, fixed idea, and all the insanities of the learned. For them, the earth should stand still, for me, it turns round, and shows me a new face every day. . . . I desire to do entire justice to every fibre of my brain, every nerve and muscle of my body" (95). Laurence's tutelage involves consideration of the restrictive roles into which culture shoehorns women. In society, says Berto, women are educated not to strength or virtue but rather "to triviality and routine. . . . They are taught to appeal to our indulgence, not to command our esteem" (99). Apart from society, the options are even worse. Berto acquaints Laurence with Eleonora, a young girl bred from an early age to a religious vocation. Now she is a novice, and the two are witnesses as she takes the veil, Laurence reflecting morosely on the sour underside of lives lived in sequestered devotion to the church. An extended sequence then focuses on a childhood friend of Laurence's, Rösli, now a ballerina, whose life offstage consists of fending off advances from dissolute men.

In the major story line in this section, Laurence, dressed as a woman, is living familiarly in Rome with Berto's three sisters. Regarding Rome as a setting for this segment of the story, it is important to note that Howe's first two published collections of poems—*Passion-Flowers* (1854) and *Words for the Hour* (1857)—heavily invest Rome as a site of liberation and insight for her. This investiture of meaning arose mainly from her sojourn there in 1850–51, when she was sharing a villa with her sister Louisa's family and considering a more permanent separation from her husband. Howe's first visit to Rome, however, occurred during her wedding journey in 1843–44; she gave birth there to her first child, Julia Romana, in March 1844. During this time she first visited the Villa Borghese with its "Sala dell' Ermafrodito" (Hermaphrodite Room)—the source for an observation in the first section of the narrative that Laurence resembles "the lovely hermaphrodite in the villa Borghese" (16). The reference is to the Sala's copy of a celebrated Greek statue, *The Sleeping Hermaphrodite*; the chamber also features paintings by Buonvicini illustrating Ovid's story of Hermaphroditus and Salmacis.[25] In putting Laurence into women's clothes, Berto's intention is to enable him to "see men as women see them" and also "see women as they appear to each other"—"divested," says Berto, "of the moral corset de précaution in which they always shew themselves" when men are present (133). The situation reverses that of Madelaine in Gautier's *Mademoiselle de Maupin*—so pointedly, in fact, that it is hard to imagine that the work wasn't part of the "enlargement" Julia associated with her brother's return from Europe. (The character of Berto serves Laurence precisely in the way Sam Ward served his sister, and the resemblance of Berto and Sam is nowhere more striking or provocative than in the later scene in which, following Berto's return from a sojourn in Naples, he and Laurence gleefully burn Laurence's female disguise—as if to suggest Sam's collusion in liberating Julia from the bondage of gender masquerade.)

From the vantage point of 170 years later, *Mademoiselle de Maupin* is among the nineteenth century's most influential works of fiction, partly because of the author's joyfully impudent defense of art for art's sake in the preface. Swinburne loved the novel, as did Baudelaire, Huysmans, and above all Oscar Wilde. But the work was assuredly not on lists of reading appropriate for young antebellum American women. As late as 1868, a writer for the *Atlantic Monthly*, reviewing Gautier's career, frequently interrupted his descriptions of works to remind readers of the "voluptuousness" of Gautier's values: "We must frankly admit that Gautier outrages the common sentiment of the American mind; . . . Gautier represents what has no place in our literature, still less in our life. He represents the supremacy of the artistic." As for *Mademoiselle de Maupin*, the novel "holds a series of pictures of more than questionable taste; in some pages it outrages all the delicate and modest instincts of human nature." Similarly, Henry James in the 1870s named Gautier "of literary artists the most accomplished," but was dismissive of *Mademoiselle de Maupin*, finding "a painful exhibition of the prurience of the human mind" in the fact that, in notices of Gautier's death, critics had focused exclusively on this earliest work as representative.[26] Undoubtedly, part of its continuing outrage-quotient was Madelaine's claim to belong to "a third, distinct sex," having "the body and soul of a woman, the mind and power of a man" (Gautier 282). The novel was not published in an English translation until the 1880s, fifty years after its initial appearance.[27]

xxix

Of course, the quantity of genuinely salacious detail in Gautier's novel is remarkable, as is the level of religious heterodoxy (itself a kind of pornography, presumably). The Chevalier d'Albert relishes not just the form of his love-object, "Théodore," but also the pagan quality of his own fantasies, as in this passage about the very statue of the sleeping hermaphrodite that Howe references in her own tale:

> Since the time of Christ there was not been a single human statue in which adolescent beauty has been idealised and represented with the care that characterises the ancient sculptors. . . . This son of Hermes and Aphrodite is, in fact, one of the sweetest creations of Pagan genius. Nothing in the world can be imagined more ravishing than these two bodies, harmoniously blended together and both perfect, these two beauties so equal and so different, forming but one superior to both, because they are reciprocally tempered and improved. To an exclusive worshipper of form, can there

Speaking with the Voices of Others

be a more delightful uncertainty than that into which you are thrown by the sight of the back, the ambiguous loins, and the strong, delicate legs, which you are doubtful whether to attribute to Mercury ready to take his flight or to Diana coming forth from the bath? The torso is a compound of the most charming monstrosities: on the bosom, which is plump and quite pubescent, swells with strange grace the breast of a young maiden; beneath the sides, which are well covered and quite feminine in their softness, you may divine the muscles and the ribs, as in the sides of a young lad; the belly is rather flat for a woman, and rather round for a man, and in the whole habit of the body there is something cloudy and undecided which it is impossible to describe, and which possesses quite a peculiar attraction. (146–47)

Nothing in Howe's narrative goes quite this far, although in scenes between Laurence and Emma and between Laurence and Ronald there are equivalently suggestive interludes. Once Gautier introduces Madelaine's narrative voice, however, the novel strikingly resembles the central situation in the second long portion of Howe's work, in which Laurence contemplates the world through women's eyes. Madelaine dresses as a man because she is hungry to know what men talk about when women aren't present: "Their real existence is as completely unknown to us as if they were inhabitants of Saturn or of some other planet a hundred million leagues from our sublunary ball; one would think they were of a different species" (152). She recognizes that the world will think her mad for relinquishing the comforts and protection of her gender, but, as she observes, "the truly mad are those who fling their souls to the wind, and sow their love at random on stone and rock, not knowing whether a single seed will germinate" (158). In the late 1840s Julia Howe certainly would have resonated to that sentiment.

Madelaine's ruse affords her exactly the kind of liberation that, earlier in the novel, her admirer d'Albert has likewise longed for: "I have never wished so much for anything as, like Tiresias the soothsayer, to meet on the mountain the serpents which cause a change of sex, and what I envy most in the monstrous and whimsical gods of India are their perpetual avatars and their countless transformations" (49). Howe's Laurence seems to pick up the train of thought suggested by Madelaine's emancipation. He speculates that it is "natural" for women to want to acquire cross-gender knowledge, even though it is also marked as "dangerous":

> Women . . . are very naturally glad now and then to throw off their chains with their petticoats, and to assume for a time the right to go where they please, and the power of doing as they please. What a new world does this open to a woman! what a delightful, dangerous abyss of novelty! It is a world of reality in exchange for a world of dreams—it is dealing with facts instead of forms, with flesh and blood, instead of satins and laces. . . . According to her own powers of feeling and perception, she may find a keen pleasure in new investigations of men and things, a mischievous delight in the usurpation of rights not her own, or a philosophical satisfaction in intellectual relations divested of the dangerous attraction and repulsion of sex. (131)

Developing the character of Laurence provided access for Howe to this "delightful, dangerous" new world, as well as sharpened understanding of the "bondage of . . . narrow life" that Laurence submits to by going the other direction. "How would I bear the endless tedium of its trivial details, or mimic a sympathy with its microscopic interests?" he wonders. He expects the strictures to feel like Hercules' vest, "full of uneasiness and of torture" (136)—an apt metaphor for Julia's own despair at the somnambulistic half-life she lived during the early years of her marriage.

Interestingly, part of what Laurence learns through the ruse of his disguise is the opposite of his expectations: female life can proceed on terms established by women and can offer a measure of liberty. Two of Berto's sisters, Briseida and Gigia, are extremely worldly—enlightened, expansive, and "too proud to present themselves as candidates for selection in the great woman market of society" (136). They resemble Gautier's heroine in their mental and sexual independence. Laurence's conversations with them acquaint him with the various means they have devised to live rich lives, and he concludes that women "are like the vines that ripen on the sides of volcanos—it is only on the perilous brink of destruction that their finest qualities are called out" (154–55).

Howe likely recognized a version of this same sentiment in Margaret Fuller's comments on George Sand in *Woman in the Nineteenth Century*, then recently published. Fuller had first read the literature of the French romantics in the summer of 1839 and immediately urged Sand's novels on Emerson. Her journal from that period records astonishment at Sand's "insight into the life of thought"—almost exclusively (in Fuller's experience to that time) the province of male writers. In *Woman*, Fuller regards women like Sand as "rich in genius, of most tender sympathies, capable of high virtue and a chastened harmony," but born into "a place so narrow that, in breaking bonds, they become outlaws." So positioned, they lose force as world-reformers, whose lives, to be effective, must be "unstained by passionate error."[28]

In her 1883 biography of Fuller, Howe, recounting Fuller's enthusiasm for Sand, describes a response that was probably as much her own as Fuller's: "To the literary merit of [Sand's] work was added the interest of a mysterious personality, which rebelled against the limits of sex, and, not content to be either man or woman, touched with a new and strange protest the imagination of the time."[29] This evidence of shared intense response to the Sand phenomenon suggests that the impact Sand had already made on Julia in the 1830s was perhaps reinforced for her by witnessing the workings of Fuller's own hermaphroditic mind on Sand's significance. I am inclined to see the image of George Sand, shadowy, behind Fuller's story of Mariana in *Summer on the Lakes*. Mariana has long been regarded, of course, as Fuller's masked self-representation, and this is certainly true of the younger Mariana. But Fuller's heroine marries—something Fuller was not to do until five years later. There is a sense of gender-displacement in Mariana's falling in love with Sylvain: *she* loves first, and her love excites his. But, says Fuller, "it is a curse to woman to love first, or most. In so doing she reverses the natural relations, and her heart can never, never be satisfied with what ensues." And so it proves. The marriage is a disaster: "There was absolutely a whole province of her being to which nothing in his answered." He is kind but preoccupied, usually out with his male companions; she is solitary and wretched, and eventually dies. Fuller notes that had Mariana been a man, many resources would have presented themselves to distract and fulfill her. Mariana reminds her of the heroine of Henry Taylor's *Philip van Artevelde*; each has "a mind whose large impulses are disproportioned to the persons and occasions she meets, and which carry her beyond those reserves which mark the appointed lot of women."[30] The script of Mariana's married life is closely a forecast of the marriage of Julia and Samuel.

Yet it is also clear that Briseida and Gigia, the older sisters, do not inspire Laurence's admiration, and the turn that the narrative takes in its final section toward the youngest sister, Nina, signifies a third way in which Julia's work on The Hermaphrodite helped her deal with the space she inhabited. If Gautier and Sand are plausible pilot lights for Howe's contemplation of the ambiguously gendered figure, to the range of possibilities they may have ignited we must add another kind of inspiration—one explicitly named toward the end of The Hermaphrodite: Emanuel Swedenborg (1688–1772). During Laurence's final illness, a doctor is called in and is asked whether the suffering being is man or woman. "I shall speak most justly," says the physician, "if I say that he is rather both than neither." Briseida understands this assessment in Swedenborgian terms: Laurence, she says, is "a heavenly superhuman mystery, one undivided, integral soul, needing not to seek on earth its other moiety, needing only to adore the God above it, and to labour for its brethren around it" (195).

The role of this Swedish theologian and mystic in the blooming of transcendental thought in the 1830s has been extensively chronicled (Emerson heard Samson Reed's "Oration on Genius" in 1821 and began reading Reed's articles on Swedenborg in 1827), but his larger cultural impact on Americans began with the translation into English in 1841 of a collection of letters and testimonials by friends. This was re-edited and printed in the United States six years later and gave rise to a spate of biographies. Henry James Sr., who had learned Swedenborgian thought from a series of articles by J. J. Garth Wilkinson in the London Monthly Magazine, began publishing on Swedenborg in 1846; Emerson delivered his lecture on Swedenborg (published in 1850 in Representative Men) in late 1847. Howe's Reminiscences records her deep interest in Swedenborg, and her letters show that she was already something of an authority on his work by 1847. She also knew of Balzac's deep fascination with Swedenborg's thought, displayed most evidently in Séraphîta (1834), the main character and conclusion of which bear sharp resemblance to aspects of Laurence's story.

The issue invoked by Briseida's comment and Balzac's Séraphîta is Swedenborg's views about the role of sex in heaven. These were understood in approximately opposite ways by different readers in mid-nineteenth-century America. In the eyes of some, Swedenborg was scandalous for insisting on the preservation of sexual difference after death—indeed, for his too-graphic-for-polite-sensibilities depiction of the marriage bond among heavenly souls. Others, however, understood Swedenborg to be saying that sexual distinctions vanish when we die—that (in Emerson's formulation, for example) "in the spiritual world we change sexes every moment."[31] Whether Laurence, like Séraphîta, is intended to be understood as an earthly incarnation of a Swedenborgian hermaphroditic angel is unclear at the narrative's end. But the moral import of Howe's concluding scene feels heavily determined by her reading of Swedenborg.

Berto's third sister, Nina, who has spent many years waiting for the return of her absent lover Gaetano, is nearly an object of veneration for Laurence. Her eerie, vatic response to Laurence's reading of the fable of Eva and Rafael, "Ashes of an Angel's Heart," is one of The Hermaphrodite's most arresting scenes. Like Nina, Eva is an icon of patient, unshakable devotion to her single love, and she is rewarded by heavenly consummation with Rafael, blessed by God. "Now, truly, are we wedded and inseparable," says Rafael; their voices blend "in one harmonious strain" and they vanish from sight (181). In her wild singing of Eva's song, "Release thou, the prisoner of hope," Nina seems, to Laurence, Eva's incarnation. Her exaltation evokes a similar state in everyone listening: "We were borne with it to unseen realms, to unexplored depths of feeling and of foreboding. . . . There was a rapture in her anguish, and an anguish in her rapture. Perhaps the two are ever thus indistinguishably blent, in the intense moods of intense minds" (184). This dual intensity, anguish and rapture, likewise describes Laurence's final moments.

The reappearance of Ronald, now a melancholy but dutiful member of the landed gentry, seems to generate a possibility of renewal. Ronald is apparently hoping for re-ignition of "that holy love which your heart gave me, and of which your will defrauded me" (190), and Laurence, in a frenzy equivalent to Nina's, appears ready at last to give it. Ronald has come only to say, however, that the two are now to part forever. His leave-taking renders Laurence a "beautiful monster . . . mute and dead" (193);

he falls ill, and in his delirium has a vision in which a woman and a man are fighting for possession of his body. He feels his bowels torn asunder by his love for both, a pain that finds expression in an image of crucifixion. A voice whose imagery recalls Eva's angel of despair tells him, "A cross is not formed otherwise than of two loves or two desires which cross each other or conflict" (196).

It is illuminating to consider Laurence's failure to achieve the harmony emblematized by Eva and Rafael in light of an 1848 letter from Howe to Louisa, written about their sister Annie two years after her marriage. "Like all of us," Howe says, Annie "has had to sacrifice many illusions—marriage is not what she expected, and men still less. Like us, after dreaming of perfect union of minds, intimate sympathy etc, she will have to fall back upon her own resources, and to find that, after all, the soul has but two possessions, itself & God." As Howe explains the ethos that enabled her continuing commitment to her husband, Swedenborg is explicitly on her mind:

> I do not see why one should pretend to be excessively happy when one is not, or why one should try to say to oneself "I love this man," when love is a matter out of the question. But marriage is not an affair simply of happiness, it does not promise us a boundless gratification of any taste or feeling. . . . I cannot pretend to say that I am perfectly happy, or that there are not vast and painful longings of my soul which, in this life, will never be satisfied, but I am to live forever, and I shall be more likely to attain happiness hereafter, by cultivating in this life, a spirit of humility, of gratitude, and the love of *uses*, upon which my Swedenborg so insists. . . . I still bear in my heart the traces of much suffering, but there was good in it for me, and there shall be good for others. This life is eminently one of duties, of thought and of action; in another world, we shall know more and love more, and these two worlds comprise for me all of happiness—for the having is little to us, it is what we are to others & what they are to us that constitutes our well-being. [32]

If this rhetoric is somewhat less exalted than that which Howe gave Eva and Nina, the position is very near theirs. Each of us is a "prisoner of hope"; we all desire release, but satisfaction derives from embracing the challenges set for us here. In her life, although it gave rise to the notes of "hoarse despair" her brother Sam heard in her poems, Julia Howe managed this embrace.

In the end, however, *The Hermaphrodite* discards this sort of pious resolution. Howe's protagonist, dying, is patently *not* the "undivided, integral soul . . . needing only to adore the God above it." Rather, s/he is the embodiment of a cross—"two loves or two desires which cross each other or conflict"—and the last image is of irreducible doubleness, irresolution, pain. Like Margaret Fuller's Mariana in *Summer on the Lakes,* like Gautier's Madelaine de Maupin, Laurence vividly instantiates the being trapped by the conventions of gender. S/he is an apt emblem (as is the text itself, in its unresolvable duality) for all ardent, multivalent nineteenth-century creatures, male and female, caught between their symphonic richness of spirit and an age attuned, for the most part, to a monotone.

I have found no indication that Howe ever attempted to publish the Laurence manuscript, or even that anyone else, while she was alive, actually read it in its entirety.[33] It is nearly unthinkable that she *would* have approached a publisher. Her trepidation regarding *Passion-Flowers,* expressed in letters from the fall of 1853, suggests that even that much tamer literary project (volatile though it, too, is) posed a substantial emotional challenge. And certainly her husband's fury after the appearance of that book would have imposed an additional deterrent. Finally, though, I think that it was her own determination to accommodate herself to her culture, to be useful within its strictures—*not* to become Fuller's Mariana but rather the best Eva she could be—that caused her to lay aside *The Hermaphrodite.*

Thankfully, however, she did not destroy the manuscript. A passage embedded in the second long numbered section speaks to the need for disguise in articulating such matters as these. Berto observes that people during the carnival season relish the opportunity to wear masks that, in fact, express the truth—hiding their faces in order to show their hearts. The man in the mask is "far less disguised than the man one meets every day face to face." Laurence sees this truth in "a wider and a sadder sense": "So intolerant, so incomprehensive is society become, that fervent hearts must borrow the disguise of art, if they would win the right to express, in any outward form, the internal fire that consumes them. There is scarcely one great passion of the soul which would not, if revealed, offend the narrow sense and breeding of the respectable world, and the few who are capable of these powerful emotions, and who must express them, must speak as with the voices of others" (121). Howe's Laurence was a product of a time in her marriage not only when her husband's affection for another man seemed to displace any he might have had for her, but also when culture-wide premises about her appropriate role in patriarchal structures seriously threatened her intellectual and emotional survival. Howe saved herself with this "history of a strange being"—a projection of both her husband and herself, and thus hermaphroditic in yet another way—which apparently brought her a measure of clarity sufficient to carry her through a rough time. The writing of it permitted her to occupy a speculative region otherwise inaccessible in her historical moment, especially to American women.

While its personal significance to Howe is an important consideration in this edition's effort to make the text available to twenty-first-century readers, The Hermaphrodite merits attention for another reason—one suggested by the indication in Sam's poem to his sister that her voice will be important to those in future ages suffering under similar strictures. One evening while in female masquerade, Laurence is called upon to perform musically for guests of Briseida and Gigia. Weary of trivial conversation, he does so willingly, and while playing and singing falls into a "musical reverie" that lifts him altogether out of his surroundings. "And here let me ask," Laurence reflects,

> what true artist ever sings to the audience actually present before him? . . . His soul breathes for the time a wider, purer atmosphere than that of theatre or concert room. To somewhat infinitely above himself, yet also infinitely within himself he addresses those deeply breathed passages, those daring flights, those high notes which seem, like the song of the soaring lark, to drop, full of liquid light, from the empyrean. He could not sing thus for money—he could not sing thus for patronage. He may be needy and desirous of both, but for the moment he is not venal, not vulgar. He is lost in the impersonality of art. (149)

At the climax of the performance, completely possessed by the passion of the moment, Laurence reprises a melody he has heard sung that morning in St. Peter's, but as he concludes he overhears someone compare his voice to that of Uberto, the Pope's famous castrato. Panicked by the possibility that such singing will betray who he really is, he determines to sing no more in Rome.

The incident, I would argue, encodes Howe's own sense of the danger of discovery and perhaps explains both the manuscript's unfinished state and its obscurity for these 150-plus years since it was furtively written. Sam's poem, with its supplication to his sister not to stop singing, is in sympathy with Laurence's conviction that a song takes the singer to "a wider, purer atmosphere" than that of his or her own moment. It foresees the value of such texts, the encouragement they might offer to others struggling to sing their full natures with passion, without inhibition, despite cultural interdictions perceived or real.

Notes

1. Samuel Ward, *Lyrical Recreations* (New York: D. Appleton, 1865), 101–2.
2. Describing her writing in the decade 1860–70, Howe said "it was borne in upon me . . . that I had much to say to my day and generation which could not and should not be communicated in rhyme, or even in rhythm" (*Reminiscences 1819–1899* [Boston: Houghton Mifflin, 1899], 305). It should be noted, however, that Howe did not altogether stop writing or publishing poems; her third volume, *Later Lyrics*, appeared in 1866.
3. Howe, *Reminiscences*, 242. A detailed account of the woe reflected in Howe's early poetry, based on her unpublished letters and journals, is to be found in my *Hungry Heart: The Literary Emergence of Julia Ward Howe* (Amherst: University of Massachusetts Press, 1999), chapters 5 and 6.
4. The manuscript's Houghton Library catalog number is *51M-283 (320), box 4. It is published by permission of the Houghton Library, Harvard University. See "A Note on the Text" regarding editorial practices in this edition.
5. Julia Ward Howe (hereafter JWH) to Louisa Ward, 15 May 1847 (bMS Am 2119). The poem is not part of the text of Howe's letter, but it is preserved on page 25 of a diary Howe began in 1843 and used as a repository and scrapbook at least through 1853 (bMS 2214 [321]). The poem and other diary notes seeming to refer to the Laurence narrative appear in appendix 1 of this volume. These notes were originally written on other paper and then pasted into the diary. This passage and others quoted from unpublished letters and journals are reproduced by permission of the Houghton Library, Harvard University.
6. I refer to Laurence throughout as male because, although he evidently has both male and female physical characteristics, he informs us that his parents raised

him as a male in order to give him freedom "to choose [his] own terms in associating with the world, and secure to [him] an independence of position most desirable for one who could never hope to become the half of another" (3).

7. Letter to Mersch, 23 July 1837; quoted in Maud Howe Elliott, *Uncle Sam Ward and His Circle* (New York: Macmillan, 1938), 160–61.

8. *Catalogue de la bibliothèque de Samuel Ward, Jr.* (n.p., n.d.). Currently in the Manuscripts and Rare Books division of the New York Public Library. A 24 November 1837 letter to Charles Mersch indicates that these books were not purchased until after Sam's return to the United States; see Elliott, *Uncle Sam Ward*, 164–65.

9. *Jacques* and *André* were published in 1834 and thus might have been among the books sent home, but *Les Sept Cordes* and *Spiridion*, both dating from 1838, must have been purchased after his return.

10. The spirit of *Jacques* is well conveyed in Jacques's unorthodox view of marriage:

> I am by no means reconciled to society, and marriage I still regard as one of its most odious institutions. I have no doubt that it will be abolished when the human race shall have made some further progress toward justice and reason: a tie more humane, and not less sacred, will take its place, and will insure the well-being of the children who shall spring from the union of one man and one woman, without fettering the freedom of either. But at present men are too gross, and women too cowardly, to seek a nobler law than the law of iron which rules them; beings destitute of conscience and virtue need heavy chains. The improvements of which some generous spirits dream, can not be realized in such an age as ours: those spirits seem to forget that they are a hundred years in advance of their contemporaries, and that before they change the law they must change mankind. (trans. Anna Blackwell [New York: Redfield, 1847])

The novel chronicles Jacques's marriage (despite misgivings of this kind) to Fernande, a girl eighteen years his junior, and climaxes in his decision to release Fernande from her vows when she falls in love with another man.

11. "George Sand," *Atlantic Monthly* 8 (November 1861): 514. The article illustrates Howe's familiarity with other early works not named in *Reminiscences*, in particular *Valentine* (1832) and *Lettres d'un Voyageur* (1834–35).

12. Julia Ward was probably familiar with a well-known poem by Schiller called "Die berühmte Frau" ("The Celebrated Woman"), in which a husband complains at great length to another married gentleman about the horrors of being married to a woman who has become famous as a result of her literary publications. The poem is an apt expression of the early-nineteenth-century's attitude toward any woman whose ambitions reached beyond the domestic fireside. The speaker's wife, he says, "belongs to the whole human race . . . she is exposed for sale in every shop, / And may be handled (more's the pity!) / By ev'ry pedant, ev'ry silly

fop—." Startlingly (in light of the Laurence narrative), near the end of Schiller's poem, the (in)famous woman is explicitly likened to a hermaphrodite:

> What have I now?—What sad exchange is this!—
> Awaken'd from my madd'ning dream of bliss,
> What of this Angel now remains to me?
>   A spirit strong with a body weak,
>   Hermaphroditic, so to speak;
> Alike unfit for love or mystery—
> A child, who with a giant's weapons rages,
> A cross between baboons and sages!

This translation of the poem appears in *The Poems of Schiller*, trans. Edgar A. Bowring (Chicago: Belford, Clarke, n.d.), 95–99.

13. In Ian Fletcher, ed., *Romantic Mythologies* (London: Routledge, 1967), 1–95. Busst uses the terms "androgyne" and "hermaphrodite" interchangeably, as he explains: "The distinctions established from time to time between the terms 'androgyne' and 'hermaphrodite' have always been purely arbitrary and consequently often contradictory. . . . Rather than attempt to choose from or add to the already excessively long list of extremely doubtful distinctions, it is preferable to consider the two terms exactly synonymous by accepting their broadest possible meaning: a person who unites certain of the essential characteristics of both sexes and who, consequently, may be considered as both a man and a woman or as neither a man nor a woman, as bisexual and asexual" (1).

Other useful studies of the image and phenomenon of the hermaphrodite include Marie Delcourt's *Hermaphrodite: Myths and Rites of the Bisexual Figure in Classical Antiquity* (London: Studio, 1961); Michel Foucault's introduction to *Herculine Barbin*, trans. Richard McDougall (New York: Pantheon, 1980), vii–xvii; Diane Long Hoeveler's *Romantic Androgyny: The Women Within* (University Park: Penn State Univ. Press, 1990); Vern L. Bullough and Bonnie Bullough's *Cross Dressing, Sex, and Gender* (Philadelphia: Univ. of Pennsylvania Press, 1993); Gert Hekma's " 'A Female Soul in a Male Body': Sexual Inversion as Gender Inversion in Nineteenth-Century Sexology" in Gilbert Herdt, ed., *Third Sex, Third Gender: Beyond Sexual Dimorphism in Culture and History* (New York: Zone, 1994), 213–39; and Alice Domurat Dreger's *Hermaphrodites and the Medical Invention of Sex* (Cambridge: Harvard Univ. Press, 1998).

Dreger's study provides useful information about Isidore Geoffroy Saint-Hilaire and Sir James Young Simpson, early-nineteenth-century scientist-physicians who studied and wrote extensively on the phenomenon of hermaphroditism (140–44). Dreger also recounts the story of Gottlieb Göttlich, raised as a female until, at age thirty-three, she was examined by a professor at the University of Heidelberg and pronounced male. Göttlich became a "traveling hermaphrodite" between 1833 and 1835, touring medical schools in Europe and England and offering him/herself for examination (see Dreger 52–53). See *Hungry Heart* for additional medical issues that may influenced Howe's thinking about hermaphrodites (95). But I have found nothing to indicate that Howe was interested in hermaphroditism as a physiological phenomenon. As with other writers discussed here, her response seems to have been to the metaphorical suggestiveness of two sexes joined in a single body.

14. Théophile Gautier, *Mademoiselle de Maupin* (New York: Heritage, 1944), 95.

15. See Tennant, *Théophile Gautier* (London: Athlone, 1975), 88. The connection between Sand and Gautier's novel is also mentioned by Enid Starkie in *From Gautier to Eliot: The Influence of France on English Literature, 1851–1939* (London: Hutchinson University Library, 1960), 29.

16. Quoted in Patricia Thomson, *George Sand and the Victorians: Her Influence and Reputation in Nineteenth-century England* (New York: Columbia Univ. Press), 11.

17. Isabelle Hoog Naginski, *George Sand: Writing for Her Life* (New Brunswick: Rutgers Univ. Press, 1991), 22.

18. "We find in this, as in many of his other productions, flat lines, and obscure phrases. The tale is, as it were, too much spun out. . . . De Lamartine should study conciseness, and cultivate more concentration of thought. He is too apt to dwell upon details which should be passed over, as they become tedious, and diminish the dignity of his style. He weakens by elaboration that which would be much more forcible and energetic if simply expressed" (*Literary and Theological Review* 3 [December 1836]: 559–72).

19.
> each soul is sister to a soul;
> God made them man or woman, and left them to stroll;
> The world may for a time separate them in vain
> Their fate is, sooner or later, to meet again;
> And when these heavenly sisters here below meet,
> Invincible instinct each to each draws their feet;
> Each soul its other half attracts with all its force,
> And friendship or love of this attraction's the source,
> By a diff'rent name called, union one and the same,
> In the sex or the being where God lights the flame,
> But 'tis truly the flash which reveals to each one,
> The being which completes him, of making two one.

Alphonse de Lamartine, *Jocelyn*, trans. F. H. Jobert (London: Edward Moxon, 1837), 122.

20. Julia Ward to Mary [Ward] Dorr, 17 September 1839 (bMS Am 2215 [350]). A fuller account of this friendship and the other biographical details summarized here is to be found in the first three chapters of my *Hungry Heart*.

21. *Letters and Journals of Samuel Gridley Howe*, ed. Laura E. Richards (Boston: D. Estes, 1909), II, 388.

22. S. G. Howe to Charles Sumner, 11 September 1844 (bMS Am 2119, #920).

23. JWH to Louisa Ward, 31 January 1847 (bMS Am 2119, #465).

24. The phenomenon of same-sex affection may have impinged on Howe's life around the time of the writing of the Laurence manuscript in the person of the actress Charlotte Cushman. Beginning in the mid-1840s, Cushman became a

celebrity on the basis of her portrayal of Romeo—a performance that was (in the words of one recent historian) "redolent with same-sex eroticism." Howe knew Cushman; she was a dinner guest at the Howes' home on more than one occasion in the late 1840s, and a decade later she was slated to perform the role of Phèdre in Howe's unpublished play *Hippolytus*.

Cushman's lesbianism (never, of course, so named during her lifetime) is the subject of two studies: Denise A. Walen's " 'Such a Romeo as We Had Never Ventured to Hope For': Charlotte Cushman," in Robert A. Schanke and Kim Marra, eds., *Passing Performances: Queer Readings of Leading Players in American Theater History* (Ann Arbor: Univ. of Michigan Press, 1998), 41–62 [the quotation above appears on p. 43]; and Lisa Merrill's *When Romeo Was a Woman: Charlotte Cushman and Her Circle of Female Spectators* (Ann Arbor: Univ. of Michigan Press, 1999). Cushman's portrayal of Romeo may have suggested the scene in *The Hermaphrodite* in which Laurence is unexpectedly thrust into a college production of Shakespeare's play, in which he plays Juliet and thereby arouses Ronald's jealousy.

25. I discuss the Villa's art works in greater detail in *Hungry Heart* (95–96). Reproductions of the Sala's *Sleeping Hermaphrodite* statue and Buonvicini's illustrations of Ovid appear following page 133.

26. Eugene Benson, "Théophile Gautier," *Atlantic Monthly* 21 (June 1868): 664–71; Henry James, *French Poets and Novelists* (London: Macmillan, 1878), 32, 36.

27. Charles Brownson has produced an authoritative list of English translations of Gautier's works; see "Les Traductions en langue anglaise des oeuvres de Théophile Gautier," *Bulletin de la Société Théophile Gautier* 13 (1991): 161–216.

28. See Fuller's letters to Emerson regarding Sand in Robert N. Hudspeth, ed., *The Letters of Margaret Fuller*, vol. 2 (Ithaca: Cornell Univ. Press, 1983), beginning on page 99. Fuller's journal quotation is from R. W. Emerson, W. H. Channing, and J. F. Clarke, *Memoirs of Margaret Fuller Ossoli* (Boston: Phillips, Sampson, 1852), 1:247. Fuller's comments about Sand in *Woman in the Nineteenth Century* may be found in Jeffrey Steele, ed., *The Essential Margaret Fuller* (New Brunswick: Rutgers Univ. Press, 1992), 284–86. Fuller also wrote about Sand on three separate occasions in 1845–46 for the *New-York Tribune*; see Judith Mattson Bean and Joel Myerson, eds., *Margaret Fuller, Critic* (New York: Columbia Univ. Press, 2000), 54–64, 227–32, 457–63.

29. *Margaret Fuller (Marchesa Ossoli)* (Boston: Roberts Brothers, 1896), 135–36.

30. *Summer on the Lakes* in Steele, *The Essential Margaret Fuller*, 126, 131.

31. *The Collected Works of Ralph Waldo Emerson*, ed. Douglas Emory Wilson (Cambridge: Harvard Univ. Press, 1987), 4:72. The confusion is understandable. Here is one of Swedenborg's several efforts to explain this principle (from *The Delights of Wisdom Concerning Conjugial Love, after which follow The Pleasures of Insanity Concerning Scortatory Love*, trans. William H. Alden [Bryn Athyn: Academy of the New Church, 1915], 42):

> Since man lives a man after death, and man is male and female, and
> the masculine is one thing and the feminine another, and they are

so different that one cannot be changed into the other, it follows that after death the male lives a male and the female a female, each a spiritual man. . . . The difference essentially consists in the fact that in the male the inmost is love and its clothing is wisdom, or what is the same, he is love veiled over with wisdom; and that in the female the inmost is that wisdom of the male, and its clothing is the love therefrom. But this love is feminine love, and is given by the Lord to the wife through the wisdom of the husband; and the former love is masculine love, and is the love of growing wise, and is given by the Lord to the husband according to his reception of wisdom. It is from this that the male is the wisdom of love, and that the female is the love of that wisdom. Wherefore, from creation, there is implanted in each the love of conjunction into one.

It should be noted that Emerson's attitude toward Swedenborg in the 1840s was essentially hostile. He was annoyed at, among other things, the literalness of Swedenborg's discussion of marriage and seems to have determined to rewrite his subject to reflect his own sense of the meaning of the conjugal bond. For an expression of annoyance at Emerson's alleged misreading, see Captain W. J. Underwood, *Emerson and Swedenborg* (London: Spiers, 1898). Other useful windows on attitudes toward Swedenborg in antebellum America include Leonard Woods's *Lectures on Swedenborgianism* (Boston: Crocker & Brewster, 1846), J. J. Garth Wilkinson's *Emmanuel Swedenborg: A Biography* (Boston: Otis Clapp, 1849), and George Bush's *Statement of Reasons for Embracing the Doctrines and Disclosures of Emmanuel Swedenborg* (New York: John Allen, 1846).

32. JWH to Louisa Ward, 13 June 1848 (bMS Am 2119, #486).
33. The Houghton folder containing the first long section includes a sheet bearing the name "Joseph Willard" and a date: "Feb. 1851." Joseph Willard (1798–1865) was recording secretary of the Massachusetts Historical Society from 1835 to 1857. In light of his political and religious associations (Whig, Free-Soiler, abolitionist, and Unitarian) and social ties, he was no doubt a familiar of the Howe family, but I can find no other reference to him in connection with either wife or husband. Why this manuscript would have been in his possession in 1851 (if indeed it was) is unclear. In February Howe was in Rome on her own; her husband had returned to Boston three months earlier. This mysterious note, and the scrap of a letter to an unidentified recipient accompanying a "history of a strange being," suggest that other eyes may have seen the manuscript, but corroborative evidence has yet to turn up.

Two other scholars have studied and written about the Laurence manuscript. Mary Hetherington Grant examined the box for her 1982 history dissertation at George Washington University, published as *Private Woman, Public Person: An Account of the Life of Julia Ward Howe from 1819 to 1868* (Brooklyn: Carson, 1994). Her account of the narrative, which she names *Eva and Raphael*, discovers "repressed sexual yearning, the beginnings of feminist thinking, and anxiety about death" (see 121–25, 227). Valarie H. Ziegler's more comprehensive and insightful reading in *Diva Julia: The Public Romance and Private Agony of Julia Ward Howe* (Harrisburg PA: Trinity Press International, 2003) also emphasizes the Eva-Raphael story, seeing the work as portraying "an ideal of man and woman moving beyond separate spheres into romantic and ethical partnerships" that are transformative for both (see 61–71 and detailed notes 181–84).

A Note on the Text

The "Laurence manuscript" is actually several manuscript fragments, written probably over a period of years in the late 1840s, possibly extending into the early 1850s. It was evidently envisioned as a single continuous narrative, although it is now impossible to say with certainty how Howe intended to pull the disparate pieces of the story together. Many segments are missing—destroyed, or not preserved with the rest of the manuscript fragments and not yet come to light, or possibly never written. It is unlikely that Howe intended to publish it, at least at the time it was written. It is unique among her preserved manuscripts both in size and genre.

The bulk of the text is comprised of two lengthy sections. The longer of the two—section 1 of the current edition—is numbered in manuscript 2–163 (but is missing pages 118–132); the shorter—section 2 here—is numbered 50–171. Section 3 is constituted from seven much shorter manuscript segments, only one of which—the Eva and Rafael story—is numbered (1–27), and two of which are variant versions of the same scene. In preparing the fragments for publication, I have created a sequence for them which is defensible in terms of the chronology of the story, but which has no claim to authorial sanction. When I first read this work in July 1995, there was no discernible order to the arrangement of the fragments in their Houghton Library storage box, and the pages within some of the fragments were out of numerical order. The sequence that appears in this volume is entirely my construction; while it aspires to accuracy in transcription, it does not lay claim to being a definitive textual edition. I have been concerned to create a readable text, not one closely observant of the precepts of the Modern Language Association's Center for Scholarly Editions. Appendix 2 is a direct transcription of sections of manuscript from which I have excerpted to create the narrative of section 3.

Perhaps because of its "closet" nature, the work was written without great attention to the niceties of spelling and punctuation. Inconsistencies abound. For the most part, I have left the punctuation and other mechanics exactly as they appear in the manuscript, with two classes of exceptions.

First, when a word is inadvertently repeated in the manuscript (as in "I was was ordered to wear my wreath . . ."), one has been deleted. Obvious misspellings have also been corrected. Second, for one long stretch of the manuscript, Howe consistently wrote "it's," "her's," "your's," and "their's"; these I have silently emended to "its," "hers," "yours," and "theirs," which reflects her practice elsewhere in the manuscript and in her letters. Similarly, where the character Briseida's name has been abbreviated "Bda," I have spelled it out. If a word is obviously missing in manuscript, I have interpolated the most likely choice, enclosing it in square brackets. Questionable readings of words are also square-bracketed. I have silently regularized many of the punctuation marks surrounding dialogue, for the sake of clarity. I have also silently capitalized the initial letter in a sentence, in a few instances in which the manuscript uses a lowercase letter. (However, in two passages in which Berto relates a story in past tense that uses dialogue, I have left manuscript punctuation as is.) Underlinings have been reproduced as italics. Howe numbered only the first three chapters but designated many other chapter breaks; I have provided sequential chapter numbers in square brackets. Finally, I have provided brief notes at certain points to bridge lacunae.

The Hermaphrodite

[. . .] ration on the part of my parents, it was resolved to invest me with the dignity and insignia of manhood, which would at least permit me to choose my own terms in associating with the world, and secure to me an independence of position most desirable for one who could never hope to become the half of another. I was baptized therefore by a masculine name, destined to a masculine profession, and sent to a boarding school for boys, that I might become robust and manly, and haply learn to seem that which I could never be.

learn to seem

At school, and afterward at college, my career was more prosperous than could have been anticipated. I learned quickly, was sensitive to reproof, and ambitious of approbation. I became a favorite with my tutors, and ranked among the first in my class. Even my rough comrades learned to play more gently with me than with each other—in my intercourse with them, I instinctively appealed to their generosity, rather than defy their force. "Laurence is tired, poor fellow, do not hurt him, he is not so strong as we —" thus they spoke of me, and the most hardy among them agreed to protect and defend one superior to themselves in grace and agility, but greatly their inferior in force. I was distinguishable from them chiefly by a stronger impulse of physical modesty, a greater sensitiveness to kindness, or its reverse, more quickness and less endurance, a more vivid imagination, and a feebler power of reasoning. But a child has, properly speaking, no sex, and my time of trial came not until childhood had passed—then only did I learn all that I was, and was not, and this fearful lesson has occupied my whole life.

"instinctively"

a child has no sex

I saw my parents only at long intervals during the years I passed at school. They were cold and reserved towards me, and seemed always to feel a certain relief at the termination of my short and infrequent vacations. I learned at last to dread rather than desire the arrival of those periods so golden in the lives of most children, and was scarcely sorry to learn that my visits at home were to cease with the beginning of my academic career. The college for which I was destined was remote from my father's residence, and on entering it, I saw him for the last time in several years. He came, on this occasion, to announce to me the birth of a younger and only brother, the death of my mother, and his own intention of being absent from the country for the space of a year or more. He seemed to me more cold and repulsive than ever, and I was surprised to find that he had taken pains to inform himself of the minutest details bearing any relation to my character and conduct. His approbation and his counsel were briefly summed up in these words: "Laurence, you have studied well; continue to apply yourself, and to avoid all unnecessary intimacies."

"Yes, Sir."

"Embrace your father, Laurence," cried my old preceptor, who was present at this laconic parting.

"It is quite unnecessary," said the frigid Paternus.

"I am deuced glad of it," rejoined I, with a long breath.

My father fixed his eyes on mine with an expression of some astonishment—he read in my face an indifference and pride which might have seemed the reflection of his own. He coldly bade farewell, and left me— young as I was, I had at least determined that he should never know the pain he had given me.

At this period of my life, I know not how an impartial judge would have decided the doubtful question of my being—my powers of intellect had shot beyond those of my compeers, while yet my form threatened to take a strongly feminine development. My complexion was singularly delicate, and my hair, though continually cropped, would retain its silky softness, and fell in many curls around my neck and brow. At long intervals, my usually robust health was interrupted by fits of indisposition, each of which seemed a sort of crisis, a struggle between death and life. Strange to say, nature had endowed me with rare beauty. I grew tall and slender, my limbs were finely moulded, and my head might have been cited as a perfect model of classic grace. This beauty, under other circumstances, might have been a blessing; as it was, it proved the curse and torment of my life. In vain would I have shrunk into obscurity—I could nowhere show myself without being observed and pointed out of all. Women often gave me proofs of a stronger interest than any inspired by mere benevolence, while the eyes of men so scrutinized me that I was fain to hide myself from them with a perturbation for which I could scarce account to myself. I was anxious to propitiate

The Hermaphrodite

the good will of all, but any intimacy beyond that of ordinary friendship was incomprehensible to me. For man or woman, as such, I felt an entire indifference—when I wished to trifle, I preferred the latter, when I wished to reason gravely, I chose the former. I sought sympathy from women, advice from men, but love from neither. Like all other young creatures, I was gladly in the company of the gay and of the gentle, but I could not be in it long without learning that a human soul, simply as such, and not invested with the capacity of either entire possession or entire surrender, has but a lame and unsatisfactory part to play in this world.

5

In the village that surrounded us, my college companions had many female friends, among whom I gradually became known. These pretty moths consumed no small portion of our learned leisure, and our holidays were entirely consecrated to their service. On these occasions, we often arranged parties of pleasure to various caves, ruins, and woods in the romantic neighbourhood, in which every youth was cavalier to some fair maiden, and the time was improved by most of them for the establishment of relations of a more or less intimate nature. Of these, some were passionate, some sentimental, some transitory, some of life long duration, but all partaking of a feeling which was to me utterly incomprehensible. I enjoyed as keenly as any one a gallop on the greensward, or a ramble in the woods—our feasts and frolics, our songs and dances were all delightsome to me then in vivid reality, as now in softened remembrance—my eye was gratified by the grace and loveliness of the young girls, and my heart expanded in the sunshine of their gentle, happy nature, but they were to me even as the flowers, their sisters, and as the birds, their cousins, and as the distant clouds of heaven, and as all things else that were changeful and beautiful like unto them.

feeling

It was sufficiently easy for me to vie with my fellow-students in rendering every courtesy to these fair creatures. Like all the rest, I led their gentle feet over rocks and mountain paths, or bent my knee that they might spring from it into the saddle—I twined chaplets for their festivals, and verses for their songs, but no passionate thought or wish was interwoven with either. The enthusiasm expressed in my verses was vague and abstract in its character, and though of warmer blood and more generous nature than most of my fellows, I yet in comparison with them seemed cold and statuelike. The innocence and purity of the young girls did not however lead them to suspect any peculiarity of kind in me. They found me ever gay,

The Hermaphrodite

affable, and gracefully bold—they often turned from the amorous gabble of a stupid lover, to seek amusement from me, and I can still recall the rage of a sentimental youth whose disdainful sweetheart, wearied, angry, or alarmed at the suit he was pressing, broke from him, and took refuge beside me, saying: I shall go to Laurence, for he never makes love.

absence/ lack 6

Chapter 2nd

The relations which I have described lasted through a series of quiet, pleasant years, devoted otherwise to study, and marked by a gentle growth in the powers of thought and of action. Happy and golden do those days now look to me, though at the time, I was conscious of little more than a vague bien être, sometimes interrupted by deepest melancholy, and a hope of some thing far brighter and better, which methought time must soon bring me, but for which I am waiting still. Thus it is that we begin life in the expectation of positive enjoyment, and look impatiently for the day which shall see us very great, very rich, or very happy. It is reserved for the positive evils of life to teach us that the negative happiness of early youth has in it more of actual delight than any thing else that awaits us; and that, from the toils and responsibilities of active life, and from the satiety of luxurious indulgence, we are fain to turn back, and remember with longing the days in which we were neither oppressed with business, nor worn out with anxiety nor ennuyé by the absence of either.

Yet the struggle from childhood to comparative maturity had had for me its secret agonies, its hours of depression and desolation—of these, I do not speak—I have never revealed them—I have never willingly laid upon another the lightest portion of the burthen which it was given to me to bear through life. Thus far, at least, God has ever been my friend, he has ever given me courage to support it.

interruption

It was in the last year of my Academic course that my quiet and harmless life met with a strange interruption. At this time, a handsome and sprightly widow, some twenty eight years of age, had added herself to the little circle of our neighbourhood. She came from a gay metropolis, where her life had been embellished by station and wealth, and, as some said, by a little gallantry. She appeared as something new and rare to all of us, a revelation of some thing as yet unseen and unimagined by us, and I fear

The Hermaphrodite

me that maidenhood, with all its tender blushes, seemed to us quite tame and crude in comparison with the ever varying powers and beauties of the all accomplished, fully developed woman. The prettiest of our girls had perhaps the advantage of her in freshness and fragility of form and feature, but on the other hand, her beauty was heightened by her wit, displayed by her toilette, and rendered irresistible by an abandon which was not levity, a tact which was not worldliness, and a self-possession which was not impudence. As one may well imagine, the young ladies envied and imitated her, the young men vied with each other in their adoration of her, and I, occupying a middle ground, admired her at a respectful distance, giving her no reason to complain of either presumption or neglect on my part. But Emma von P. was not to be treated in this way. She was accustomed to see herself the queen of every circle in which she moved. The homage of the least was as necessary to her as that of the greatest, and while one heart remained unconquered by her charms, her triumph was incomplete.

One by one, rather in a body, the youths of our division had surrendered themselves at discretion. For her were the flowers, for her the verses and the serenades—it was who should ride beside her, who should drive or walk with her, who should go furthest and labour hardest for her pleasure. For such is the generous ambition of youth, it is who shall give most, and its day dream is to deserve the affection of one beloved by devotion and true service. Men of a riper age are better calculators—it is their business to receive as much, and give as little as possible, and the vision with which they delight themselves is one of fond, beautiful women, driven to distraction by their indifference, and vying with each other in their endeavors to win the worthless love of one who loves himself.

But let me do justice to the heroine-worship of our young gentlemen. I have seen the fools quarrel for the possession of a glove, or a faded flower from her hand, as they scramble for gold and precious stones at the largesse of some Eastern despot—bets were made upon her ribands, and duels were fought for her smiles. Nevertheless, as all human beings are said to esteem lightly that which is lightly got and as women especially are piqued by the indifference of a man and rejoice more in the subjugation of one rebel than in the loyal devotion of ninety and nine faithful ones that need no subjugation, so Emma von P. turned from the crowd of her admirers to look upon the unapproachable Laurence, whose greatest merit may have been that he seemed to trouble himself very little about her.

"Why does he never bring me any flowers?" said she, one evening, when her appearance in the ball room had been hailed by a perfect ovation of wreaths and banquets. A magnificent Camelia from my boutonnière was the only possible reply—it was honoured by a place in the bosom of the fair one, in which, however, I had no desire of succeeding it.

They were comparing several lyrics addressed to her on her birthday— she turned carelessly to me.

"I suppose that you have not the gift of writing verses."

"None worthy of being offered to Madame von P."

"He slanders himself," cried my fellow students: "Laurence is the best poet of his class—if he tries for the University prize, his poem is sure to receive it."

"There are other prizes worth striving for," said Emma von P. demurely looking down, and lancing to me a glance fuller of meaning than a thrown gauntlet. I hastily improvised some verses, and wrote them in pencil, the crown of my hat serving me for a desk. She received them triumphantly but having read them, her countenance expressed a certain disappointment.

"They are beautiful, but cold," said she.

"They are at least sincere, I say only that which I feel, and feel only the little that I know."

"Then you have still every thing to learn," said Emma, and bit her lip.

The challenge was now fairly given. I must either quarrel with Emma, or make love to her. The latter would be by far the most agreeable alternative to her, and the most advantageous to me. The incipient attacks were hazarded on the one side, and met on the other, with a skill & caution truly military— I cannot say that the same circumspection characterized all that followed. There is something of coquetry in all human beings, and mine could not but experience a certain elation when Emma repulsed for my sake a crowd of suitors, and when I marked that, in the admiring world of which she constituted the centre, she was seized with sudden blindness, and had no eye, no ear for any but me. My place was henceforth ever at her side in the salon, or in the green-wood. I was her chosen knight, and never have I been promoted to more gentle service. Many were the tête à tête wanderings

The Hermaphrodite

arranged by herself, in which the charms of all that is loveliest in Nature, and in woman were combined by her, to give the fair picture the fairest surroundings, to place her image in the innermost shrine of my heart and to gather around every association of poetry and beauty. Long were our interviews, endlessly varied, our conversations. Unlike most women, she possessed the twofold gift of being graceful alike in speech and in silence—her voice was full of music, her words full of power, but when she listened, her features all spoke; and you read the eloquent answer in her eye long before you heard it from her lips, as lightning travels more swiftly than thunder. Gradually the charm of our intercourse deepened, the tone of coquetry grew into that of deepest feeling, and the eyes that had once flashed such proud defiance at me now sought mine with an expression by turns enthusiastic, tearful, even agonized. When we met, and when we parted, her hand lingering in mine, each finger seemed to interrogate each of mine, asking why its pressure was so slight, and so easily relaxed. Often, at the termination of a moonlight walk, or of a long session à quatres yeux in her little boudoir, she would fix her eyes on mine, as if in earnest interrogation and entreaty—not reading there the response she wished, she would turn abruptly from me, or push me from her, and close the door upon me with a nervous energy bordering on irritation.

The epoch of our last collegiate examination had arrived—we were all occupied in preparing for the exercises. Among various prizes had been announced one, to be adjudged to the author of the best poem, and this concurrence was to be crowned by the most imposing ceremony of the week of trial. For this, the last day had been chosen, a numerous company would be invited. The rival poems were to be read aloud, each by its author, and the successful candidate should receive the prize from the hand of Emma. The last clause in the prospectus of arrangements gave the keenest edge to the eagerness of the young competitors. They had all envied me the preference shown me by their new divinity, they were all determined to snatch from me, if possible, the crown made doubly precious by her hand. There was great agony of preparation throughout the college, and a sighing and groaning as of parturient mountains preparing to bring forth mice. During the last month of the term, all spoke in rhyme, thought in verse, ate and drank in strict measure. Those who had neither been born poets nor bred orators hoped in a few weeks to possess the attributes of both, not knowing that it needs a whole lifetime to acquire an art, of which the germ has not been given with life itself. They had each chosen themes suited to their various tastes and studies. I had written my poem without labour, almost without any fixed design—it was but a piece of my every day thought, more neatly fashioned than the crude jottings down which often recorded my soul's life, and which always spoke of states of feeling, not of events. I had only followed the guidance of the voices which, in those days, came to me at morn, at noon, and with the holy eventide, bringing me as from another world, thoughts and images of thoughts, which could only utter themselves in song.

"Here we are, all talking, consulting, and disputing about our poems," cried the students one day, "and no one has heard a syllable from Laurence, in any way explanatory of his intentions. Confess now, Laurence, that you have not yet thought of a subject."

"Not much in truth."

"Ah! for the first time, you will be behindhand. Know, gracilis puer, graceless boy, that moonlight rambles and metaphysical discussions with pretty women will not help you to the Muse."

"And tears will bedew the nose of the sweet old preceptor when, at the critical moment he shall thus interrogate you: 'Laurentsi, ubi est carmen tuum?' "

"Yet the poem has somehow written itself," said I.

"Has it so, and already? Then it is probably something brief and personal—to memory, hope, despair, or your mistress's eyelash."

"To the blessed wig of our chancellor?"

"Or to his ox, the Latin professor, or his ass, the Greek professor, or to his man-servant the chemist, or to his maid-servant, the old woman who presides over our theological studies and gives us, hebdomadally, a foretaste of damnation?"

"To nothing and nobody," cried I, stunned by their noise.

"Ah then, to one who is not a thing nor a body, but a heavenly essence, radiance, and effulgence—to the witching Emma?"

"I do not jest about Madame von P." said I, with some coldness, and turning to depart.

"Is he not shy, this Laurence?" said they, as I left them.

The Hermaphrodite

Chapter 3rd

On the evening that preceded the last day of trial, Wilhelm, a student who might have been my friend, had he not been Emma's lover, came to my room.

"Laurence," said he, "you have passed, thus far, a better examination than any of us. Are you not satisfied with your success? Do you still intend to present your poem for the prize tomorrow?"

I replied in the affirmative. He continued: "I implore you to listen to me. You are sure to receive the prize, and from Emma's hand. But for you, this happiness would be mine, but for you, I should still be as once I was, her favored one." *but for you*

"As once you were?" repeated I, with contemptuous disbelief.

"Yes, but let me say all that I have to say. You do not love this woman, you have never loved her, you are but playing with her, and here stands one who would peril his life to obtain the boon which to me were blessedness, which to you will be but a trifling and transient gratification."

"What is the end and aim of this discourse?"

"It is briefly this—name your price, and sell me your poem."

"I am no Judas, to sell my soul for thirty pieces of silver."

"It shall be no mean price, my patrimony is large, ask whatever you will."

"If I should sell it thrice over, I could not make it yours," said I, with some haughtiness. "Children will claim their own parents."

"Then thus do I commit your first born to the flames," and before I could spring forward to prevent it, the excited youth had held my manuscript, which lay upon the table, in the blaze of the lamp—he waved it, flaming, around his head until nearly consumed, and then threw it from the window with a yell of triumph. *burns poem*

I stood and smiled upon him. "I will give you your revenge, if you wish it," said he.

"À demain," said I, courteously waving my hand, "I am in no hurry about it."

He looked at me in embarrassment and surprise, and was glad to seek the door.

That very evening and late into the night, I sat and talked with Emma von P. Our conversation had wandered hither and thither, as freely as our thoughts, but these, though widely discursive, ran ever in parallels. She had sung her sweetest, looked her beautifullest, and her discourse had been, as it ever was, full of point and of meaning. We had entered into a playful battle, tilting with golden lances, and pelting each other with rose leaves. At length, we became silent, she from very weariness, while I grew absorbed in painful forebodings. The conviction had forced itself more and more upon my mind that beneath Emma's jests there lurked a deep & dreadful earnest. I had begun to experience a malaise, an anxiety in her presence, for I felt the hidden strength of her nature, and I knew that it would soon be turned against her own happiness, and my peace. It was well, methought, that the hour of our separation was so near at hand.

"We have been very merry, and yet I am so sad!" sighed my companion from her corner of the causense.

"Your ladyship has then a fearful habit of deception, for I have observed that whenever you have been gayest, you turn to me with the smile yet on your lips to tell me that you are so sad!"

"Sadness and mirth are ever as near to each other as life and death," answered she musingly, "and there is always something of the one in the other."

Another pause: "What am I like?" said Emma to me.

"You are like a beautiful flower on an iron stem. The flower will fade, the iron will kill, so that you are mortal in yourself, and mortal to others."

"Thanks for a very bad compliment—shall I tell you what you are like?"

"Most certainly."—"You are like this marble against which I lean my head, whose pulses throb so that there seems to be a pulse in the cold stone itself—thus, a heart that is near you may think to feel the presence of one in you, but it is all marble, only marble."

After a moment's silence, she continued: "How old are you, Laurence?"

"Nigh upon twenty one."

"Nearly twenty one? quite a man then, and still a trifler." Exquisitely touching was the tone in which this gentle reproach was uttered. I durst not betray the emotion it caused me, and my reply was cold and almost rude. "You have always invited me to trifle," I said, "and I thought that it was altogether to your taste, but since you have had enough of it, good night."

Oh, Emma! this should have been our last good night. As I left the house, she called me back. I heard her steps as she ran to overtake me, but

The Hermaphrodite

I hastened mine, and did not look back. She returned and closed the door abruptly, but I heard a sob, as I passed near her window, on my way home.

On the afternoon of the day following, we were marshalled in the chapel of the college, for the reading of the prize poems. As we entered, we found the area filled by the members of the junior classes, the faculty of the college, our young friends of the neighbourhood, and some distinguished guests from the castle. At the upper end was the rostrum from which, by turns, we were to make our appeal to the favour of the audience—upon either side of this was a raised seat, on one of which was seated the chancellor of the University, and on the other, as upon a throne, our fair queen of love and beauty, Emma von P. to whom men forgave the pangs she sent to their hearts, for the delight she gave their eyes. It is so great a pleasure to see a woman finely trained and developed in person and in character. Your crude ore is cumbrous to carry, and difficult of estimation, but though Emma bore the guinea stamp of high breeding, she was yet of virgin gold, for a' that.

The compositions were really of a more respectable order than I had anticipated. There was unavoidably some pedantry displayed in the choice of subjects, and the young authors were obviously more familiar with their humanities than with humanity. It is true that we had a disquisition on the sufferings of Dido, and an ode commemorative of the constancy of Penelope, but I have often seen both of these heroines much more unkindly treated. There were several other productions, of which the theme alone could be called classic. A revolutionary poem followed, flaming and captious, at which the venerable Chancellor and other wigs there present winced somewhat. Then came a theological argument in blank verse, dogmatical, ambitious, and exceeding tedious to the young girls, delivered by a youth of pale complexion, red nose, and very indifferent digestion. After these exhibitions, Wilhelm really appeared to the greatest advantage, as he recited with a feeling voice a graceful lyric upon the ever old and ever new subject of love, into the closing lines of which was wrought an unmistakeable tribute to the charms of Emma. Universal applause followed his performance. He looked at Emma and at me, and seemed surprised to see a smile on my lips, and none on hers.

"I am the last, at least," said Wilhelm, with an air of satisfaction.

The Hermaphrodite

"You forget that the best and worst is yet to come, here is Laurence—"
Wilhelm hastily replied: "Laurence has no poem."

Emma overheard him, and changed colour, while she stole at me an

anxious and inquiring glance.

"How know you that, Wilhelm?" said I—the countenance of my rival was instantly darkened. As my name was called, I ascended the platform, stated to the audience that my manuscript had accidentally been destroyed and requested permission to repeat memoratà, instead of reading my poem. This was granted me, as a matter of course. Then, with a voice of silvery sweetness, and in a measure peculiarly my own, I sang the sufferings of a soul exiled from heaven, and sent into this world invested with the semblance, but not the attributes of humanity. I told of its solitary wanderings on earth, how it could nothing make, nothing possess—how its abstract orphanhood could establish no relationship, and extort no sympathy from the souls of men, veiled in a flesh of whose wants and powers it knew nothing. The alternative was then offered to it of becoming utterly mortal, or of returning to its ghostland, and I closed with some thrilling numbers descriptive of the noble scorn with which the pure spirit refused to bear the unworthy burthen of the flesh, once contemplated and understood, and the free and fearless courage with which it spread its wings, and flew back to the bosom of its God. My audience was deeply and attentively silent, and when my voice ceased, one long-drawn breath betrayed the interest with which I had been heard.

The committee appointed to decide upon the adjudication of the prize did not include (Deo sit gratias) the faculty of the college. It was composed of several gentlemen of the neighbourhood, among whom was the well accomplished Baron L——, who was present with several foreigners, his friends, and guests. The committee retired into an anteroom, whence they shortly returned, having been quite unanimous in their decision. The Baron, as foreman of the Jury, addressed the chancellor, and informed him that they had agreed, without one dissenting voice, to adjudge the prize to M. Laurence de ———. The Chancellor at first replied by a well bred stare and the whole Council of Pedagogues unhesitatingly expressed their disapproval.

"The poem of M. Laurence bears no marks of historical research," murmured the expounder of Sallust.

"In a theological point of view, it is an entire fallacy," growled the Doctor Divinitatis.

"There is nothing in it which would lead one to suppose that the author had been thoroughly grounded by me in trigonometry, integral calculus, conic sections, et alia," remarked the man of cubes and decahedrons.

"It is at least highly, beautifully poetical," rejoined the Baron, in his courtliest manner, "and as we came hither to listen to poems, and to decide upon their merits as such, you must allow me in the name of my friends of the Committee, to announce to the company the name of M. Laurence as the recipient of the prize, and to offer him our warmest thanks and congratulations upon his public desert of it."

A loud burst of applause confirmed the sanction of the whole assembly upon his decision. Some reply on my part seemed necessary, but I could only say to the Baron: "I have as yet small pretensions to knowledge of any kind. Thanks to you, who have recognized in me the presence of the poetic power."

Turning from him, I knelt at Emma's feet to receive the prize—it was a crown woven of velvet oak leaves with golden acorns. I felt the tremulousness of the hand that placed it on my head, I saw by the tearful smile with which she greeted me, that her heart was moved at once to joy and grief. She was proud and happy in my triumph, but that another should have dedicated his services to her, while the poem of her chosen one bore no trace of her, this grieved her deeply. Yet she was alike incapable of feeling or of showing a petty vexation, and when she spoke to her [sic], her voice and her words were deeply sympathetic.

"Oh, Laurence, your flight is lofty, and the heaven you dwell in is beautiful, but why do you take no one with you?"

"Could you not follow me then, Emma?"

"Did you expect it?"—"Yes—at least I hoped it. I have often wished to talk with you of the relations of pure spirit."

"Laurence, I hope that you are not one of those unsexed souls."

"Have you never been one?" said I.

"Never," she replied, "since I have learned what it is to be a woman."

These words made a strong impression upon me—"what is it to be a woman?" I asked of myself: "It is obviously a matter of which I have small conception."

The Hermaphrodite

As I looked from Emma's countenance, I saw that Wilhelm stood near, and glared on us with angry eyes. I went up to him, and offered him my hand.

"Come, Wilhelm, you cannot be angry that I have taken my revenge—I am at least glad that it is one which involves no injury to you"—"Why do you look so savagely upon me?" I continued. "I have entirely forgiven your foolish freak of last night."

"I shall never forgive you," muttered Wilhelm between his teeth.

I was ordered to wear my wreath through the evening. Music now sounded in the hall, and couples stood up to dance. I gave my arm to Emma, and led her to the head of the Quadrille. Her momentary sadness had passed away, and as she began to tread her graceful measure, she turned upon me a look of love and delight so radiant, that it sent a strange thrill to the very core of my frozen heart, and again I asked of myself: "what is it to be a woman?"

As we stood together in an interval of repose, I could not avoid overhearing the conversation of two strangers who occupied a place behind me, and of whom one spoke with a strongly marked Southern accent.

"What a beautiful antique head is this of the young Laureate's," remarked one, "so delicately chiselled, so finely set, one might say an Antinoüs, a Mercury, almost an Apollo."

"None of these," replied the Italian. "His beauty is of a more vague and undecided character—it is a face and form of strange contradictions—the eye and brow command, while the mouth persuades."

"The motions and gestures too are peculiar."

"Do you not see a striking resemblance to the lovely hermaphrodite in the villa Borghese?"

I heard no more—a mist came before my eyes, and a deadly faintness over my heart. With a hurried apology, I resigned Emma to the eager Wilhelm, and staggered to the open air—some minutes passed before I could recover strength to regain my room.

Chapter 4th

Once alone, in my own room, I could breathe more freely, but my whole being had received a shock, an impetus that hurried it to some deed, some resolution, I knew not what. A sort of galvanic agony had taken possession of my body, and forces foreign to itself were playing wildly with it. My vestments seemed to gird in my swelling heart, and I tore them off, half resolved to wear them no more. I was incapable of thought or of reason, but my brain was in a state of the highest spontaneous action, and a thousand horrible images of disgrace, despair, and utter confusion crowded each other in and out of my mind, like figures in a fever dream. Every thing around me seemed instinct with life—the very walls had eyes to spy out my secret, and tongues to betray it. I hurried hither and thither to escape the scrutiny of mocking spectres, who, all unseen, were yet present to me, and with hideous laughter followed me every where. At length, in very desperation, I threw myself, half undressed, on my bed, and drawing its covering around me, attempted to close my eyes, and compelled myself to lie still. Gradually, the confusion of my thoughts became greater, but less painful—the sounds of music and laughter became fainter in my ears, and soon ceased altogether. I know not how long it was before a light footstep at my bedside, told me that I must have been asleep.

A light footstep? oh how light! a gliding form, a gentle but fervent voice. Could it be? I rubbed my eyes, I was fully awake, and Emma, in all her brilliant beauty, stood before me.

"You were ill, dearest Laurence, and I could not rest until I had seen you—you are to leave tomorrow, and I could not live without one kind farewell from you. Oh Laurence, Laurence, do not look at me thus—you know well, you have long known what I am here to tell you."

I raised my head from the pillow and looked into her eyes. That look must have expressed the horror I felt, for it seemed to destroy the momentary courage which had given firmness to her step, and clearness to her voice. She sank upon her knees beside me, she buried her face in the curtain that hung near us, and was silent for a moment—then, raising it again, she clasped my knees, and spoke with a rapid, unequal, faltering intonation, as if she feared that her strength would desert her before she could speak out her meaning. "Listen to me Laurence," she said: "two deaths were before me. If I sought you not, I died of longing, if I came to you, I died of shame. The first I have long endured, it is slowly feeding upon my life—if the second fate must be mine, be merciful, and kill me quick." In stony silence, I sat and listened—she continued: "I do not ask you to marry me, Laurence,

I am still young, rich, and perhaps handsome, but I do not pretend to be worthy of you—had I such a hope, I should scarce be at your feet, but look you, I am here alone, in your room, in your power, at dead of night—you cannot misinterpret this, it must convince you that I love you better than life, better than honour, better than my own soul and God. Give me but this one night, but this one hour—do you ask where I shall be tomorrow? I can die tomorrow—I shall have been happy."

I roused myself at length from my stupor—"Emma," said I, laying on hers a hand so cold that she started. "Emma, as you value your soul's peace, fly—fly from me, and think of me only as you think of the dead."

"Never!" cried Emma: "you may smite me, you may kill me, but I will die here at your feet—my last look shall be on you—my last prayer shall bless you."

I pointed to the time piece on the mantel, and said: "Emma, this is madness—to yield to it would be fatal to both of us. One of us must leave this room for the night, I give you five minutes to decide which it shall be."

She sprang to her feet, and stood before me, a beautiful impersonation of scorn and fury. Lightnings flashed from her eyes—a curse rose to her lips and died there—those lips were made for blessings only—tears and convulsive sobs burst forth instead, and brokenly these words: "you cannot cannot—cannot!"

"Listen to me, dearest Emma," I said, and drew her to a seat beside me—"listen to me—can you bear to hear the truth? will you hate me for telling it to you?"

"Tell it gently," she replied, with averted eyes. I continued: "Emma, your love is too beautiful, too glorious a thing to be thrown away upon one who can never make you his. There lies between us a deep, mysterious gulf, seek not to fathom it—with me, your human destiny would be hopelessly imperfect—were I to wed you, I should indeed deserve your curse." She was silent, and I proceeded: "there are between human beings relations independent of sex, relations of pure spirit, of heavenly sympathy, of immaterial and undying affinities—such are the only relations that can exist between us, dearest Emma."

While I spoke, here eyes were suddenly turned upon mine with a look of almost superhuman intelligence. A new and dreadful suspicion seemed to dawn upon her mind. When I had ceased, she came slowly up to me, and

The Hermaphrodite

uncovering my arm, held it up to the light—it was round and smooth as her own. With the same deliberation, she surveyed me from head to foot, the disordered habiliments revealing to her every outline of the equivocal form before her. She saw the bearded lip and earnest brow, but she saw also the falling shoulders, slender neck, and rounded bosom—then with a look like that of the Medusa, and a hoarse utterance, she murmured: "monster!"

"I am as God made me, Emma."

A shriek, fearful to hear, and thrice fearful to give, followed by another, and another, and a maniac lay foaming and writhing on the floor at my feet.

§

Over the memory of that night, I would gladly draw the thickest veil of oblivion. Like Job, I could pray that its name might be blotted out from the fair annals of the year, that no evening star might smile upon its birth, and no morning star weep for its departure, that its dews might bring no blessing, and its shades no rest. Methought it was a night on which God had slept, and permitted the power of evil to possess even the fairest of his creatures, for her own destruction. Yet it was not so—behind the worst that had happened there lurked an unfathomable *worse* from which the barriers of heavenly love and watchfulness had separated us. Emma was doomed, marked for her grave, but it would be a spotless one, and we were both guiltless of any crime against ourselves and God.

But for the moment, I was incapable of consolation. The curse of my nature had fallen upon another more heavily than upon myself—the shattered being before me was at once a monument of my past, and an earnest of my future: and kneeling over her, I almost prayed God to smite me with her madness. She heard me not, saw me not—a wild and frenzied smile distorted her features, and her lips were parted in incoherent ravings, of which I could only distinguish these words: "like the hermaphrodite in the Villa Borghese," followed by a hideous laugh, after which she relapsed into broken and unintelligible mutterings. Almost as wild as herself, I struggled in vain to summon counsel for the exigency of the moment. The only idea that clearly presented itself to me was the necessity of restoring Emma at once, and unseen to the retirement of her own walls—there was but one way of effecting this—scarce knowing what I did, I raised her in my arms, and carried her down the staircase, and in the direction of her dwelling. My

The Hermaphrodite

strength, though doubled by the energy of desperation, was scarcely adequate to so great and long continued an effort; and as I staggered, nearly fainting, under the burthen, it was almost a relief to hear the approaching footsteps of a man. This feeling vanished, however, when I recognized the voice of Wilhelm who, in no very happy or friendly mood, was wandering about the precincts of the college.

"Whom have we here?" he cried, at the unusual sight of a man bearing an inanimate form in his arms.

"You had better not interrupt me," I said, endeavouring to pass him, but he had recognized my voice, and planted himself in my way. A straggling moonbeam broke at that moment through the thick shade of the avenue, and fell upon the changed and convulsed countenance of Emma. Alas! he had seen her, she was in his power.

"Laurent, in the name of God, what means this?"

"Wilhelm, if you are a man, help me to bear Emma to her own house— she is ill, she is delirious, and every thing depends upon her being immediately at home, and under proper care."

Wilhelm spoke not, but placed his arm with mine around the form of Emma—together, and in silence, we carried her to the home that she would leave no more. We summoned her domestics, and ordered them to seek the promptest medical aid. We laid her on her couch unconscious of the presence [of] others. I knelt beside her, I clasped her hand, my eyes silently implored from hers one look of recognition and of blessing, but in vain. I was aroused by Wilhelm, who laid his hand upon my shoulder and pointed to the door. The surgeon had arrived, our presence in that chamber of despair was worse than unnecessary, and Wilhelm was impatient to demand of me an explanation of my mysterious conduct and position.

When we were alone, and out of sight and of hearing, Wilhelm, who had forced me to walk at a pace as rapid and nervous as his own, drew his arm from mine, and abruptly said: "Now Laurent, you must account for this either to me, or to the world."

"I am ready," I said, and drew my rapier.

"That will not suffice," he replied: "There are some things known to me which the shedding of your blood or of mine will scarcely elucidate—how came Emma in your room tonight?"

"How dare you assume that she was there?"

The Hermaphrodite

"Liar!"—"Slanderer!" Such words are not often exchanged with impunity. "I will die in defence of Emma's honour," cried I. "You shall die to avenge it," shouted Wilhelm. Another moment, and we closed in mortal combat.

Wilhelm fought with the ferocity of a tiger, almost it seemed to me, with the strength of one. At first, I was quite overwhelmed by the fury of his attack, yet scarcely daunted by it for I felt that his very rashness and violence must, in the end, defeat themselves. I cannot say whether it was by greater coolness, quickness of eye, or agility of body that the struggle was decided in my favour—this only I remember, that Wilhelm lay before me, prostrate and disarmed while with the point of my weapon at his throat, I held him at my mercy. At this moment, I paused. The steel that had let out our blood had perchance let out with it some of our madness, but, be that as it may, I could not slay the man now that I held him, defenceless in my grasp. I looked earnestly in his face, it was not the face of a coward. Even in the presence of death, his cheek blanched not, his look quailed not, and in his desperate danger, he even strove to taunt me.

"Don't be afraid to kill me," said he, with a bitter laugh: "It is safest, dead men tell no tales."

I threw away my sword: "I am not afraid to let you live," was my only answer. Wilhelm arose, and stood in silent surprize.

"Ask any thing of me but thanks," he said at length. "You have made the boon of life too worthless to me that I should thank you for it."

"I have nothing to ask of you for myself, but Wilhelm, as I have spared you, so I pray you to spare one whose reputation is in your power, even as your life has been in mine."

"Curses on her! she has trifled with me, scorned me, ruined herself. Is there any earthly reason why I should spare her?"

"Because you have loved her, because she is dying, most of all, because she is innocent."

"Prove to me her innocence, and I swear to respect it," replied Wilhelm.

I was silent. I saw clearly that the fates demanded an expiatory sacrifice, but the victim appointed was neither Wilhelm nor Emma. It was my own pride, almost my own life that I was called upon to immolate in behalf of one who had not hesitated to give up every thing for me. I must myself endure that fearful crucifixion. I must tear off that innermost sacred veil that shielded from scorn and pity the secret of my fate, and wrap it around Emma's defenceless honour. I was silent, but only for a moment. Oh Truth! oh Emma! thank God, in that hour of trial, I loved you better than myself.

"Prove it—" repeated Wilhelm, in a defiant tone.

"I will do so," I replied, "but let me first tell you that the secret I am about to impart is not entrusted to you as a mark of confidence, you have deserved nothing of the kind from me. It is my desire to do justice to Emma alone that induces me to inform you of a fact, which, but for her unhappy position, would concern none but myself. Tell me now, Wilhelm, have I fought like a man?"

"Certainly."

"Have I treated you like a man?"

"I must say that you have."

"Have I, in all my college life maintained the integrity, the courage, the honour of a man?"

"Truly, I think so."

"Wilhelm, in all save these, I am none."

I did not repent me of my words, once spoken, but I felt that time, that eternity could never wring from me a confession more agonizing.

I turned me to depart, but I had not gone far, before Wilhelm came up to me, and laid his hand on my arm. He looked earnestly in my face, with an expression of doubt and wonder.

"You are no woman," said he, after a deliberate survey of my face and person.

"No," I replied, with a horrible sort of calmness: "I am no man, no woman, nothing. Let me go," and I pushed him from me, but he again seized me by both hands, and I saw in the cold moonlight that tears stood in his eyes.

"Laurence," he cried: "the sacrifice you have just made is heroic, and however lightly you may esteem me, I fully appreciate it—you have spared me, you have shielded Emma, and you cannot know that you have not ruined yourself. Hear me then while I swear, by the bloody agony of Christ, that the words you have spoken are, to all save me, as though they had never been uttered."

The Hermaphrodite

Wilhelm spoke in a tone of the deepest feeling, and as he did so, raised his right hand to heaven, so that his promise had all the solemnity of an oath.

"The vow is now registered in heaven," continued he, "and now tell me, what can I do to evince my gratitude for your forbearance, my appreciation of your noble conduct?"

I pointed, as nearly as I could, in the direction of Emma's dwelling—Wilhelm well understood the signal. "Remember her, and forget me," I said.

We parted sadly, but in perfect kindness.

Cold as duty, and stern as fate, the moon looked down upon me—and I was alone. *no such place*

Home! I might indeed have been wise enough to know that no such place existed for me. What hearth, what heart would welcome me as its cherished guest? The only breast that had ever harboured my love had been as fearfully punished for its fondness as though it had opened its doors to a fiend, in the form of an angel.

Dim and vague indeed were my impressions of the scenes and companions of my childhood; cold and repulsive my remembrance of those who had borne to me the relation but scarcely the love of parents. The mother that bore me was dead to me long, long before the day that bade me mourn her death. And my father? It was with reluctance that I gave him even the name. In many years I had not once seen him, or heard from him otherwise than through the medium of my tutor. He had indeed written to order that I should return to him immediately upon the close of the term, and had enclosed a sum of money amply sufficient for my expenses, but his letter was perfectly innocent of any hypocrisy of affection, and on reading it, I could not but acknowledge that he at least was entirely candid and constant in his indifference to his child. His parental tenderness, if any thing in his horny heart deserved the name, was doubtless monopolized by my younger brother, in whose person, but for my rights of primogeniture, would have been combined the succession of two princely estates.

Still, in my slowly weaned heart there dwelt the vision of a place where I had played in happy freedom, before I had borne the burthen of life, and learned how doubly heavy it was destined to be for me. There came

doubly heavy

to me images of trees that I had climbed, of waters that had held me in their sunny embrace, of grassy meadows on which I had laid me down to watch the gorgeous glory of sunset or the quiet beauty of a starry night. There lingered yet in my ear the echo of merry voices, and I thought that the laughing playmates who had so often caressed and tormented me still formed a rosy garland, of which I was the only blighted flower. The horrible event too which was still too fresh in my mind to be a memory, how did it chase me to some ark of safety, some spot sacred to kindest affections, to some heart whose sympathy should be spontaneous, whose love should be the involuntary tribute of nature. It was then with feelings of a mingled nature that I sought my father's house, yet in them hope predominated, and the very desperation of my condition, the sore need of my heart inspired me with a certain confidence in the ready succour and compassion of those nearest to me.

Once arrived, it needed little observation to dispel these consoling illusions. Cold and brief was my father's greeting, icy cold seemed the family circle that had been gathered to receive me. If the dinner that followed was not cold, it was at least utterly chilling and ungenial in its effects. The wine warmed no one, the food nourished no one—there were long pauses which nobody dared to interrupt, and brief remarks to which no one cared to reply. Paternus seemed to be the Evil Genius, the master magician of the feast, and one could have dreamed that the other figures around the table had been so many automata, animated only by his will. When he ate, the company ate, their very knives and forks keeping time with his. When he spoke, they listened and replied—when his voice ceased, they subsided into sympathetic silence. The dessert having been got through with, my health having been formally proposed and mechanically drunk, I wondered whether he would leave them rooted in their places until the next day, at the same hour; but he gave the signal of command, and they rose in concert, and marched like well drilled soldiers back to the drawing room.

I found my sisters changed past all remembrance, the world, matrimony and maternity having had full sway over them. The elder of them had married money, the younger had married love. Money was of course stupid and tedious, Love was a pretty man, but had probably seen his best days. Lady Money was cold and haughty, and iced me with a glittering smile. Lady

doubling

The Hermaphrodite

Love was shy and timid, yet she glanced kindly at me when Paternus was not looking. Their children were not introduced at dessert, kept away doubtless in the fear lest they might catch their death of cold of their grandfather.

After having endured for an hour or two this purgatorial entertainment, it was a relief to hear a bounding step in the entry, and to see on the opening of the door, the glowing countenance of a beautiful boy. This was my brother, Philip, whom I had never before seen. The grim visage of Paternus relaxed into a smile at his approach, and patting him on the head, bade him go and shake hands with his brother. The boy glanced around the room, and having singled me out from the company, ran up to me, threw his arms about my neck and gave me, after his childish fashion, the heartiest welcome. Having hugged me to the extent of his ability, he drew back and took a survey of my person. It seemed on the whole not to displease him.

§

"Is your name Laurence?" he asked. I nodded affirmatively.

"I thought so; my name is Philip, but they call me Phil. I have been wanting a brother for a long time, but I am afraid that you are too old to play with me."

"No indeed, I can shew you many fine games."

"Then you will be very kind—pray tell me what you have brought in that big trunk."

"We will go and see, Phil," and by a sort of joint diplomacy of the child's and of mine was effected a speedy escape from the forbidding presence in which, as no one seemed to be wanted, it was scarcely possible that any one should be missed.

"Somehow I have never much to say before papa," observed Phil confidentially, when we were once out of sight and of hearing. "He doesn't talk much himself and it seems to me that he does not like to have other people talk."

"Is he in one of his best moods tonight? I carelessly inquired.

"Verbs have moods," said master Phil, proud to show his newly acquired grammatical knowledge. "Father is a common noun."

"Thank heaven, an uncommon one. Is he as pleasant as usual tonight?"

"I don't think that he ever is pleasant."

"Well, is he in a good humour, or in a bad one?"

The Hermaphrodite

"Why, brother Laurence, there is little difference in him when he is in a good humour and when he is not that I never can tell how it is." Truly, a satisfactory answer.

But we were not to be so easily let off from the family penance. Phil was soon deep in the mysteries of my dressing case and busied himself in opening every box drawer and inquiring its use. I was gazing with a mournful pleasure upon his fair face, and as I drew him to me, and looked in his eyes, I said to myself: "Thou art indeed my own brother, my eyes and heart tell me so; but are we, can we be the children of that domestic iceberg?"

At this moment a summons came to us from the drawing room, where coffee and cards awaited us. Excusing myself from the latter, I entered into conversations with a young man, the chaplain of the family, and Phil's tutor. He seemed to me an amiable and genial person, and was anxious to be informed of my course of life and of study at the University. Thankful to pursue any subject which should lead me away from the unpleasant realities by which I was surrounded, I answered very fully all his questions, related anecdote after anecdote, and became so entirely emancipated from the yoke of the present that I was quite surprised at the end of the evening to find a knot of listeners gathered around us, and had been equally unconscious of the fact that Paternus, ensconced behind his evening gazette, had not lost a word of our conversation.

Welcome indeed was the nod of the master that released us all from further attendance upon us [sic] and dismissed us like a band of culprits, silent and ashamed, to the shelter of our bed chambers. I said to myself as I bade him good night: "I am glad that I do not love him—if habits of early intercourse had rendered him dear to me, I should feel a pang at every cold word and look of his."

I had been glad to leave the formal salon, but in the solitude of my own room, what fearful visions awaited me! The frantic ghost of Emma rose before me. I heard again the footstep that had roused me from my last dream of peace to my first real sorrow. I saw again the pleading look, the gesture of indignation, the tears of despair—again I heard, oh! I heard it all night long, the shriek of the agony which had rent asunder the mortal veil of that most beautiful temple. Now, with glowing countenance, with eyes

The Hermaphrodite

suffused, she told me of her love; now, rising in the might of her beauty, she spurned me from her foot like a crushed worm—now, her white arms sought to wind themselves about me, and now the lightning of her angry eye withered my very soul within me. And then I saw the strength of love, of courage, of anger, all give way beneath the weight of hopeless anguish, saw her totter, faint and fall, and the abyss of madness closed over her. Was it sleeping, was it waking? alas! it was one wild dream of wretchedness, a dream of many nights and days, and yet no dream.

Chapter [5]

The morrow brought a decisive interview with my father, and one that completely emancipated me from every filial relation towards him. Of him and of his words I wish to speak as briefly as possible, for many years and many thoughts have quite obliterated the painful impression then made upon me. Looking back from the varied experience, the wide range of thought through which life has led me, and viewing all things in the light of God's love, it seems to me a matter of infinitely small consequence that one who called himself my father was once cruel and unjust to me. He did not injure me, he had not the power to do so, but the evil intention in a father's heart—ah! it made an orphan of me at once and forever.

My father commenced the conversation by asking me if I had any preference in the choice of a profession. I told him that I had not thought of adopting one. He spoke of the church, of his influence among its dignitaries, of the livings within his gift. I looked at him in astonishment—what inducement did the priesthood offer to me, the heir of a noble estate? I briefly replied that I abhorred the clergy and would never willingly enter their ranks. My father adroitly turned the current of his remarks upon the subject of my college life, and questioned me concerning my standing in my class. In reply, I presented to him the medals I had received, accompanied by various written commendations of my scholarship and good conduct from my college instructors.

"I am satisfied that you have, on the whole, done much better than might have been expected."

"I have done my duty, sir, I hope that you did not expect anything less of me."

The Hermaphrodite

Paternus looked at me for a moment and then fixed his eyes upon the credentials I had shown him.

"You seem to have been a favourite with your tutors," he remarked.

"They have never complained of me."

"You have had a duel; what was the occasion of it?"

"I fought to defend the honour of a lady from an unjust imputation."

"Let me advise you to trouble yourself as little as need be about women, for the future."

"Your advice is quite needless, sir, I have never given myself any unnecessary trouble about them."

My father did not relish the sharpness and decision with which I spoke, and we entered into an altercation—not at all calculated to establish a good understanding between us. Paternus, nettled by some profession of independence on my part, threw off at length his diplomatic *équivoque* and appeared in his true colours.

"You stand there, and dictate terms to me, presuming yourself the heir to my fortunes and estates. You know not, young sir, that I have power to disinherit you, *if the inclination should not be wanting.*"

"You the power?"—"Yes, the power to strip you of name, fortune, and position, and to hold up your assumed manhood to the scorn of society."

"That is a point susceptible of some discussion. I shall take legal and medical advice upon the subject; but supposing that you possess the power, have you also the right?"

"You give me the right when you refuse me the respect due to a father."

"That can only be given in return for the kindness—the humanity due to a son."

My father's coup d'état had failed. He had hoped to astonish and overwhelm me, but he had not found me unarmed. I was better informed upon the subject than he imagined. I knew that difficulties, that impossibilities [lay] between him and the accomplishment of his wishes. He could not, he would not dare attempt to prove my incapacity to inherit his estate. There was danger and disgrace in the endeavour, and its result would be defeat. I told him so, I defied him, and in the bitterness of my heart, I laughed him to scorn.

Feeling the weakness of his position he endeavoured to fortify it by various statements. He told me that my mother had borne him many daughters

The Hermaphrodite

in succession. His estate was entailed upon the heir male. At the epoch of my birth he was attacked by sudden and dangerous illness, and death appeared to him doubly formidable from the thought that his cherished lands and title must pass from his own family to that of a distant relative. At this critical moment, my birth had been a welcome event.

"You were born imperfect," related Paternus. "It was difficult to determine your sex with precision, it was in fact impossible. No time was to be lost however, and the exigency of the case decided for us. Under the circumstances we deemed it most expedient to bestow on you the name and rights of a man."

"It was expedient only because it was right," said I, "but having once decided thus, what has induced you to contemplate a change of purpose?"

"The desire to assure the integrity of the succession," replied Paternus, after some hesitation. "You can never transmit it to a lawful heir, but having once been permitted to represent it, you may see fit to abuse the trust confided to you, and bestow upon the son of another the heritage of your brother Philip."

These words fully roused my indignation: "Can you then suppose me so vile?" I cried. Paternus smiled grimly.

"We must be prepared for such things—it is easy to know men better than they know themselves."

I was cruelly angered, I was cruelly wounded—my father had confounded me, not by his threats, not by his arguments, but by the display of his wickedness. Encouraged by my silence, he went on to propose a compromise.

"Were you, instead of Philip, a younger son, your yearly income would be (he named a sum fully equal to my wishes). The enjoyment of such an income, I shall be happy to secure to you, and will add to it the sum of ten thousand pounds from my private fortune, in consideration of a formal relinquishment on your part of the expectations in which you have been brought up."

Before I could reply, my father had left the room. I sat and mused in silence. The pang of those harsh words once over, my resolution was quickly taken. The succession so much dearer to my father's heart than his own child appeared to me a worthless bauble. Richly endowed and ancient as it was, it was in my eyes irrevocably degraded in his person. I had no ambition to represent him. The income he offered me was my right—it was shame enough that I should have to thank him for life, for aught else, I would never thank him. My reflections were interrupted by the reappearance of my father, who now returned, holding a paper in his hand.

"Here is the deed of the property I offer you," said he. "My terms are handsome, you will do well to accept them."

"From you, Sir, I will accept nothing. Let my brother Philip be summoned, and if he thinks fit, let the deed be made out in his name."

"Philip is a child!"—"Thank God, yes—he has the purity and the wisdom of a child."

Philip was sent for, and soon bounded into the room. There was a whole revelation in his manner as he eyed Paternus askance and nestled close at my side.

"Philip," said I, "your father wishes to have no son but you, and I am not going to be his son any longer."

The child looked at us both in wonder. I went on: "If you had been born before me, you would have been many times richer than I, you would have been called by a title, and the castle would have been your home; but now, as I happened to be born first, all these things are mine."

"I'm glad of it," cried Phil. "I'm very glad of it. I don't want anything except my pony, and Grandfather's sword, and the little lodge down by the lake."

"If I should die, there would be an end of my rights; you would be the rich and titled man, and there would be no one to stand in your way. Would you not be glad?"

"Brother Laurence, don't talk so!"

"Now Phil, I cannot die, but I am going away, and you will never see me here again. Your father wants to give all these fine things to you—I am willing. I leave them all to you, Phil, may you live long to enjoy them."

As the child looked upon my face, his beautiful countenance became pale as marble, and his dark eye grew eloquent with sadness, still, he spoke no word.

"Your father does not love me, and he has taught me not to love him. He wishes to give me money, to pay me for going away, for not being his son any more. I have told him that I would not take any thing from his hand.

The Hermaphrodite

I will receive it from you, if you are willing to give me something to live upon."

Paternus, black with rage, beckoned Philip to him, and bade him write his name in several places upon the deed. Pale and speechless, the child obeyed, and scarce understanding wherefore, brought the paper to me. A bag of gold stood on the table, Paternus pointed to it, and Phil lifted it with all his strength, and laid it at my feet. My father now produced the deed of renunciation, which was signed and duly witnessed.

"Dear Philip, go and tell the servant to carry my luggage to the inn; I will follow on foot."

The child had, thus far, obeyed in passive silence, but as he listened to these words, his face flushed painfully and tears gathered in his eyes. I repeated the order, but instead of leaving me, he sprang into my arms, and hung weeping and sobbing upon my neck.

"Laurence, dear Laurence, don't leave me here! Take me with you!"

The child's heart already pined for sympathy and affection—in all his ignorance of life, and of human nature, he knew that the father who preferred him above me and who had despoiled me of every right in his heart and fortune, to lavish all upon his more favoured child, was yet an unlovely and unloving being.

"Laurence, don't be afraid to stay here—papa shall love you, if he does not, I will not love him."

At this threat, so likely to be fulfilled, Paternus and I exchanged a look of dreadful intelligence. I felt that for the sake of Philip's future peace, the scene must end. I held the boy near to me, and spoke a few quiet words to him. I was cold and immoveable as marble, and the child was somehow awed into tranquillity and obedience. Sadly and reluctantly he kissed me, and slowly went to do my bidding. I had a few words to say to Paternus, and walking nearer to him, I looked him full in the face.

"Now Sir, understand me. I do not give up the succession because I love my brother. He is very dear to me, but I know that he will be none the happier for the rank and wealth I resign to him—these I lay down because I despise them, and still more because I scorn to derive them from you. I will not even thank you for a name. As you disown me, I disown you, but your feeling may change, may soften with time, not so mine. God shield my brother from all harm—God preserve him long to life and its best happiness. But

The Hermaphrodite

should any evil overtake him, should he die childless, and your old age be desolate, and your succession vacant, then never send for Laurence, then raise up an heir from the stones beneath your feet, for you will never find one in me—I swear—"

"Stop, stop, maniac!" cried Paternus arresting my words.

I left him without any other farewell than this. I hurried down the stairs, and out of the house. On the lawn I was met by the young tutor, who seized my arm, and attempted some expostulation. I broke from him. "Watch over Philip," I cried. "He has gained an inheritance, and lost a brother."

And farewell, and farewell, and farewell forever.

Chapter [6]

I had wished to travel by night as well as by day, partly to beguile the long hours of painful wakefulness, partly because my way led me through the scenes of my former peaceful life, and of the tragedy which so abruptly ended it. I dreaded to look upon those familiar spots in the daylight, and desired to avoid all encounters with my late associates. The weary day had sighed itself to rest, the twilight had deepened into the gloom of night before we reached the village. Post horses were ordered and instantly attached, but not quickly enough to satisfy my feverish impatience, and it was a relief to me when the postilion sprang into his saddle, cracked his whip, and gave his beasts the word of command. On past the Manor and its grounds—on, past the venerable college, and the shade of its rigid avenues—there was no light in the window of my old room, it needed none to make it painfully visible to me. I leaned back and closed my eyes to shut out the sight of things once lovely, but now harrowing to my soul. It was in vain—within my carriage, within my brain presided an attendant spirit that traced for me every landmark of my mournful way, and compelled me to measure with thought and remembrance, each step of my painful progress. Imagination grew worse than sight, the darkness of the carriage was frightful, its atmosphere oppressive to me—gasping for breath, I again leaned forward to the window that the real presence of objects might put to flight their monstrous phantoms.

Where was I? what was this? had I forgotten that pretty, fantastic mansion with its lovely shades and shrubberies? That window, who had stood

The Hermaphrodite

beside me there? that threshold, how had I last crossed it? On, on, good postilion we dare not think, dare not look, dare not stop to ask of any one the dénouement of that tale of horrour! Ah! such secrets soon make themselves known. The oracles of evil wait not to be inquired of and propitiated—they are glad and in haste to scream their dreadful tidings in our ears. On, on, let us not pause to listen lest the wail of death and the sound of endless malediction make themselves heard to us. On, on, I say!

"But I cannot, good Sir—a funeral procession bars the road." Do you not hear the De Profundis? do you not see a form arrayed in white, borne on its flower crowned bier to its bridal bed? On, on! no—stop, stay—undo the door—let me out! let me fall prostrate in the way! let the icy car of death pass over me too, and offer up an expiatory victim to the manes of the unwittingly betrayed, of the irrevocably lost. Here is a solemnity in which I have a part to play, here is the only matter in which I shall have any interest for many years to come. Let me down, let me down, and thank God if He will give me tears!

An hour later, and the dirge is hushed. The mourners have gone their way to sleep and to forget—the saddest of them shall arise tomorrow, glad that the dead is buried out of their sight, glad that the mystic being they love and dread has no longer any claim upon them, any fellowship with them. Can you blame them? God himself—is not a God of the dead.

Did I say that she was buried? not yet, thank God, not yet. She lies before the high altar—its consecrated torches lend a gentle, life giving light to her dead beauty. She lies here alone with God, and the faithful priest who watched her remains, who will ask no reward to pray for her sweet spirit. Yield thy place to me, holy man—thou cannot pray for her as I can, thou art not bound to her as I am. Dost thou ask where I shall be tomorrow? I may be mad tomorrow.

A desperate man knelt at Emma's feet, as Emma had knelt at his—tears, groans and prayers he offered up at that holy shrine—when these were exhausted, he was mute and listened to voices heard never before. It is long but blessed, a night that we pass with the dead we love, and the dawn that succeeds it may usher in a better day than that which follows upon a bridal feast. No lover in the arms of his mistress ever received consolation so divine as that which came to me from the lips of that silent one, that night. Promises of divine guidance, of angelic companionship, assurances

reversal

of immortal blessedness, and encouragements to a life of earnest striving and hope—all these were poured upon me as from a full urn, from the heart that had so loved me. Does any one doubt whether the souls of the dead have power to bless us? Let me tell such an one, solemnly and truly, that in my best hours, when the passionate music and the angry discords of life have been hushed and silent enough for the soul to hear other sounds than those of earth, then the holy dead, the living dead have walked with me, have spoken with me, and my heart and life have borne the record of their heavenly messages.

Let me say moreover that to these our periods of reception are appointed corresponding periods of reproduction. The sacred fire shall not merely afford us light and heat—it is like the genial warmth of Nature, quickening, fruitful, life-giving. The abstract truth revealed to us in our hour of agonizing prayer, of rapt meditation, grows into strength and courage in our day of trial and of action, and heavenly wisdom, the soul of our soul, becomes mortal and visible in heroic conflict in holy words and deeds, in patient labour, in calm endurance.

Thus did I pass the night. When the grey light of dawn warned me to recommence my journey, I arose and went on my way with gladness. I had laid down at Emma's feet the burthen of my humanity. I had taken up the heavier but more precious one of immortality. Upon her bosom I laid my poet's wreath—upon her lips I imprisoned the first, last kiss that woman and woman's love ever wrung from mine.

Chapter [7]

Come, earnest labour, earnest thought,
Life must fulfill, and not destroy;
A noble sorrow, nobly borne
Is better than a vulgar joy.

I wearied of my travels ere they were well begun. The unrest of the soul is fed, not subdued, by change of scene and of place. Go where I might, I sought always something that I could not find, and carried with me something that I could nowhere lay down. Cities, churches, palaces, the pride and show of the ancient world, spread themselves in vain before me. I wandered among them with listless gaze and languid movements, wondering only to find each new place so like the last, so unlike any thing that I wished or cared to see. It was a new thing to me, the utter despondency, this worm feeding at the heart and ever devouring, and never satisfied. I asked myself why I had never before known it—Nature had wronged me from my birth, my father's heart had repudiated me from my early childhood, how was it then that I had hitherto been happy? Ah! it was that I had been a child, and the kind Providence of childhood had surrounded me with its bulwarks of ignorance and innocence. Now, I had been loved, and the sweet dream was gone. I had been wronged, and the cruel sting remained. Was there aught that could fill the void of the one, or heal the wound of the other? I shook my head, shut back the proud tears in my heart, and went sullenly on my way, scarce knowing or caring whither.

I had left my father's house filled with a burning desire to win for myself no common fame. I longed to throw back in his teeth the odious slur upon my manhood, and to distinguish myself in the eye of the world as he and his had never done—then, when I had made myself illustrious, when my favour and influence were become great enough to be courted, then would I meet my father, and proudly say to him: "You are welcome to the name you took from me. I have made for myself a better one."

Not thus did I part from the ashes of that which had been all beauty, all delight. I was solemnized, chastened, subdued. Oh God! since I must live, I will live, since thou hast made life such as it is, I will bear it as well as I can—but if there be any good for me to accomplish in it, oh guide me to it, help me to it quickly, and let me die.

At length, I felt myself unable to proceed any further on my aimless journey—my body must have rest, my mind must have scope and leisure to work out the new and strange thoughts that came to it, unbidden. Oppressed with physical lassitude, I thought to take root like a tree in some quiet beautiful spot, and wait, and grow there quietly until fate should mark me to be cut down and the axe of death should accomplish my destiny. Coupled with my longing for repose was the craving for mental labour. I remembered that the tasks of my childhood, the studies of my riper years had borne me a perennial harvest of good, and of contentment. And yet all these were but child's play. Oh! there were mighty thoughts to think of these souls of ours, and the spiritual world which had given them birth. Let us have solitude and silence to deal with these vast themes. I am weary of

The Hermaphrodite

conning the deeds of man, I would fain fathom the thoughts and intuitions of God.

It was not long before I found the very spot I sought. Having stopped one day at a village inn to repair some damage sustained by my travelling carriage, I was tempted by the beauty of the surrounding country to leave the dingy atmosphere of the Gasthof, and stroll forth to the green shades that lay beyond the town. I did not long continue to hold the fair landscape in my eye. That introversion of thought which is called absence of mind had grown so habitual to me, that I wandered in this lovely place even as in a desert waste, or crowded street, glad only of the cool air, the loneliness, and the silence that permitted me to hold undisturbed converse with myself. I had followed a narrow side path that led me into the recesses of the wood, and ere I was well aware, I had wound myself deep into its gentle secrets. The little path still hurried me on, now dodging behind the trees, now showing itself again, like a shy but friendly fairy, till having conducted me to a little wilderness of shade, it made an awkward bow and left me. Here was shade so deep that the sun scarcely pierced it, and I reluctantly abandoned the idea of proceeding further, lest I should quite lose myself in the leafy labyrinth. I was about to retrace my footsteps when I caught a glimpse of something like a stone wall, beyond the thick screen of underwood. With some little trouble, I forced myself a way between brambles, bushes, and low hanging boughs and soon emerged into an open space in the midst of which stood the object that had attracted my attention. This was a low and ancient structure of unhewn stone, overgrown with mosses and ivy. It stood in the centre of the little lawn, a neglected garden was on one side of it, on the other a spring of pure water flowed into a venerable stone basin. It appeared to me the very beau-idéal of a hermitage, and before I had crossed the threshold, I longed to take possession of it. The main entrance to the building was open to wind and weather, but it led only to a ruinous gallery on the left. On the right my progress was impeded by a solid oaken door, which resisted all my efforts to force it open. Nothing remained for me but to find my way back as well as I might to the little path, and then to the high road, and then to the village inn, where I straitway began to question the host concerning the history of the Lodge in the Wilderness. I learned from him that it had been for many, many years the property of a noble family holding large possessions in the neighbourhood. The right

The Hermaphrodite

wing of the building had been fitted up and occupied from time to time by the late Count ———, an eccentric representative of the family, who had died unmarried, bequeathing his large estates to his nephew. The Count had been, said the Host, a man of wondrous learning, but much study had made him mad. He had distinguished himself in public life, but often retired hither from the cares and tumult of the great world, to enjoy the silent companionship of books. He had done so too often for his own good, the host mused, and quoted the authority of the village priest, to the effect that the noble Count would have enjoyed a longer life, and would have made a more edifying death, if he had married a wife, gone to mass, and settled the affairs of his soul with a jolly confessor over a flask of Rhenish, instead of choosing to settle them alone with the devil as (he opined) had been the case. It had even been thought by some that the Count did not rest quietly in his grave—here the narrator doubly crossed himself, and waited for a word of encouragement to pour forth a flood of ghost stories bottled up to suit the demands of his customers. I carefully refrained however from drawing the cork, and proceeded to inquire for some one who should be able to unlock for me the oaken door, and let me into the secrets of the solitary abode. The present Incumbent had long been travelling in foreign parts, they told me; and had rarely if ever visited the spot in question. His agent was easily found, and persuaded to accompany me thither, and having provided ourselves with the key, we set forth together for the wood, whose outskirts by this time were softly tinged with the golden light of sunset.

We were soon there, and my sudden conceived passion for the little spot returned with renewed force, as I saw it in the lovely summer twilight. The door once opened, we passed into an apartment of moderate size, but of beautiful proportions, fitted up as a study. The pointed windows, curiously carved woodwork, and ancient furniture of the room were all in perfect keeping with each other. The walls were adorned with well filled bookshelves, a massive writing table occupied the centre, and a few heavy chairs of the most antique fashion completed the appointments of the room. Beyond it lay a small bed chamber, scantily, almost meanly furnished, and from the further door of this, a narrow corridor led to a chapel of small extension, finished in the old Gothic style.

This chapel bore the only traces of luxe to be found in the whole anchoritic establishment. Its floor was paved with precious marbles, and its screen was richly and wondrously carved. Behind the altar, a window of magnificent stained glass shed throughout the place a truly magical light; but the altar itself was scarcely such as one might have expected to see there. It was simply hewn of pure white marble, and upon it stood only a marble cross. No portraits of saints, no luxury of religious symbols appeared on the walls, but that upon the left of the altar supported a strange monumental conceit. This was a sculptured bas-relief, describing the head and bust of a female figure. The forms of the neck and shoulders were delicately chiselled, and the graceful hands were tenderly clasped upon the rounded bosom; but a strange caprice of art concealed the features that should [have] given the charm of soul to such perfect physical beauty. The sculptor, and his patron, had kept their secret—a marble veil covered the face, as hopeless as the grave. Beneath it was simply inscribed the name: Angela.

My companion was a man of some understanding and had seen something of the world beyond the bounds of his native village—he seemed anxious to show himself superior to vulgar prejudice and superstition. "You know, Sir," said he, "the follies of these poor rustics who have had neither experience nor education—this appears in nothing more than in their judgements of those above them. The Count was one who dwelt much alone, ergo, he was mad. He followed his own ideas in matters of religion, ergo, he was a skeptic and an infidel. He studied late into the night and his light always appeared at midnight in the chapel, ergo, he was in the habit of practicing unlawful arts, and had evil spirits for his familiars. I remember him only as a boy remembers one greatly his superior in years and in rank, but the image I have of him in my mind is so noble and so stately that I should grieve to lose it."

"Did you ever speak with him?"

"He has often spoken with me. My father was his agent and I have brought many a message to him here. I found him sometimes at his books, sometimes walking in the garden. His face was often pale and haggard, and his eye looked sometimes bloodshot and sleepless, but he always greeted me kindly."

Further conversation shewed that the Count had been an earnest and thoughtful man, grave and at times devout. Yet had he led a varied life, and

The Hermaphrodite

had done the state good service with sword and with pen. He had been familiar alike with court and camp and in his ancestral castle was wont to exercise a generous hospitality. By a scrupulous and exact division of his time and his duties, he had accomplished much in many ways. A part of every year he devoted to his Sovereign—part to society, a part to travel, and a part to prayer, solitude, and abstinence. In this little retreat, he kept his yearly Ramadan. Flying alike from luxury and from worldly labour, he found here a welcome refuge, green, cool, and melodious with the songs of many birds. During his annual visit to this sacred spot, he had ever lived in entire seclusion, and with the most ascetic simplicity. The garden and the spring supplied his frugal meals, his own hands administered to his necessities, and he slept upon a bed to the hardness of which my aching limbs were able, after one night, to testify. A cursory glance at the bookshelves confirmed the statement that this had been a place specially devoted to religious study and devout contemplation. I saw there no maps or charts, no books of history, political economy or romance. The library was a collection of tracts and treatises, metaphysical and theological, of all ages and in all languages.

Platonics and Mystics of the ancient time were there, and the early Christian fathers. The chroniclers and expounders of the Roman church had their niche, but near to them in flagrant contradiction were the works of the sturdy Reformers, who had been to them Anathema Maranatha—these, in their turn were forced to submit to a close juxtaposition with the doubting, questioning speculations of the modern Teutonic theologues. The Revelations of Jacob Boehme, and the visions of Swedenborg seemed to be as much at home here as Papist, Calvinist, or inspired Heathen. It was quite impossible to gather from the Count's choice of books any satisfactory idea of his creed—one thing only was evident therein, and this was the fact that upon the mysterious questions of the soul's relations with God, he had studied and thought for himself. It was strange enough to behold assembled here such a Congress of all Saints, and as I mused upon their mutual differences, and excommunications, I imagined that the Count had spoken thus with himself:

"God hath sent them all into the world, why should I not receive them into my library? He hath seen them in his garden as so many various seeds of good and wisdom, why should I not gather the harvest they have borne? All of them that was not peace and love is dead, and the truth which they have illustrated and which still survives is one on earth as it is one in heaven."

Methought too that these silent Saints had each a voice, and that each spake to me, and all invited me to come and dwell there, and be acquainted with them, and all promised me that I should find peace and comfort in so doing. The mystic said: "I will teach thee how to believe—" the reformer said: "I will teach thee how to reason—" the sublime heathen and the Godlike Nazarene said: "I will teach thee to suffer, to love, and to forgive." And I replied to each and all of them: "I will come."

Towards the little chapel too, my heart felt a peculiar yearning. The white altar and the white cross that consecrated it were to me the emblems of a pure and simple faith, while the mysterious entablature on the wall appeared to me a monument of expiation. Was Angela a victim, and had the Count wept and mourned and agonized, even as others?

I was aroused from my reverie by the voice of the Intendant, who warned me that it was growing late, and suggested that as there would be no moon, it would be wisest for us to make our way through the forest before night should be further advanced.

In reply, I communicated to him my desire of fixing my residence there for a time, and inquired of him the terms upon which I might hire the hermitage, for my own use and occupation.

"The hermitage cannot be hired," answered my friend, "but it is free to any one who will comply with the Count's terms as recorded on the wall before you."

As he spoke, he directed my attention to a wooden tablet fastened upon the wall. I looked, and read an inscription in Latin verse, which I have rendered thus:

> "Who would inhabit this cell of mine,
> "He must eat no flesh, he must drink no wine.
> "No goodly garment his state shall shew,
> "No steel his locks and his beard shall know.
> "No menial here his hest shall wait,
> "In his stall no steed, in his bed no mate.
> "In holy study his days must pass,
> "At the noon of night, he shall say his mass.

conditions

The Hermaphrodite

"To gold and blood he must bid farewell.

"Who liveth thus may keep my cell.

"In body and soul shall good betide him,

"And the angel of peace shall watch beside him."

"And is this intention carried out in the Count's will?"

"It is."

"I joyfully accept the terms, but how shall I first procure for myself the simplest food in this place?"

"Bread and pulse can be daily supplied you from the village. When you shall feel that you require more generous diet, it will be time for you to return to the world."

"Let me then enter into possession this very night," I said. "You can easily send my baggage from the Inn, with a provision of bread, a lamp, and some oil. I think that the dead branches in the wood will supply me with material for a fire."

The good Bourgeois expressed some surprize at my determination. Finding me inclined to persist in it, he kindly aided me to gather some branches, and to kindle a blaze on the long vacant hearth. Having thus imparted an air of some comfort to the somber apartment, and recommending me not to expose myself heedlessly to the damp night air, he took his leave. When he had left me, I drew my chair near to the hearth, and sat watching the fire, until its bright flame died away. As I looked listlessly into its embers, I reasoned thus with Life.

Oh Life, lie thou behind me for a time! terrible angel of Life, restrain thy fleet footsteps, do not overtake and destroy me in my hour of weakness. I am no coward, but I fly and fear thee. At our first encounter, thou hast disarmed and cruelly wounded me, thou hast stripped me of that thou canst not restore. When my unripe manhood shall have put on maturity—when the rainbow robes of Hope, of which thou hast despoiled me, shall have been replaced by the armour of faith and of conscience, then the voice that now bids me kneel and pray, will command me to go forth and meet thee. But now Childhood is gone, and Youth and Love have slain each other, and I am here to weep for them, and to wait for the spirit of consolation. Wherefore spare me, I pray thee, that I may recover my strength before I go hence."

The Hermaphrodite

I am to thee as one that's dead,
And thou art as the dead to me;
Yet twixt thy sometime love and mine
Methinks, strange difference must there be.

For thine is dust to dust returned,
Corruption, buried out of sight;
A *mortal* feeling, born to die,
And dead, to be forgotten quite.

But mine's the disembodied soul
To heav'n, that gave it life, returned;
It gleams for me a star on high,
That once, on earth, a torch light burned.

And in my bosom garnered up,
Its gentle ashes gently rest,
While its pure essence dwells with God,
And waits for death to make me blest.

Chapter [8]

The death of those we love often imparts a strong impulse to our spiritual nature. It is long ere we can believe in the permanence of such rude dis-severance between ourselves and them. They still live, but where, but how? Are we wholly parted from them, are they forever lost to us? For a time, faith and imagination are quickened by our suffering to the development of powers unsuspected before. Weak and defenceless as we are in the grasp of sorrow, we find to our surprise that we have courage to question the secrets of eternity, and to ask of Him who has made us immortal that our love shall be deathless as our souls. Anxiously and earnestly do we strive to follow their unseen flight through regions imagined, and blessings fondly invoked by us, until that ancient solemn voice from the olden time enters into our hearts: "he shall not return to me, but I shall go to him," and we come back to life, saddened but satisfied.

Even thus did sorrow lead me from the world. Turning away in very heartsickness from the aims and pursuits of actual life, and shrinking painfully from the lonely and desolate future, I tried to fathom the problems of the world that lies beyond our sight, and to anticipate its revelations. Methought I held there an invaluable treasure, the inalienable sympathy of a devoted heart. Methought I had there an object of unceasing, of boundless interest, the destiny and happiness of her who had laid down her beautiful life, a willing sacrifice, at my feet. Thus she who would have led me into the inner sanctuary of earthly love, still held me in her power. Death had not relaxed, had but more firmly locked her hold upon me; and as the priestess of mysteries yet more divine, and as the Genius of love that could not die, she grew to me an object of mystic reverence and wonder, devoutly shrined in my inmost soul—revered and worshipped, perhaps, all the more for being no longer seen, for having never been possessed. Yet, as study succeeded to vague imagining, and reflection to emotion, my ideas of another life gradually lost somewhat of their personality. Truth soon became to me greater than hope or happiness, and in the pursuit of it I lost much of myself that I never found again.

[It is a matter of no small interest to watch the origin and progress of religious faith in a world,] a nation, or an individual—the conception of the mighty idea of immortality in the narrow breast of man—the pigmy, un-equal to the subjugation of his toy-world, and yet claiming a share in infinite capacities, and endless existence—the child, trembling in the power of the elements and yet raising his rod of compulsion to draw down, harmlessly to himself, the fire of heaven. It is a history of various orphans, in which blind reverence and daring or sorrowing doubt succeed each other, till from the ruins of these is reared the structure of an earnest and reasonable belief, which neither doubt nor fear can destroy. Nor can this be easily obtained, without a severe struggle against our own cowardice, and against the despotism of other minds. The time for this struggle comes to all when belief is thoughtful, as well as sincere, but few meet it bravely—the most shrink terrified away, and after one look at the enemy, are well content to leave the field uncontested. Spiritual cowardice has ever been the virtue most extolled by the church. But what then? Shall Conscience be afraid, and Reason ashamed? Shall we dare to derive our creed from the teachings of one like ourselves? Shall we be satisfied to perceive the highest truth through the cloudy medium of other men's superstitions and prejudices? Ah! no one of the great processes of life can be performed by proxy. That soul only is alive in God which has had its own revelation from Him, upon which He has graven in the characters of its own experience, the law of Fear, the gospel of Love, the Apocalypse of infinite Hope that were appointed to it.

Such a revelation I sought in all my readings, in all my musings, in all my efforts of mind and of soul; for my studies were all thoughts, and my thoughts were all prayers, and my prayers, at first dim, chaotic, unutterable, gradually took to themselves form and distinctiveness and breathed themselves in such words as these:

> "Oh God! grant me a new baptism,
> The baptism of the new Jesus, of the living Jesus,
>> Of the victor, not the victim.
> Shew me the human rising to the divine,
>> Not the divine vanquished, destroyed in becoming human."

It is not my purpose to dwell in detail upon all that I learned, enjoyed and suffered during the period I am attempting to describe—neither can I give a definite idea of its length. It is marked in my remembrance by states, rather than by days; and its light and darkness were other than that of the evening and of the morning. A few words suffice for its history, because it is one for which we possess few words. It is not always easy to find fitting expression for matters which are open to the experience and comprehension of all men, but for those truths which then tasked my weak powers to the utmost, I feel that thought is inadequate to think them, and speech to utter them. The eternity which will make these Divine ideas clear to us, will give us also a Divine language in which to clothe them.

Though I can neither comprehend nor explain the unseen influences to which I was, at this time, subjected, yet I can never disown or disclaim them. The whole state of painful blessedness has since then become as a dream to me, and I have by turns doubted the infallibility of many of the propositions which then seemed to be announced to me by such superhuman authority, while yet my whole life has been insensibly molded by them. Like all else to which man can attain, my religion was imperfect in theory, wild and exaggerated in practice. The temple of thoughts, deeds and aspirations which I raised to the unknown God was utterly defective, unsound, and tottering as a child's palace of cards, but the God has been there, and has overthrown the altar only that I might worship at a holier one.

The charge of inconsistency is ever brought alike by the bigots of the world and of the church against those in whose lives the religious idea has shewn itself under various and contradictory phases. "Fie upon you!" they exclaim: "You once thought and acted thus and thus, you were the pillar of such a congregation and a polished corner in the sanctuary of the Reverend Father Bosh!" Ah! my friend, my ideas of divine architecture differ from yours. I cannot think that living temples are well supported by *dead* columns. Remember that in the days of ancient rites, the sacrifice was consumed by fire, in token that God constantly desires from us new sacrifices of new thoughts, new capacities, new views; whereas thou keepest thine offering hermetically sealed up, like a saint's relic, and takest it out to shew how well it is preserved and straightway puttest it back into thy bosom again. Think too a moment whether in the mighty and endless progress of His laws and of His Providence, it can be altogether agreeable to His intentions that thou shouldst stand immoveable for a score of years or so, blocking up the way and insisting that all who would pass beyond the ground thou occupiest shall stumble over thee. The very globe on which thou dwellest was not, by any sudden conversion admitted into the church of the heavens. Its growth in grace was very slow and moreover very changeful and revolutionary. For ages ere thou wert thought of, it was the unshapely habitation of unshapely creatures, and experience is unable to declare how many eternities elapsed ere from its chaos of organic and inorganic life were evolved the divine ideas of Earth and Man. Thou thyself in thy most brilliant sainthood art but a very imperfect sketch or botch of what thy race should be—It remains to be seen whether all the teachings, shewings, and scourgings of life will prove sufficient to make a man of thee.

Not thus did I reason in those days. My mind was too fully occupied with the first conviction which had taken possession of it to be very receptive of new ones. I had read largely and eagerly of the New Testament, and among all its rules of life, had instinctively seized upon those of its precepts inculcating prayer, fasting, and the mortification of the flesh. In my zeal for the entire subjugation of the body, I studiously neglected every necessity of physical life, while in fancied imitation of the vigils of Christ and his apostles, I carried almost to insanity my pursuit of divine guidance and communication. Having once fully adopted the conviction that the commands of God must be obeyed to the utmost, my fevered imagination took its own license in determining the extent and bearing of those commands, and the wildest promptings of my overwrought brain were often received and obeyed by me as the dictates of one too holy and too mighty to be disobeyed. These tendencies were all stimulated to an incredible degree by my unnatural mode of life.

From the day of my entering the deserted hermitage, I had never walked an hundred paces beyond its walls. Its shade and stillness were become utterly necessary to me, and my whole being had contracted a sort of harmony with the sombre monotony of its interior. My only changes of place and of scene were from the study to the chapel, and from this in turn to the little garden, whose bounds were become a sort of charmed circle between the living world and me. My habits of diet, always simple, were grown austere. Of food and of fire, I allowed myself only so much as was strictly necessary to support life. Of my appearance, I had grown utterly forgetful—convenience had guided me to the assumption of a long, loose garment, while my neglected hair had quite outgrown all bounds, and rolled about my shoulders its long golden waves. The curse of my existence, the cruel injustice of nature had for the time quite faded from my remembrance—my body was become a matter of such small consequence to me, that I cared little after what manner it was made; only when by chance one day I saw my face in the mirror, I was glad to observe in it a diaphanous, mortified look which seemed to assure me that the spirit was now lord absolute, and that the flesh had at last learned its place, and would keep it. If common sense sometimes ventured to expostulate with me upon my disobedience to the laws of physical well being, I reasoned with it after this fashion.

God hath appointed that trees should grow and flourish, that animals should wax fat, and increase—their existence and its ends are alike material and finite, but it were shame that the soul of man should be satisfied with pleasures and destinies like theirs. To him also it is allowed to choose whether he will be a simply sentient and material creature, or the brief embodiment of a spiritual essence. Shall the Godlike look toward the dust, or towards heaven? Shall it crumble and decay, like the plant, or shall it soar upwards like the golden angel of the chrysalis? What obligation binds me to languish in patient subjection to the gross laws of animal being? This

The Hermaphrodite

blood which should glow with high and ethereal electricity, why should it be degraded to meaner offices, and checked in its upward course to aid in the assimilation of superfluous food? This feeble stomach, why should it command the brain whose thrall and servant it was born to be? This brain, why should it heavily adapt itself to the lower impulses and necessities of life when it may be developed and perfected into a tool fit for the noblest uses of God himself? Colour is pleasant to the eye, and music to the ear, but why should they distract my thoughts from the pursuit of that supreme truth of which they are but the outer husk and shell? Let me have no sights, no sounds, no soft bed to tempt me to repose, no fire to awaken the physical pleasure of warmth. I am choked with the solid, asphyxiating gases of your materiality—give me the pure atmosphere of the upper regions—let me once breathe the air of sublimated spirituality, even though that breath should forever dissolve the link that binds me to the visible and tangible. I have been long enough buried with the dead forms of things. I am now in frantic pursuit of the soul of the Universe. My course leads me ever upward and onward, past all the warning outposts of this poor, feeble, hysterical nurse of ours, called Nature—she was good in her way, but I demand to be released from her jurisdiction. I will no longer suffer her mediation between the God of my love, and my love for Him.

religion/ God as an answer

. Nature's

'And thus might common sense have replied.

"Stop, my friend—not quite so fast, if you please. Whither are you bound, do you know whither? Remember that the father's house has many mansions, and this is one to which you are not bidden. Providence has marked out paths in the upper air for the summer and winter flight of birds, which are hardly intended for your guidance and accommodation. Your way led you across a mountain—having reached the summit, will you cast yourself from it into the unfathomed abyss of nothingness, or will you quietly descend the other side of the hill and journey along until you shall come to another? Take heed lest, having been urged beyond all right and reason, your poor wits may not take leave of you like post horses breaking from a carriage, leaving the poor traveller to lumber along with his heavy luggage, as best he may. Clearly, it is God's will that you carry this poor mortality with you as far as you are able. Your mother Nature is not to be turned off with a pension. Dutifully and with filial piety must you provide for her wants and pleasures, nor desert her until she shall be gathered to the things that were. Otherwise, when you deem her slain, she may rise up against you with horrible energy, and avenge to the death the wrong you have done her."

Chapter [9]

The boy was very beautiful,
Very beautiful to see;
And in his eye a deep light shone,
And in his voice there thrilled a love
That fastened like a spell on me.

After those days there fell upon me a sort of trance, and for a time I had no more thought or perceptions like to those of other men. Whether I was awake or sleeping, I know not, but while my body was unconscious and incapable of motion, my mind seemed to penetrate with rapid progress into regions unknown before. It was to me as though I were approaching the end of a long journey; and fleeting glimpses of light and beauty announced to me the proximity of another world than this. The silence of my cell became harmonious to my ear and from every side voices of wondrous sweetness spake to me words of comfort and of encouragement. The gentle ministration of spirits was vouchsafed to me, and I thought that a shining band of them had gathered closely around me, admitting me into their fellowship and tendering me their guidance and protection. Methought that they were leading me with soft music to the very threshold of heaven, and that its golden portals would soon unclose, and receive me into the light of divine love. Already it was given to me to understand their language, and to share their ethereal emotions. They repeated to me in ever varying tones the words of Christ, and though they spake them again and again, the modulation of their voices was so changeful and melodious that it seemed to me like a rainbow of sound. Full of hope and of confidence, I advanced with them to what seemed the entrance of heaven, and my heart thrilled with joy, for I looked to be admitted in their company. But even while I waited, they were gone, they had passed through, and the gate had not opened to receive me. And lo, in place of those bright ones, there stood at the gate a dark and frowning angel, bearing a flaming sword whereon was written *madness*. He waved it over me, and I shrank away in terror, he smote

The Hermaphrodite

me with it, and I fell on my knees and cried to God for help, but all around me was darkness thronged with horrible shapes while my ears rang with the discord of dreadful sounds.

In my agony, I bethought me of Christ. I called upon his name, and to it grew light once more, and a gentle form stood before me. With one hand he motioned back the angel saying: "spare him for my sake—" with the other he touched me, and said very graciously, "child, come hither no more till I call thee"—then, it became as though I slept.

49

Again, I dreamed in my frozen sleep. I thought that I stood alone, suspended between the elements. Above were the heavens, gorgeous as in the glory of sunset; beneath, and parted from me by the frailest bark, were the waters, wildly beautiful. But my eyes rested not upon them, for a mighty volume was spread open upon the clouds above me, and I read therein as it were the words of truth, illustrated by the visions of faith. My thoughts were rivetted upon the page, and I wished that I might read and read forever, so great was the delight of the wondrous and beautiful things that were written thereon. But even while I looked upon them, the book was gently closed before my eyes, and it was as though an angel received it up into heaven, for it was veiled from me not in darkness, but in light, which my sight could not endure. And as I stood in sorrow and in wonder, a voice spake to me from out the cloud, and said a little child shall lead thee. I looked down, and a beautiful child arose from the deep—its garments were dripping with colours, and the water that it shook from its locks glistened like golden rain. It took me by the hand and led me, even as Christ led Peter on the water. The waves changed to dry land and the ground grew form beneath my feet, and mine eyes beheld once more the beauty of the earth, as it is when the trees and shrubs are bearing their fullest and fairest.

I awoke, but I could hardly believe myself awake. I was lying before the cross, upon the cold pavement of the chapel, but my head was supported by one who had raised it from the marble floor, while a sudden thrill of terror made me aware of the presence of a pair of stranger eyes, that looked intently into mine. Incapable of speech or motion, I silently returned their gaze until their gentleness had subdued my fear, and their beauty had sunk into my soul. That first look was not the last, but had it been, it would have contained in itself the germ of something not to be forgotten.

The Hermaphrodite

The eyes in question belonged to one whose sex disclosed itself in a form of perfect beauty. It was of youthful proportions, but its lightness and grace gave the promise of manly strength, even as the ingenuous features gave their earnest of steadfastness and truth of soul. The white forehead so serene and unmarked seemed to defy life to put any save her noblest stamp upon it. The hair was of dark hue and strong growth, and the mouth, crowned with its nascent line of black, seemed as yet to have drunk only at the cup of innocent enjoyment—but the eyes of deepest, mournfullest blue were the glory of the face. Oh! if truth, if love, if soul have a colour, it can be none other than the blue of those mysterious eyes.

The boy (he could scarce have outnumbered sixteen summers) still watched in my countenance the fluctuations of returning life—he held my frozen hands in his, and warmed and chafed them until I had recovered strength enough to withdraw them from his hold—this done, I made a feeble effort to raise my head from his knees, and aided by him, sat upright on the ground, looking at him and at all things as through a mist.

At length returned to me the power of speech, but scarcely that of thought. My brain still wavered between its symbolic visions and the sights and sounds of earth, and my first words were:

"Art thou human?"

"If you could see yourself," replied the boy, "you would think that I might far better ask the question of you."

"I found you here," he continued, "quite alone, stretched on the floor, stiff and cold as the marble itself. At first I was terrified, and would have called for help, for I thought you dead. I looked in your face, and could not leave you. I felt of your heart and found that it had still a little motion; then I knelt down by you, and tried to recall you to life."

"I wished to die when I lay down here, yet I thank you."

"But come, you must not remain any longer in this icy vault, let me lead you into the outer room—the fire there has died out from the hearth long ago, but I can try to kindle it again." And leaning on him, I left the haunted chapel for the study. My guide gathered upon the hearth some fragments of decayed pine, and struck a light from his flint and steel, but I impatiently interrupted his labours.

"Not here, not here!" I cried, for the air of the place was grown baneful to me, and I longed to escape from it as from a tomb; "not here—nothing

The Hermaphrodite

can live, or breathe, or burn in this dwelling. Do you not see that the quiet which prevails here is the repose of death? Do you not see that I have been living with the dead until I am almost become one of them? Let me go forth into the living world once more—let me hear once more the voices of living men."

"Come home with me then—my father will gladly receive you as his guest, and all our household will wait upon you—come with me, Madam."

"Madam?" cried I, starting back, "do you take me for a woman?"

The boy replied not, but led me to a mirror that hung upon the wall. I was terrified at my own appearance. It was not the long hair, nor the deathlike countenance, nor the wild, haggard eyes that startled me, it was that in my long robe de chambre, and with the wild profusion of my locks, I looked a woman.

I turned to him and spoke. "I am weak as a child, and as you have well said, I look like nothing human, but I swear to you that I am no woman—can you help me to cut off my hair?"

"Do not, do not cut it off!" exclaimed the boy, "it is the most beautiful hair that I ever saw. I can aid you in concealing it, but I will not suffer you to cut it off."

Half pleased, half vexed, I allowed him to gather my hair in a sort of knot, and to conceal it beneath the collar of my robe de chambre. He next bethought him of my clothes, and charged himself with the valise which contained my sometime wardrobe. Thus equipped, we set forth together, at the quickest pace compatible with my state of weakness. Phantom voices seemed to ring around me as I crossed the threshold, and the clang of the ponderous door as it closed upon us had for me something supernatural in it. I breathed more freely when we had passed the outer enclosure, and clung to my young guide, feeling that he had rescued me from deadly peril.

How changed was the world without! how little had I heeded or recked of the change! The green leaves of summer had changed, and withered, had fallen and been swept away, the diamond snow fruit hung in their place. Like to a festal carpet, the green covering of the lawn had been drawn away, and in its place appeared the icy pavement of winter. As I looked mournfully upon the frozen earth, there struck me a thought more sharp and bitter than the frost itself.

The Hermaphrodite

This was the first snow that had fallen upon Emma's grave. But I smiled as the dreadful remembrance smote me. I made it welcome to my heart— horrors were at home there. The boy saw the smile, and shuddered. "If you look so, you will make me mad," he said.

"Pardon me; I will do so no more."

As I walked on, I trembled before the physical discomfort of life, even as I had once shrunk from its spiritual burthens. The keen air that called up the blood to the fresh cheek beside mine, struck to my heart the deadliest chill. His elastic step scarce broke the crust of the snow, while my heavy feet sank continually below the glittering surface, and soon grew wet and benumbed. Fitfully there came to us a cold wind from the North, that visited every part of my feeble body, like a cunning champion whose lance seeks every where to pierce the weak joints of his adversary's armour. No combatant was I, but a willing victim. There was no strength in me to oppose to the pitiless force of nature, and soon, yielding to utter discouragement, I sank upon the ground, and prayed that I might be left there.

"Come on, come on—it is madness to delay here."

"No, no. I am struck with a mortal disease. Death has long been busy with my heart, I will struggle with him no longer. I could not die in that fearful place, where every thing was already dead; but here in the free air, I can lie down on this pure winding sheet of snow, and depart in peace."

Tears stood in the gentle eyes of the youth, as he persuaded me to rise and resume my journey.

"Do not, do not talk so," he said, "you are too ill to reach my father's house today, but you cannot think that I will leave you here to perish. There is help nearer at hand than the castle—we are not far from the dwelling of Lischen, my old nurse, who lives hard upon the skirts of the wood. She will tend you like a mother until you shall be able to set forth again, and then I will bring the carriage for you."

"No woman shall tend me," said I eagerly: "I cannot suffer the presence of a woman."

"But Lischen is an angel of kindness."

"I will rather die here, than look upon a woman."

"What a strange fancy! I have then but one other resource. Yon little path on the left leads to a sort of hut, inhabited by one of my father's huntsmen.

52

The Hermaphrodite

It is but a rude place, and he is a rough man for one so delicate as you, but if you will, we can but try his entertainment, such as it is."

Silently assenting to his proposition, I rose once more to my feet, and essayed to follow the gentle guidance of my companion. It was not long before we reached a narrow path, half dug, half trodden in the snow—my progress now became less difficult. We were soon in sight of the little hut, a few moments more of pain and weariness, and we stood before the door.

"Who waits without there?" cried a sturdy voice from within, in reply to a rigorous knock.

"One who needs your aid, good Rudolf. Come, stir yourself, be quick, unbolt, unbar."

"Can it be you, Master Ronald?" exclaimed the huntsman, as he threw back the rude door.

"Yes, good friend, and I bring with me a sick stranger whom I found lost in the wood. Provide for us straitway fire, and food, and wine. He is faint with hunger and half dead with cold."

"Fire, food, and wine, I have them all at hand," cheerily answered the forester, whose strong arm now relieved Ronald of his burthen. He carried me as if I had been a child to the warmest seat beside his hearth, stripped off my wet buskins, and wrapped me in a generous robe of furs. This done, he poured wine from his hunting flask, and held the cup to my lips.

"What have you there?" asked Ronald, "is it wine that a Christian may drink?"

"It would not disagree with the stomach of an angel. It is of the castle vintage, and my Lord your father filled my flask with it from his own table yesterday, when I brought him a leverett and a brace of pheasants."

Of the merits of the wine I was not, at that moment, a competent judge. I drank with all the eagerness of exhaustion and received new life from the genial draught.

"What have you for supper, Rudolf?" next inquired the considerate Ronald.

"Venison, black bread, and an excellent broth, most appetising for a weak stomach. It is ready this very minute, you shall try it yourself, Master Ronald."

The Hermaphrodite

The forester hastened to serve the broth he so highly praised, in a wooden bowl, with an iron spoon. Ronald eyed the mixture doubtfully—"can you eat of it?" asked he.

"Willingly," I replied, and the few drops that I was able to swallow seemed to me like the food of angels.

Having eaten and drunk, I suffered myself to be laid on a rude couch which Rudolf and his master had arranged for me. I was utterly overpowered with sleep, and my eyes soon closed alike upon the rugged countenance of the forest-bred and the radiant presence of the Porphyrogenitus. Yet ere I had entirely yielded to forgetfulness, I heard the latter renew the charge of watchful attendance to Rudolf, to which the huntsman returned ready promises of obedience, adding however in a tone half of jest, half of expostulation, these words:

"Your will is mine, Master Ronald, and it were a sin and shame to refuse aught to a stranger and a sick man, but you must remember that it is an ill omen for any of your race to hunt in the Count's wood."

"Fie, Rudolf, you are a man of sense, and above such idle superstitions."

"Why truly, I hope so."

"I will return betimes in the morning, and I bid you remember that I shall reward any kindness you may shew to this stranger, as if it had been shewn to myself."

The silvery tones of the young Baron's voice still rang in my ears as I entered the world of dreams.

Chapter [10]

Unmarked The days that, passing, found me still in the forester's lodge were unmarked by any event, almost by any thought. They were occupied simply in the renovation of my exhausted physical energies. A large portion of my time was consumed in sleep—when awake, I sat listlessly before the fire, and caressed the huge hunting dogs, or watched with a sort of indefinable pleasure the movements of the good Rudolf. Among these my most confidential friend was a noble stag hound, who had taken me under his especial protection. His master was often about at the chase without him, and on these occasions he faithfully kept me company. When we were alone together, he seemed quite unwilling to lose sight of me, and watched over me with

The Hermaphrodite

the same jealous care with which he would have mounted guard over his master's coat or game pouch. He evidently considered me an object of some value, but quite incapable of self preservation or defence. He allowed [me] to indulge without interruption in reveries many hours long, but as 55 regularly as the hour for the repast came round, he would pull at my skirts, and emphatically remind me that it was time to feed him and myself.

The beast seemed to be endowed in some sort with a healthy magnetism which exercised over me a soothing power. He and his rude master were more congenial to me for the time than even the gentle Ronald—there was in them such a vigour and fulness of animal life, and in the uncouth gambols and savage endearments constantly exchanged between them was all the rude grace of untutored strength. When Rudolf, exhilarated by close and repeated consultations with his pocket flask, would discourse to me of woodcraft, and the noble science of venery, I listened in deferential silence, as if to the *dicta* of an oracle, and when the huge hound lay crouched at my feet, I would gaze long and dreamily into his dull, drowsy eyes until his lethargy had proved contagious, and we sank simultaneously to sleep. He was licking my hands, one day, when Rudolf, who was looking on, carelessly remarked:

"There is a deal of healing in a dog's tongue—I have known this beast to cure an ugly wound."

"He cannot reach mine," I said, thinking aloud, "or if he could, he would die of it—the venom would kill him."

Rudolf fixed on me a doubtful, inquiring glance, and shook his head in pity for my supposed insanity.

"It is a pity that you waste your time here with me and my dogs," said Rudolf gruffly, but kindly, on another occasion. "I know little more than they, and perhaps not as much—you, they say, are book learned and scholar-bred. Sure I am that you would find yourself in far better company at the castle than here."

"Who is at the castle?" I asked.

"Much company, chiefly of learned men—there are some that come and go, and some that always live there. My Lord keeps them for the instruction of my young master. Pity it is that they make such a monk of him—he would take to the hounds right well, if they would but give him a chance—let him come to his growth, he would make a gallant huntsman."

The Hermaphrodite

"He has not been here in many days," I said, musingly.

"You took small enough heed of him when he did come," answered the huntsman *brusquely,* "yet he is here at the gate daily to inquire after you—why should he come in? you do not care to see him?"

The remark shewed too much penetration on the part of Rudolf and his young master to be controverted.

I awoke one morning, and to my surprise found myself well. The iron band was unloosened from my brow and brain—my shoulders stooped no more as beneath an invisible burthen—from my heart a nameless load was lifted. Once more, I breathed and spake like other men, and the mist which had made all things dim and formless before my eyes had suddenly vanished. My limbs longed once more for action, my brain for thought—my lungs panted for the keen, frosty air of the woodland—my ten fingers all rose up against me and clamoured for work. It was early, and my host was not yet astir—urged by a strong impulse, I ran to the borders of the half frozen spring, and leaped gladly into its icy waters. Emerging from my plunge, all glowing with life and warmth, I hastily dried myself, and drew on over my own clothes the furred hunting frock of Rudolf—thus equipped, I rushed out from the Lodge, followed the first footpath that presented itself, and ran about at random through the forest until my quickened breathing and aching limbs reminded me that my strength was not as yet wholly restored. Having reached an open space, I clomb a hill that I might look upon the ruddy glow of the winter sunrise. I leaned against a tree, and pleasant tears rose to my eyes. "Oh dear Father God," I cried, "thou hast not been asleep all these dark and weary days. Thy sun has risen every morning upon the fair world, and thy glory has flashed upon the eyes of all save the dead and blind. I have been as one of these for many months, but now even unto me have health and strength returned. The deadly disease has healed itself. Like a leper, I hid me for a time from all men, but now at thy bidding, I will go forth to the battle of life again." Heavenly comfort streamed in upon my soul with the morning rays—my heart turned to God in the fulness of confidence and love, and He spake to me through the double medium of soul and of sense. Distinct as pearls, yet noiseless as raindrops falling in a lake, were the words uttered by the Divine voice. I listened, and then as one refreshed with wine, I turned upon life and cried: "Come on now, for I am stronger than thou." And Life replied: "If it be so, I am thy foe no more.

The Hermaphrodite

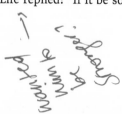

It is given to me to overthrow the coward and the craven but to him who conquers me, I become as a servant, a friend, a brother."

Swiftly, gaily, with limbs now strong and a heart newly attuned, I sped back to my rude lodging place. Rudolf had commenced his daily career, and was occupied in preparing a frugal breakfast on the hearth. Disdaining the door, I leapt in through the open window, seized his stout arm from behind, and shook it with an energy that startled him.

"Why, whom in God's name have we here?" was his gruff salutation, as he turned to look upon his unbidden guest. "What, Sir monkling, has your craziness taken a new turn, and have you taken advantage of this fine morning to go roaring mad?"

"Not in any degree, good Rudolf, the change that you see in me is nothing more than the difference between a sick man and a well one."

"But your recovery seems to me wondrous sudden. Last night I made your gruel for you and tucked you up in bed like a sick baby, and—"

"And now the gruel does not exist that will satisfy me. If you would have me bear myself like a Christian, you must feed me like one. In the words of the Psalmist, 'stay me with collops, comfort me with Rhenish, for I am sick of slops.' "

"That is a very excellent Scripture," gravely remarked the hunstman, who at the mention of the sweet singer of Israel had reverentially uncovered his head. "I wonder I never heard it before, but I am sure that it was said by some wise man and not by the rascal who came home from hunting, and took bean-porridge for his breakfast."

"What food is that which you are preparing over the fire?"

"Tea, blue groats (blaue grötze), a slice of toast, cursed stuff indeed," answered Rudolf, with a distasteful smirk.

"Yes indeed, let us give it to the dogs. But what have you got in the cupboard for your own breakfast, lovely Rudolf?"

"Let me see—there is a good bit of venison, cold boar's ham, black bread, and Universal Consolation."

"The last, I suppose, is derived from your grandmother's Bible."

"From my grandfather's hunting flask, you mean," glibly returned the forester, holding up to view the article in question, from which his reverence for his grandfather's memory barely allowed him to separate himself.

"Well, I shall breakfast with you this morning."

The Hermaphrodite

Rudolf speedily arranged the meal upon his coarse wooden table, and for the first time in many months, I sat at meat with a being of my own kind. We fell to with a good grace. I was half famished by my unwonted exertions, and if I had ever before feasted on more sumptuous viands, the fact did not at that moment suggest itself to my remembrance. Rudolf eyed me with a sort of savage glee, and encouraged me both by precept and example to make a blessed repast. It would hardly have been for the advantage of his larder that I should have made many such.

The day passed after quite a new fashion. I wandered forth again and occupied myself by gathering mosses which here and there pushed up from beneath the melting snow. I gathered up in my mind some fragments of botanical knowledge, as one may gather from a tomb the scattered bones of a friend. "Is it possible," I asked myself, "that there was ever a time in which I knew anything that it was not sorrow to know? This lesson of anguish has lasted so long that I have forgot all else—but now I remember my poor professor of Physical Science, that rusty high priest of nature—I remember his well-marshalled army of suns and stars, of laws and affinities, of elemental substances, primitive forces, e tutti quanti. I can remember how my head has ached with the jangle of his learned words and how my limited powers of memory have endeavoured to accommodate themselves to the length of his endless sentences—how difficult it was to know at once what he was saying, and what he was talking about, and how often I deemed it a pity, even a cruelty that God had made the world as it was, if I must needs understand it. I meditated upon these things, they gradually rose up before me clothed in a majesty, and invested with an unity which in earlier days, had never been revealed to me. Seen as a multitude of disconnected facts, they had confused and frightened me. But as they now appeared to me, the various members of one great body of truth, I saw their grandeur, their harmony, and thought it quite time that I should renew my acquaintance with them. Thus is it ever. The child must dissect, the man is able to combine—analysis is the task of the first, synthesis that of the second—the one stimulates to unrest, the other elevates to peace—the one is the legitimate gratification of the child's destructiveness, the other is the exercise of the Creative principle which constitutes one of the strongest sympathies between the narrow mind of man and the infinite mind from which it emanates.

The Hermaphrodite

As for the first time, I was able to reason upon those days gone by. I marvelled that the thoughts which had filled them now seemed to me crude and childish, while the emotions that animated them were still too mighty, too terrible for me to look back upon. How was it that when I had understood and reasoned as a child, I had felt as a man? Why was it that long ere experience had taught me to rein in the fiery steed, he had been loosed from his stall, and sent flinging madly about at wildest random, as if commissioned only to fling his rider to destruction?

Oh feeble child, sent weeping to the great school of this world, learn there thy lesson even as thou mayst. To learn it diligently, to get it by heart is thy business. For the modus-in-quo, thank God, thou will not be held responsible.

Wearied with my morning ramble, I returned to the Lodge, and threw myself upon the rude settle that always stood before the fire.

"Shall I bring you some of your books?" said Rudolf, "the young Baron sent them here, long since, but you have not even unpacked them."

"Not those books!" said I, with an involuntary shudder. "Have you nothing of your own that one might read?"

Rudolf's library, fairly mustered, made but a sorry show. A very primitive treatise on woodcraft, a battered collection of Psalms—the spelling-book from which the good forester had not learned to read, and a few odd volumes of Legends and Romances constituted the sum total of his literary possessions. Taking up one of these last, I turned listlessly over its leaves and coming at last to a long-winded story of the incredible hardships undergone by one Sir Gunther, for the love of some beautiful virgin largely endowed with golden locks, I followed conscientiously the progress of the affair, and fell asleep just as the happy pair, united in the sacred bonds of wedlock, were presenting their first born at the baptismal font.

Unlike the mystic visions of my ascetic life, my dreams were confused and common place enough—only at the last I became conscious in my sleep of a soft, warm light that stole through my closed eyelids, and won its gentle way even into my very soul. Bathed in this peaceful glow, my brain began slowly to unravel the fanciful web that had gathered around it in its repose as the frost work gathers on a pane at night. Lazily, languidly, I opened my eyes—was it the light of the setting sun, streaming broadly upon my face, that had so wrapt my soul in heavenly radiance, or was it that a pair of starry eyes were fixed lovingly upon my face?

Chapter [11]

"What were you dreaming about?" asked Ronald.

"What were you thinking about?" asked Laurence.

"I was thinking," answered he, "that sleep is sometimes life-like, and sometimes deathlike. The slumber in which I first found you was horrible to look upon—you were stretched upon the floor, your limbs were stiffened and icy cold, your blood was all white; but now."

"And what now?"

"You had thrown yourself down like a tired child, you were flushed and smiling in your sleep—you were happy, and I was happy in watching you."

I started up—"My pretty young Baron," said I: "shall we try a walk?"

"Willingly," was the reply, and yet he spoke as if he had something more to say.

"Come, speak out. I see by your face that you have some other engagement on hand, and we can as well take our walk tomorrow."

"You mistake me," said Ronald, after a moment's pause. "The truth is that I came here from the castle an hour ago, commissioned by my father to bring you straitway to dinner—I found you asleep, I had not the heart to wake you, I would not return without you, and by this time dinner must be half over."

"And you have lost yours, poor youth?"

"That is a small matter," answered Ronald, with a heightened colour, "but I *promised* to bring you."

"And I promise to come—we shall at least be in time for the Nach-tisch."

"Yes indeed," cried he joyously, "the disputes never begin until the cloth is removed—they are all too busy to quarrel over their meat, but that once disposed of, their tongues begin to emulate the industry of their teeth, and they waste more learning upon each other than would educate a dozen boors like poor Rudolf."

"And who are they of whom you speak?"

"First, my father and his body guard, by name the poet, the antiquarian, and the Theologue—besides these, divers guests and friends of his, among

The Hermaphrodite

whom is the famous geologist N——, and others whose names I forget, but they are all learned men." And Ronald indulged in an involuntary yawn, at the thought of them.

Having retired to make the speediest toilette possible I opened with a hasty hand the valise which contained my vestments of former days. Alas, its glory was departed, the moth and the rust had corrupted it. Equivocal insects came flying out upon me as I lifted the dusty lid, and seemed in their angry agitation to expostulate with me after this fashion: "You have been dead these six months, and have bequeathed to us the legacy of your broad-cloth; it is an unheard of act of impudence in you to arise from your grave and molest us in the possession of your property." Moreover, nothing seemed to fit me as of old—my form had both shrunk and expanded, and as I submitted myself once more to the tyranny of coat, vest, and breeches, I breathed a last sigh over the worn out relics of my poor old dressing gown. With a little patience, however, I contrived to equip myself decently, and after an affectionate farewell to Rudolf and the dogs, I started under Ronald's guidance for the castle. We had crossed the threshold when Ronald, in boyish fashion, seized a stone of some size, and hurled it at a rude target that stood near the house. I took up one of a double size, and hurled it to a double distance. "That's no woman's throw," I said, and Ronald could not contradict me.

As we walked side by side through the wood-path, Ronald endeavoured to prepare me, in some degree, for the new surroundings in which I was about to find myself. I gathered from his words the following facts. His father was a nobleman, and the proprietor of large landed estates in the neighbourhood—he was moreover a man of genial and liberal nature, delighting in the society of intelligent men and in the exercise of hospitality. He had long known of my residence in the neighbourhood, and his curiosity had been much excited by various reports of my eccentric mode of life. The peasants had spoken of me with a sort of superstitious reverence, first as a sorcerer, then as a saint, or at least as one holy, harmless and incomprehensible. The castle was, at this time, filled with guests, and among more worthy themes of conversation, my character and habits had been made a subject of discussion. That very morning at breakfast, it had been proposed to invite me to take up my abode among them for a short time, and those present had playfully defied each other to bear me the invitation,

The Hermaphrodite

and to induce me to accept it. The youngest and bravest had accepted the challenge, and was not a little proud and happy in his success.

The castle was old and grim enough to be altogether to my taste—it was beautifully placed on a slight eminence, and commanded an extensive prospect. The eccentric outline of its exterior suggested the idea of tortuous passages, winding stairs, and turret chambers in which an owl like myself might safely take shelter, and build himself, with books and parchments, a most congenial nest. Yet as I paused on the terrace to survey all the beauty that lay spread at my feet, it occurred to me that I had played the owl quite long enough, and that my wits might be somewhat sharpened by a little communion with living things and living men. But the wide portal opened to admit us, and I followed Ronald to the dining-hall, where the guests were all assembled. As we approached, we heard the sounds of conversation and laughter—as we entered, several voices cried out: "Here is Ronald,"—they were obviously not prepared for the apparition that followed, and all eyes were turned upon me as upon something new and strange. Anxious to prevent the utterance of any word or jest which might greet me unpleasantly, Ronald led me at once to the master of the house, who sat in a capacious armchair at the head of a long table covered with wine, fruits, and confections, and surrounded by a sufficiently numerous party. He was a man of noble appearance, in the very prime of life, and clothed with a dignity far beyond that of rank or wealth.

"Father, I bring you the stranger," said Ronald and the stately Count arose to receive me.

"You are welcome," he said in the friendliest manner. "We have long desired to see you—pardon me if, by way of introductions to the company, I ask how we may name you, and whence you come."

"That I come from the Hermitage in the wood is well known to you," I made answer, "but since I have surrendered myself prisoner at your summons, you must remember that I am not bound to make any disclosures on my own part until I have been informed wherefore and by whom I have been summoned hither."

Instantly every one present, including the host, gave me in a loud voice his name, rank and place of abode.

"And we have sent for you," said they, "to laugh with us, and to drink with us and to be one of us."

The Hermaphrodite

"Gentlemen," I replied, "I am gratified by your frankness, and entirely satisfied with the statements you have made—permit me in return to say that my name, at your service, is Laurence, my nature, masculine, my habits anti-gregarious, my tastes anti-bibulous. I am your servant for all good and pleasure."

It is ever a questionable thing, the introduction of a new unknown element into a social compound already in a high state of fermentation. Who does not know that the admixture of one ungenial drop may reduce the whole distillation to flatness and acidity? A dinner as well as a kingdom, has its destiny to the which sudden revolutions are, for the most part, fatal. Let us suppose then that you have composed your dinner after the best receipt with sufficient preponderance of wit and sentiment, benevolence tempered by a slight infusion of malice, not forgetting a grand pièce de resistance of learning and obstinacy; which latter, attacked by each in turn, proves itself too much for demolition and promises to be good, cold, another day. Let us suppose all this, and who does not perceive the madness of risking the happy eventuation of the whole by intermingling with it an ingredient which has neither been tried by your self, nor recommended by others?

In the present instance, however, I cannot say that the experiment was unsuccessful. It was a company of genial men, into the midst of which I had fallen, like a man from the moon, or the stony corpse of a meteor. I found myself surrounded by an atmosphere of learning and intelligence, and I had scarce seated myself at the table before the thread of the discourse broken by my arrival was cunningly mended, and I found myself called upon to join in the discussion of questions of high and noble interest. At first, I sat among them cold and impassive—soon, I found my attention rivetted upon that which I heard—at length, my very tongue untied itself—I too entered the lists, and defended with warmth and courage the truth that was truth to me. My words were received with attention, and skilfully answered— then, the conversation assumed a lighter and merrier character—stories were told, keen jests and graceful personalities were allowed to relieve the fatigue of graver arguments—then we left the table, and the party was some what broken up. While others sought diversion in whist, billiards, books, or conversation, I ran out upon the lawn with Ronald. Finding him quite wearied with the themes of the dinner table, I made for him a caricature of

The Hermaphrodite

the whole conversation. I imitated by turns the poet, the antiquarian, and the theologian, until the youth lay upon the ground in fits of inextinguishable laughter. I ran with him, wrestled with him, sang, swore, and shouted, until our insane gaiety had exhausted itself, and we bade each other a cordial and unwilling goodnight. Ronald left me at the door of my room; it was the very turret chamber I had coveted, and beautifully from its window showed the moonlit park, the river and the outline of distant hills. Yet, as I looked out upon it all, a strange pang shot through my heart, and I asked of God why the angel with the bright wings came down to me no more from the moon, and why the brightest star sent not, as formerly, its pencil of rays to my soul, and why the fair woman in white arose no more from her bier before the altar in that old church, nor came as she was wont to clasp me in her gentle arms, and to print upon my forehead her kiss of heavenly forgiveness. As I mused thus, and sought more fondly for my sacred sorrow than I had ever sought for its consolations, I heard an unwonted voice in the corridor beyond. They were carrying the poet, incapable of independent locomotion, to his sleeping-chamber. He was sublimely drunk, and loudly declaimed various verses, among which I could distinguish this line:

"Let the dead past bury its dead."

"God, does the past die?" I cried out to heaven; "if aught that bears the stamp of thy truth and our love can die, what immortality have we?"

Chapter [12]

Let not the reader imagine that I had more sympathy with the condition than with the sentiment of the poet. I was, as I have said, anti-bibulous by inclination, if not by necessity. It had needed little experience to teach me that in my best days, any extraneous stimulus would hasten to madness the swift current of my blood. It is the cold and dull of temperament who need the genial flow of wine. For them it may quicken the fancy, warm the heart, and give to the sluggish brain the impulse of a more living life than that which tinges all their days with its somber monotony. Some men grow wise, and witty, and even generous in their wine, who without it are ever crabbed, sordid, stupid. For such, the dancing devil of the grape juice is a friendly genius, almost a ministering angel, while to finer, quicker natures, it becomes the most cruel and brutal of the tyrants.

The Hermaphrodite

I too had ever my seasons of dullness and depression, and as I have grown older, the slow torture of my torpid state has become a greater bugbear to me than were the acute suffering of my earlier life. But I have learned the nature of these slumbers of the soul, have learned to bear them patiently, and to beguile them by the exercise of the more mechanical powers of mind, memory, comparison, perception and imitation, while waiting for the divine voice to awake me to higher and nobler musings.

I have become convinced that to all the innumerable subdivisions of the human race, there are two which may yet be added. Among thinking men at least I have observed two very distinct classes—those belonging to the first are ever awakened, ever capable of thought and action; they ever possess themselves, and there will never appear any wide discrepancy between that they were yesterday and that which they will be tomorrow. In those who constitute the second class, the brain is capable only of a spasmodic action, and presents alternately the phenomena of an intense and concentrated activity, and of entire inertia. The intellectual life of the latter is marked by a series of crises, more or less remote, and ever followed by an interval of exhaustion and repose without which Nature could scarce resist the too lavish expenditure of her forces, or prepare herself for renewed exertion and fruition. I had just passed through one of these crises (and its somnambulic influences still lingered around me), veiling from me in part the reality of the external world, while the mystic visions of my introverted life still presented themselves, unbidden, before me, and seemed in their eternal truth to mock at men as phantoms, and to deride their aims and desires as dreams worthy only of children. Still, while regretting these hours of rapture and of inspiration, I knew that it was well for me that the spell was broken. Death, madness, or a return to the common life of humanity had been the only alternatives presented to me. I had not deliberately chosen the latter, but Heaven had kindly chosen for me and had sent the gentle Ronald to form a kind of rainbow bridge between my terrible ghostland and the fair earth which I am still content to inhabit.

To that earth I now returned with a terrible & exaggerated fondness. As wildly my imagination had spread its wings and soared in pursuit of the highest Ideal, so now I stretched out my hands to grasp the real, the tangible, the mathematically demonstrable. As boldly as I had ventured into the deepest mazes of speculation, hoping to conquer there the unconquerable

The Hermaphrodite

truth, so now was I content to tread the beaten track of other men, and to deem myself rich in the inheritance of their discoveries. The question had hitherto been with me: "Is it possible?" I now asked: "Is it certain?" I had clung savagely to my solitary life—I was glad now of the sympathy and companionship of one younger and feebler than myself; and the words of my dream were soon fulfilled, that a little child should lead me.

My reader may be surprised that I speak of Ronald as of a child, while yet I have said that my years scarce exceeded his by half a lustre. Still, the distance which experience had placed between us seemed to me more than that of many years. The precocity of my temperament and the strange sorrows of my early life had too soon awakened in me those dangerous powers which in Ronald's heart still slept the innocent sleep of childhood. This very ignorance and unconsciousness of his made him but the more beautiful to me. I rejoiced to think that his reason would be nobly developed ere his passions were aroused; that it would be granted him to learn the shoals and the harbours, the true aims and ends of life before he was launched on its rude and stormy waters. In this hope, I watched over myself with jealous care, that no fervid breath from my own soul should invite the budding sympathies of his to unfold themselves before their time.

Ronald became very dear to me, dear rather as himself than as a part of myself. It was not difficult for me to understand and minister to the necessities of his nature. Without knowing, without understanding, the boy had soon more than repaid the debt. He attached himself to me with almost feminine fondness, and his presence chased the phantoms from my brain, even as a nursling will often draw away the poison from the sick heart of its mother. His age was not so much removed from mine but that its wants and perplexities were still fresh in my remembrance, and claimed my fullest sympathy. I endeavoured to give him the clue to labyrinths in which I myself had sometimes lost sight of hope and patience, and to resolve for him those weary questions of the days of elementary study: "Why should I learn it? what is it good for? what shall I do with it when I have learned it?"

I have said that, at this moment, the remembrance of my recent experience of exaggerated spiritualism had given my mind a strong impulse towards the real and positive. I still sought for God every where and in all things, but methought I would now learn of Him in the records of the world He had made. I was fain to lose sight of my own soul, with its narrow

The Hermaphrodite

powers and destinies, and to think of the Infinite in His relations with the Universe. It was time that I should give myself up to the teachings of Nature, to the study of its old testament, graven on tables of stone, and its ever new testament of organic life, springing from the dead past, and bearing the living future in its bosom. It was time that I should better understand this gospel of hope and beauty and renewed life which is preached every spring in the dull ear of the sleeping earth, and which, by the Autumn, has revolutionized the world.

Ronald was as yet incapable of comprehending the true aim of these studies, but he was easily led to participate in them. He gladly became the companion of my geological and botanical excursions, and with evident benefit to himself. The exposure and fatigue attendant upon our wanderings supplied the necessary vent to the restless activity of his age, while our researches, such as they were, gave the happiest direction to those powers of perception and observation which are so clamorous for exercise in the earlier periods of life, and which suppressed or misdirected, are sources of evil and discomfort.

Ronald's father, whom I shall call Raimond, interfered little in my intercourse with his son neither to stimulate or restrain. It was nevertheless easy for me to see that he watched with interest and satisfaction the new interests which had now interwoven themselves in Ronald's life. To me, he was the kindest of hosts—he treated me less as a stranger than as one long known and esteemed. He placed at my disposal all the resources of his generous establishment, of which however, I availed myself of three only, the library, Ronald, and my own little turret chamber which had been transformed into the most charming of dens. If I ever spoke of my departure, he answered: "You are very well here, young gentleman."

But all were not as indulgent to me as the good Raimond. The poet, the antiquarian and the theologian had hither been the pedagogues of the young Baron, and had been jointly entrusted with the care of his education. They had failed to excite in him any love for the studies over which they presided, and their teachings, as well as themselves, were utterly tedious to him. They soon saw in me a dangerous rival, nor was it long before they had formed themselves into a league, offensive and defensive, against me, their animosity being all the more bitter because I had carefully avoided giving them any excuse for it. As it was, Ronald passed the first half of every morning under their jurisdiction—these weary hours once over, he bounded from them like a hound let loose, and led me forth to the woods and hills of the neighbourhood. Here we gathered plants, and dissected them; we searched for stones, and classified them; we plaited garlands, we sang, we improvised dramas—we were the gayest of all the children of the Spring. Then, at table, I would argue against the three pedants, to his great delight. I answered the poet's verses by verses of my own, and puzzled the theologian by arguments more subtle, though less learned than his own.

One eccentricity of mine sometimes troubled Ronald—one morbid impression still retained its dimension over me. I could not bear the sight of a woman. Fortunately the lord of the Manor was himself no woman-fancier, and within his walls, the fair sex had no representative, save in a menial capacity. The presence even of the maid occasioned in me that feeling of faintness and malaise which is felt by some individuals at the approach of a cat. Ronald had observed this, and had taken pains to guard against the recurrence of the evil. The women of the household were refused all access to my room, and one of the valets was induced to take charge of it. If in the course of our wanderings, I descried at a distance the outlines of a female form, I instinctively turned my steps in an opposite direction. Ronald soon learned to avoid them even as I did, a course of conduct which did not find any great favour in the eyes of the village belles, to whom the fair youth, with his graces and his expectations was not altogether unattractive. It was a pleasure to me, in all else, to show myself gentle and tractable with Ronald, and to obey his innocent caprices as if he had been the stronger, and I the weaker of the twain. I had resources for all his leisure hours, and consolations for all his discontents, only when he would have kissed me, I shrank from him with a horror quite incomprehensible to myself and to him.

Yet while it was a delight to me to yield to the gentle magnetism of his will, I was glad to find on the other hand that my mind had acquired over his a certain ascendancy. I had taught him to reason, while he had taught me to hope and to enjoy. I soon felt that he had grown, had put on strength, had learned in some measure to read the meaning of earthly things, to comprehend their uses, to feel their beauty. Encouraged by me, he had

The Hermaphrodite

caught glimpses of a land of promise beyond the driest of his studies. I had taught him to believe that from the dull chrysalid of science would come forth the lovely spirit of art, with her troop of butterflies. From childish love to manly knowledge, from manly knowledge to illuminated love, this was my idea of mental progress, and I hoped to have the happiness to see it realized in Ronald.

I learned at a later day that I had not understood all that was passing at this period in the mind of my pupil. Some seeds were ripening there which I had never desired to sow, and Nature was slowly arousing in his breast some impulses with which I could not sympathize.

One day when he was lying at my feet on the mountain side, he said to me: "Does not your brain grow weary of thinking in these long pauses, when you are still and silent, and neither hear nor see me?"

"One must have many thoughts before one learns to think."

"And what is the use of so many thoughts, is it not enough for us to live?"

"We must know how and for what we live."

"Oh," said Ronald, "I understand that full well. I know that I live because I love you, and I live to love you."

These words, and the tone in which they were uttered, struck a sudden pang to my heart. I changed colour, and Ronald's eyes filled with tears.

"You do not wish me to love you, Laurence, and yet you have changed my whole heart to love for you—you seem at once to hold me fast and to spurn me."

"Ronald, do you know that we have been out all this morning, without having found one new mineral? Take up the basket, and give me the hammer, we have played, now we must work."

He stood before me for a moment in most expressive silence, and fixed his eyes upon mine.

"Already?" said he, and his look told the rest.

"To work already? must I begin the task of life so early? Are there not scores of years for labour, and do you scourge me to it in the first hour of the morning?"

I replied to his look as well as I could: "You will one day thank me, dear Ronald, for much that may now seem irksome to you. There is no blessing

The Hermaphrodite

like the habit of employment—we have need of it in our best days, and in our worst, we could not live without it." Ronald did not dissent from my proposition, but he was silent and thoughtful as he followed me to the spot where I thought to have discovered a curious vein of homeblende.

Chapter [13]

It came to pass in process of time that the three pedagogues grew utterly impatient of my presence at the Castle. My favour with its master and my intimate relations with his son had aroused in them a thousand petty jealousies which after smouldering long, at length broke out into open flame. Strange to say, these three peaceable and conservative old gentlemen became at length quite inflamed and revolutionary, and finally rose in a body to expel me from the house. In this endeavour, well concerted as it was, they did not succeed. It is undeniable that three heads may be better than one, vide the inventor of Cerberus, and the German proverb: "alle gute Dinge sind drei"—nevertheless, three bad heads are not better than one good one, of that I will take my oath.

It must have puzzled this worthy trio to find a decent pretext for their hostility to me. I had always treated them with the most punctilious consideration. I had borne with their asperities without loss of temper, and in all our postprandial disputes, had shown clemency to the vanquished. They might accuse me of interference in their guidance of Ronald, but they could not deny that it was only since the commencement of our intimacy that he had begun to apply himself, in good earnest, to his books. It is true that he shewed in his relations with them more determination than formerly, but this was shewn simply in defence of the man's right of selecting, from the multifarious forms of science, those best suited to the wants and capacities of his own nature. I had in no wise disturbed them in the enjoyment of their rights—they were as well fed, lodged, and salaried as ever, but their absolute power was shaken, and who does not know the strength of this love of power in narrow minds?

I have said that Ronald was grown more studious but less tractable than formerly. He had discovered the fact that the pursuit of truth in some ways was clear and satisfactory to him, while in certain others little became apparent to him save names, dates, classifications, the dry dead bones of

The Hermaphrodite

learning with which the pedants had endeavoured to satisfy him. Guided by that fine intellectual instinct which leads the poet to song, and the artist to form, he had gradually chosen and marked out a course of study for himself, from which his tutors could not induce him to deviate. The determination of Ronald, and the new energy of will lately aroused in him were attributed entirely to my influence, and were treated by the three as childish contumacy and stubbornness. Their expostulations were received by him at first with firmness, then with indifference, finally, with sarcasm. They threatened to appeal to the good Count Raimond, and Ronald replied that it was the best thing they could do.

Having resolved upon this grand coup d'état, the three accordingly waited upon their patron, one afternoon, to lay at his feet a deposition of their grievances. Raimond's sense of justice would not permit him to hear us accused without allowing us to defend ourselves, and so we were sum——

> [At this point the manuscript is interrupted; numbered pages 118–32 are missing. In the intervening pages, it is evidently determined that Ronald's schooling at home has brought him as far as possible; arrangements are now complete for him to depart with Laurence to enroll in university.]

propose a toast:

"Success to Ronald in his Academic career—may he nobly continue and perfect the education of which the foundation has been so carefully laid by these gentlemen!" This was drunk with hearty goodwill. Raimond hastened to follow it up by another:

"Success to Laurence—may he become to the world all that he has been to Ronald!"

"Do not make me ashamed by your unmerited commendations," I said. "Remember how much Ronald has been taught, and how little I have taught him."

"Do you remember," rejoined Raimond, "how small a thing is the key stone of an arch, and yet what were the structure without it? Let me give you this brief formula, Laurence: laborious minds construct the arch, but suggestive minds supply the key stone."

The Hermaphrodite

Chapter [14]

There is little to be said of the time that I passed with Ronald at the University, save that it glided by, for the most part, tranquilly and happily enough. Ronald sustained with honour the ordeal of his preparatory examination, and entered upon his course under the most favorable auspices. Once admitted into his class, he was of necessity enrolled among the members of the various students' societies, and the companionship of these young men, and such friendship as they had to give, were entirely at his service. I cannot say that he was in any haste to avail himself of the privileges that extended to him—the wild, shaggy foxes of H. possessed few attractions for him, and there were few points of sympathy between their rude and boisterous manière d'être, and his own refined and thoughtful nature. Drinking, gaming, and fighting were as uncongenial to him as to myself; and these were the only amusements which beguiled the elegant leisure of those gentle beings. Still, it was my wish that Ronald should mingle with them. I sometimes thought that their follies, their passions, their very vices might in the end be less dangerous to him than those too grave and mystic habits of thought which had so grown upon me, and which I feared to communicate to him. Far from fostering the reserve of his character, I availed myself of every possible argument to induce him to make some more intimate acquaintance with the strange world by which he was surrounded. I descanted to him upon the advantages of studying men of all characters, habits, and dispositions, and even exaggerated to him the importance of the knowledge he would thus acquire. But Ronald's soul was yet enwrapped in its virgin garments of purity and tenderness, and he clung to me, like a child to its mother.

"What would you have me do among those savages, Laurence? What can they teach me that were not better unlearned? I have no vacant time, no idle thoughts to bestow upon them. Here I have you to talk with, I have my notes of today to copy, my lessons of tomorrow to prepare. If we get through in time, we can take a moonlight walk among the ruins of the old castle—you will sling the guitar over your shoulder, and we will make music as we walk, even as we were wont to do at home."

"But Ronald, you might as well have staid at home, if you intend to shut yourself up with me for your only companion."

The Hermaphrodite

"I could have been well-content to have staid there alone, alone with you forever," answered Ronald with fervour. In spite of my attempts to wean him from his too exclusive dependence upon me, I could not but be glad to retain in some degree, the guidance of his immature youth. I rejoiced in the persuasion that the destiny of this beautiful being would be all purity and love, all marked by high impulse, and earnest thought. "He need not fall," I said to myself, "he need not sin and repent. God has given his angels charge over him, he will live but to bless and be blest."

As a natural consequence of our quiet and studious mode of life, we became daily more popular with the professors and more odious to the students. They made us the subject of impertinent songs and epigrams, they invented a thousand petty insults for our daily annoyance—finally, they became such a trouble and vexation to us, that I thought it best to absent myself for a time, and to try whether Ronald, once left alone with his classmates, might not be led to cultivate more friendly relations with them. I became distrustful of my own influence—I feared to identify, in any sense, his destiny with mine, and so I availed myself of the pretext of some trifling business in a town at no great distance, and prepared for a brief removal to other scenes.

On the evening preceding my departure, I sat at my window and mused alone. There had been, of late, many things in my surroundings to recall to me the scenes of my early academic life. Half gladly, half regretfully I looked back upon the earnest strivings, the dim conceptions, the innocent pleasures of those days, and then shudderingly averted my mental glance from the dread catastrophe which lay like a black and awful gulf between that I had been, and that I had become. As I followed this train of thought, my attention was aroused by a slight noise in the room adjoining, whither Ronald had retired to prepare his thesis for the morrow. I ran to him, and found that he had fallen asleep over his task. The uneasiness of his posture had given to his breathing the unnatural sound which had startled me. I laid my hand upon his shoulder, and gently shaking it bade him awake. He started, stared around him in some confusion of mind, and finally threw himself into my arms with an effusion which, in a state of entire consciousness, he would never have ventured to display.

"Beautiful angel," he cried, "you shall not fly away!"

The Hermaphrodite

"Ronald, you are still asleep, still dreaming. Collect your senses, you do not see where you are, nor who is with you."

"Dreaming, was I? oh yes, truly, it must have been so. I see, I see that I have been asleep; but Laurence, my dream was all of you. Only imagine it, I thought you were a woman."

"That was an idle dream," I said.

"It was a glorious dream," replied Ronald with vehemence. "I saw you robed in white, crowned with flowers, and half veiled by the floating tresses of your bright hair. You were transfigured in a light which seemed to emanate from yourself, and all your motions were accompanied by a faint music. Your countenance too was altered—it was no longer grave and sad, but beaming, glowing, all life, all tenderness. Young and beautiful as the Hebe of the Gods, you glided around me, and dropped odours on my head, and poured out wine for me from a golden cup."

Astonished and disturbed at these words, I sought in a somewhat ungracious manner to put an end to Ronald's rhapsodies. "It *was* an idle dream," I repeated, "and as it can never come true, it is scarce worth while for us to waste our waking moments in talking about it."

"Why are you vexed, Laurence? The dream was involuntary. I see no reason why it should thus disturb you."

"Let us speak of other things," I said, not finding it easy to give any satisfactory reason for my displeasure.

"Speak of what you will," answered Ronald, "but do not look so coldly at me, or you will frighten me back to my father. Grimm, Grub, and Dingdongo, all concentrated into one, could not chill me as you do at this moment."

I felt the folly of my conduct, and hastened to smooth my ruffled brow. Ronald took down the guitar, and we sang together until our souls, as well as our voices, were in entire harmony with each other. After this, I occupied myself in making a list of works to be consulted and tasks to be fulfilled during the brief period of my absence. This completed, I bade Ronald bring me his thesis, that I might make any necessary corrections in the style and language of it. He hesitated to obey me for some moments. "You will not like it," he said, "it is not in the least that which you suppose it to be."

I insisted upon seeing it, and after every possible delay, and with evident reluctance, he placed the paper in my hands. It was indeed no thesis, no boyish composition, but a poetical version of a popular legend, right gracefully rendered. The verses have long since escaped from my memory, but I can well recall the meaning of the story. It was that of a pilgrim who had long worshipped the marble image of a saint, so long, that it was become to him the truest of realities. At length, in the madness of his passionate longing, he impiously prayed God that it might become human for his sake. The prayer was heard, the miracle was granted. The beautiful saint breathed, smiled, spake, and descended from her marble pedestal— the lover opened his arms to clasp her to his heart, but lo! at the first touch, it had ceased to beat—the cold embrace was death.

The tale was, as I have said, an oft-told one, and in itself sufficiently commonplace, but Ronald had treated the subject with so much grace and power that he seemed to have breathed a new soul of his own into the worn-out body of the legend. I was astonished at the harmonious klang of the versification, at the just and apt choice of expressions, but still more at the power of the mood which had given birth to the poem. I raised my eyes to the face of my companion, and diligently scanned its every feature, tacitly questioning it of the soul within. Hast thou thyself dreamed of passionate desire? hast thou too implored heaven to work the miracle of love in some cold heart that should respond to thine? But the face was either utterly transparent, or utterly impenetrable—it looked all freshness, all beauty, all hope.

Ronald knew not how to interpret my silence—with the naive impatience of a young author, he snatched the manuscript from my hands, saying with playful petulance: "You do not like it—I knew you would not."

"It has many merits, and even beauties," I replied: "but what may be the intended moral of it?"

"That it is more dangerous to love marble than flesh and blood, and that a saint may work one more peril than a sinner," answered Ronald, laughing.

"I should draw another lesson from it, which is that when we seek to wring the impossible from Heaven, we pray for our own destruction. The order of our lives, like the order of the universe, is good and beautiful, and the intervention of a miracle in the one might be as dangerous and destructive as the admission of some lawless comet in the other."

"The fulfillment of that which we most desire often appears to us a miracle, yet heaven, or fate, or chance sometimes permits it. You will not

75

Pygmalion?

Moral

The Hermaphrodite

tell me that even our most daring hopes altogether mislead us, or if you do, I shall not believe you."

"Ronald, go to bed—you are too young to reason."

"Laurence, good night. I am older than you think."

I had not confided to Ronald either the day or the hour of my departure. He knew that I was about to leave him for a short time, but I had wished to spare him and myself the pain of parting, and he knew not while we had been talking together that my trunk was already packed, and my post-horses ordered. He retired therefore to rest with the utmost tranquillity, little dreaming that he should wake in the morning, and find me gone. The door that separated our rooms had been left ajar, and it was not long before his deep breathing assured me that he was sleeping as one only sleeps at his age. I had scarcely completed my final preparations, when the servant knocked at the door, to warn me that the postillion was in readiness. I bade the man move lightly, lest he should disturb the young Baron's slumber, but why was it that I lingered behind, when he had left the room? It was that I could not go without one silent farewell to Ronald. I paused a moment on the threshold, and then shading the lamp with my hand, I crept noiselessly in to look upon him once more in his sleep. Oh! what repose was in that sleep! He had fallen upon his bed as a snow drift falls upon the earth—passive and unconscious as a babe, he rested upon the bosom of the Love that sleeps not. His cheek was still flushed with the excitement of our late argument, but there reigned in his countenance an unspeakable serenity, and I accepted it from heaven as the eternal promise of his fair soul. Scarce knowing what I did, I stooped to print the lightest, faintest kiss upon his forehead; but as I did so, his red lips parted, and he murmured: "Laurence!" I shrank back into myself. I turned away, lest a tear should fall upon his face. I spread over him hands which seemed able to compel from heaven its dearest benediction. One more look, and I was gone—oh soft bloom of adolescence, oh gentle type of nascent manhood! your remembrance will never die out from my heart.

Chapter [15]

Ronald was much altered when we met again. My absence had been pro-longed considerably beyond the term first proposed, and although I had not bound myself by any promise, my young friend was obviously disposed to consider me guilty of a breach of faith, and to treat me accordingly. I was made aware of this by the change in the tone of our correspondence, long before we met again. Ronald's letters had at first been as gushing and unrestrained as his conversation, but as my return was delayed from day to day, they assumed a more unequal tone. There was somewhat of constraint in them, somewhat of irritation, while now and then a wild burst of feeling seemed to say that this coldness was assumed, and that he who wore the mask was ill at ease beneath it. At length came a long and moody silence into which the kindest words I could devise and write dropped as stones into an abyss too deep and sullen to render back the gentle acknowledgement of sound. Days and weeks passed, and still brought no word from Ronald; until wearied with waiting, I wrote him a mournful and reproachful farewell, to the which he replied as follows:

> Laurence,
>
> Do not write to me any more of your affection for me—if you love me, come to me, and prove it.
>
> > Ronald.

I did love him—I would have proved it by the sacrifice of my life, and so, stifling every doubt and foreboding suggested by my own reason, I followed the guidance of ever loyal affection, and replied to his letter in person.

"Reason is trivial and finite," I said to myself, "but the wisdom of love is an instinct given of God."

Three days later, I stood before Ronald.

I had taken him by surprize—he had not expected me, and the cry of delight with which he greeted me was thrilling, almost startling. He sprang from his seat—he caught me wildly in his arms—he held me to his heart as though he would have crushed me. I drew back involuntarily, and in an instant his countenance had changed, and the momentary gleam of sunshine was quenched in a look of cold displeasure.

"Ronald, dear Ronald, I have come back to you."

"Yes—I see—it was quite time."

"If you speak to me thus, I will not even have my trunk brought upstairs, but will betake myself with all speed to the place whence I came."

The Hermaphrodite

"Not so—we shall not part again, alive—I swear it." It needed many hours of intimate converse to soothe the irritated nerves of Ronald—my forbearance was somewhat tried by the varying tenor of his words which were now quick and petulant, now cold and cutting, all ungenial, and by moments unkind. After some patience and some suffering, I succeeded. We sate long together, but before we parted, the acute tone had melted from his voice, and the rigidity was smoothed from his brow. He laid his hand in mine, he looked lovingly in my face, we laughed and wept together, and went forth arm in arm, as of old.

Yet another day, and another, and another convinced me that things were no longer between us as they had been. Ronald, once so calmly and steadfastly joyous, was become strangely variable in his moods. Our first interview might have served as a type of all our subsequent intercourse, which, intimate and earnest as it was, had yet on Ronald's part its fluctuations from chilling reserve, to the fullest and freest épanchement. There were days in which Ronald was content to lay down his arms at my feet, in which he seemed compelled to seek from me the sympathy which none other had ever given him. There were moments in which he essayed, with tears in his eyes, to break the seal that estrangement had set upon his heart, and to unfold to me all the unwonted thoughts that were imprisoned there—but even in these moments, the cold wind of distrust swept over his soul, and he shrank back into himself, the tears unshed, the tale untold. I sometimes asked myself whether some devil's seed had been dropped into Ronald's mind, and was ripening there into dark and unholy life, but no, I could find no evil in him—he was earnest, truthful, beautiful as ever, and though I could no longer understand him as of yore, I trusted in him, and trusted in God for him. I sought in the state of his health, an easier and happier solution of the changes that so perplexed me. Ronald's frame had grown and expanded somewhat too rapidly, he had put on the stature of manhood ere he had attained its strength. He had of late applied himself with too much intensity to his studies, and was grown careless of the hours of food and sleep. These causes seemed to me amply sufficient to account for the apparent alteration in his temper and mood of mind, and while I sought to lead him to avail himself of the few relaxations that H——presented, I looked forward to the vacation, and the subsequent change of scene as the surest remedy for the half comprehended evil.

The Hermaphrodite

The chief object of our separation had partially accomplished itself. Ronald, once left to himself, had been as it were compelled to associate somewhat with his fellow-students, and to put himself in some degree *au courant* of their pursuits and amusements. Nor did this cease on my return. We became regular attendants at some of the clubs, and sometimes passed an evening together in the dingy smoky dens devoted to drinking and gaming. Still, in this point of view, Ronald's habits of life had changed far more than his tastes. He was with these rude and sensual beings, but not of them. He frequented their haunts, and surveyed their diversions and disputes with a certain curiosity, but he took no part in them. He had acquaintances enough, and even admirers and critics among the young men, but I could not discover that he had contracted a friendship with any one of them. They could not but acknowledge his talents, and respect the dignity of his personal presence, but they could not make him one of themselves. Still less were they disposed to trifle with him. He came and went, was grave or gay, as it suited him, and no one cared to call him to account for aught that he said and did, or to interfere with his pleasure.

It happened in these days that a company of tragedians took up their abode in H. for the space of several weeks, and gave a momentary impulse to the dormant theatrical tastes of the inhabitants. Their performances were far from contemptible, and the choice of pieces in their repertory comprized some of the best German dramas, and even some adaptations of the plays of Shakespeare. I rejoiced in the hope that so intellectual an amusement might have a humanizing effect upon the Burschen and Fuchsen of the University, nor was I disappointed. They were content to forsake for a time the fighting gallery and gaming table, and organized themselves into that formidable parterre, to which the actor really plays and upon whose applause he mainly depends. Even the meetings at the drinking *kneib* assumed a milder and more reasonable character. There was much criticism of authors and actors, much spouting and declaiming of favorite passages, and even now & then a rude attempt at the performance of a scene or two from some familiar play, without the concomitant aids of dress and scenery. I was present on many of these occasions, and was always ready to aid as well as I could so instructive an amusement.

On one of these evenings, it was proposed to declaim some scenes from a version of *Romeo and Juliet* which had been lately represented on the stage.

Some pains had been taken to give to this performance a certain dignity and importance. The committee of arrangement had been at the trouble of borrowing a dress or two, and had erected a temporary platform of divers tables and planks that lay at hand. A certain youthful Freiherr Von ——— had committed to memory the part of Romeo, and was prepared at least to recite it very correctly, while a tender fox of beardless lip and diminutive proportions had been selected as the fittest representative of Juliet. At the time appointed, Romeo was summoned to the boards by the kicking, stamping, and shouting of the audience. He appeared in some sort of *demi* costume with a feather in his slouched beaver, and a short cloak draped most ungracefully about him. He prepared to commence with the opening words of the famous Balcony Scene, but instead of speaking, he looked around him in some embarrassment and remained silent. The cause of his perplexity was obvious—there was not the smallest appearance of any Juliet. The heroine was loudly called for, and impatiently sought—she was nigh at hand, but alas! in what a state? Having undertaken to fortify herself for her part by an unwonted use of stimulus, she had enjoyed somewhat too freely the blessings of beer, and had stretched herself upon the first bench at hand, fit only to be carried to the Tomb of the Capulets. The unfortunate Romeo waited for a moment or two, and then withdrew, with a disconsolate countenance. But the assembly were not thus to be baulked of their evening's entertainment—they had come together to see the play, and see it they would. Vigourous efforts were made to provide a substitute for the unworthy and unconscious Fox, but all in vain. There was but one person present who had any knowledge of the part, and that person was myself.

The tide of public indignation now turned more strongly than ever against the Fox. "We will punish him at least!" they cried, and heaven only knows what tortures they might have invented to recall him to his senses, had not some one near me mentioned my name.

"Laurence is perfectly able to personate Juliet," said this person in a loud voice—"he has written an essay upon the play, and knows it by heart."

This announcement produced quite an uproar around me. I was not only called out but dragged out. "Recite or fight," cried the ferocious public, and I thought it best, however reluctantly, to accept the gentler alternative of the two. I retired therefore behind the scenes, to array myself in such

The Hermaphrodite

tragic robes as I might find. The dress of the ill-fated Juliet was there, waiting for me, but it was with a strange foreboding that I clothed myself in its white draperies. Romeo was at hand eager to lend me any assistance in his power. He undid my queue, and marvelled at the abundance and beauty of my hair. I suffered it to fall in loose locks upon my neck, and bound some trumpery garland about my brow. A few minutes sufficed to complete my primitive toilette—we appeared on the proscenium, and as soon as the tumultuous satisfaction of the audience had subsided, my Romeo commenced the delivery of his opening speech. In this, he was more successful than I had supposed he would be. He had vanity enough to care for even the undiscriminating approbation of the very uninformed public before which we found ourselves, and he really exerted himself to display to the greatest advantage his limited powers of voice and of elocution. His zeal proved contagious, but it took in me a different form. Utterly indifferent as I was to the approval or censure of those around me, I soon forgot them, and felt for a moment a nameless pleasure in being something other than myself. My heart warmed, my voice became deeper and fuller, and I found myself giving a fervent expression to the glowing words of the Italian woman-child. Such fragments of the play as we were able to present were received with the most gracious attention, and our death was hailed by what is commonly termed rapturous applause. Even flowers were not wanting to our triumph; I found myself crowned with an improvised garland of myrtle, whether I would or no, and as the young Freiherr descended, leading me by the hand, the whole company gathered around us, to express their thanks.

I heeded little what they said, for at this moment, for the first time, I caught a glimpse of Ronald's face, turned full towards me, with a strange expression. It was entirely white and bloodless, and all the vitality that usually animated it seemed concentrated in the eyes, which were intensely dilated and fixed upon me. Another moment, and the colourless countenance became suffused with angry red—the glittering eye flashed forth its imprisoned lightnings. Ronald sprang forward, and attempted to push Romeo from my side, and not succeeding, would have struck him, had I not seized the half-raised arm, and held it back with all my strength.

"Ronald, are you mad?" I said in an undertone, "would you disgrace yourself and me by this unprovoked brutality?"

The Hermaphrodite

Ronald turned, half furious, upon me, but thank God I had still some power over him. I met his angry look with one of entire and resolute self possession and his eye sank beneath mine. The rude assemblage would have been but too much delighted to see the pleasures of the evening consummated by a bloody quarrel, but I had recalled Ronald to himself and he could not condescend to fight for their diversion. I drew his arm through mine, and would have led him from the hall, but ere I could do so, he turned aside and exchanged a word with Romeo. The young men preserved so calm an exterior that I hoped to effect a speedy reconciliation.

"What have you said?" I inquired. "I hope that you have made peace. Come, Ronald, be reasonable; Romeo, be forgiving, what earthly occasion can there be for dissension between you?"

Romeo smiled, and assured me that all was right; and Ronald silently nodded assent, and left the room with me. As no blow had been given, and no abusive words uttered, I anticipated no evil result from this momentary ebullition of temper. But Ronald was fearfully sullen, and we parted for the night in silence which weighed like lead upon my heart.

Chapter [16]

The words exchanged between Ronald and the Freiherr Von ——— were briefly these:

"You are a fool," said Ronald.

"Your Juliet is a woman," said the Freiherr.

"You have lied in saying it."

"And you in denying it."

"You are challenged."

"I accept—name the time."

"The sooner, the better—tonight, tomorrow."

"Tomorrow night, then."

"It will be quite agreeable to me."

Why did not some kind angel whisper to me that night that I was sleeping on the brink of an abyss, on the crater of a volcano?

The angel did not repeat to me one of those fierce words so coldly uttered, did not unveil to me one of the fierce thoughts which were at work

The Hermaphrodite

so near me—his task was a gentler, perhaps a kinder one. He stood at my threshold, and waved his flaming sword across it, so that no dark or dangerous thing could enter there, and on the eve of ruin, and on the verge of desolation, I slept in innocence, in peace, in safety.

There is a tide in the bosoms of men which, taken at its full, may bear them beyond the reach of guardian spirits, beyond the heavenly power of truth. Life has its moments of concentrated damnation. The cup is at our lips, and the draught is sweet to our taste—some one tells us that it is hellfire—well, let it be so—we will pledge the devil in it. The result, one fondly hopes, may still be in God's hands.

There is a prayer which I have heard strong men and brave men pray—there is a vision before which I have seen strong and brave men blanch, and fall upon their knees, with quivering lips and white cheeks, and eyes that stared upon vacancy as upon some horrid sight. And the prayer was: "All powerful One, keep me from that I am"—and this vision that overcame the brave man was that of the imprisoned devil within him. But I looked, and ministering spirits held up those quivering hands in prayer, and the All-powerful One listened, and His angels said Amen.

The morrow came, but Ronald sought me not, as was his wont. I listened for him in vain—his room was empty, and when I questioned others of his movements, I was told that he had gone out at an earlier hour than usual. The hours of study, of recitation, of exercise passed, and brought him not. Never before had it been so. As I sat down, for the first time, to dine alone, a message was brought to me to the effect that Ronald had promised to entertain some of his young friends that day at the Gast haus—he begged that I would not wait for him, he had engagements also for the afternoon, and would not be at home before nightfall.

Ronald's young friends? was I not his only friend? A certain gloom and sadness came over me at the tiding of this seeming perversity, and I found it difficult to account for conduct so unusual on his part. But I chid my swelling heart, and strove to reason down its rising regrets. "Shall I curtail for him the blessed boon of freedom? no, let him enjoy it fully and freely—in God's name, let me not play the court pedant." Thus I spake to myself, and recalled to my aid a faint remembrance of the words of some Eastern poet:

The Hermaphrodite

Youth brooks not the rein of Counsel,
Nor the curbing hand of Friendship,
Behind it, but unseen, is the scourge of Necessity.

For it, the river of Life runs wine, and all its sands are golden.

It would snatch at the clouds, it would swim upon the Infinite.
It would stake eternities on the pleasure of a moment.

Pass on, oh young man, in thy strength, in thy pride!
Who shall stay thy footsteps, or hang upon thy skirts?
The path thou hast chosen was yet traced for thee
And even thy follies are written in the book of the Eternal wisdom.

I passed the day in lonely wanderings, in solitary musings. As the twilight came on, I grew restless. I must needs go forth, and some uneasy impulse led my steps towards the Gast haus where Ronald and his companions had held their banquet. I entered the dining hall which was still redolent of wine and of good cheer. A servant was occupied in removing the relics of the feast. I walked to the seat which Ronald must have occupied at the head of the table. A bunch of violets, bought of some barefooted flower girl, lay carelessly beside his plate—half withered as they were, they had for me a certain meaning, and I placed them in my bosom. The Kellner was sweeping from the floor the fragments of glass with which it was strewn. I asked him if there had been any quarrelling, any fighting among the young men. No, he replied, they had been friendly enough, but the wine had circulated very freely among them, and at last, the toast of Liebschen (love) having been given and drunk, the convives had unanimously thrown their glasses behind them, that they might never be desecrated by any meaner service.

And Ronald, had he done likewise?

"Yes, and yet worse—he had not only thrown his goblet to the ground, but had ground it to powder with his heel, so wild was he, although he had not drunk deeply—I might see where the crushed drinking glass lay, a heap of glittering dust."

Among the Hebrews, the nuptial rite is crowned by a ceremony analogous to this. The prayers, exhortations, and vows having been duly recited,

The Hermaphrodite

the bride and her husband pledge each other in wine from the same cup, which the bridegroom then tramples beneath his feet. Tradition says that this act implies the eternal union of the newly wedded pair, which is destined to last until the shards of the shattered wine cup shall unite themselves to form once more a whole. For a bystander, it might suggest this sadder reflection. Love, the wine of life, is soon drunk out, and the empty goblet, were it of the finest crystal, or the purest gold, is fit for naught but to be crushed to nothingness, a heap of glittering dust.

But Ronald's lady love? I had never seen him so much as look upon a woman.

With that kind of indecision which loves battles, which allows the crises of fate to arrive unprepared for, and to depart unimproved, I sat in my room, and waited for Ronald. The evening closed in gloomily—the darkness of my room seemed peopled with unfriendly shapes; corresponding to the melancholy bodings which, all unbidden, thronged my vacant mind. I lit my lamp, and made various unsuccessful endeavours to amuse myself. At first a new book beguiled my attention—then, I busied myself with a long letter—finally, my uneasiness became almost insupportable. I threw aside the book, the pen, and paced my room, counting the lapse of moments by the throbs of my excited pulse. At length, I heard a step ———.

I heard a step, but I could not think it his. He had learned motion of the winds, the waves, the birds, and walked upon the earth as though he scorned it. The step that ascended my stairs was heavy and rough; the hand that undid my door was slow and unskilful, but the sound approached, the door opened, and Ronald staggered into the room, and flung himself heavily upon a chair. For a few moments, he neither moved nor spake, and I had not courage to address him; but soon, impatient of my own weakness, I went up to him, and drew the slouched beaver from his brow. Ah! upon its fair expanse I saw the first frown, indelibly written. His face was deadly pale, save a burning spot on either cheek. In his eye was a wild and wavering light—at first it shunned mine, then I saw it fixed upon me with a terrible intensity. This was not the Ronald I had known, this was not the fair child whose innocence and tenderness had reconciled me to life, who had led me, by a way which I knew not, from the giddy heights of madness to broad

The Hermaphrodite

and sunny regions of affection and delight. Yet even in that evil moment, in that evil mood, how beautiful was he!

"Ronald, dear boy, you have been drinking!"

"I believe so," he replied, speaking slowly as with repressed emotion. "They gave me wine to supply the place of the blood I have lost."

"Of the blood you have lost?" I mechanically repeated.

"Yes, blood. Does the sight of it make you sick? look here." He tore open his vest, and pointed to a bandage upon his right shoulder—his linen too was stained with blood.

"Good God, you have been fighting, Ronald, with whom? for what?"

"For a lie," was the fierce and sullen answer.

I had no words to express my terror, my surprise, and Ronald, once aroused, had so much to say that he heeded not my silence.

"Yes, for a cursed, a damned lie, for the cruel deception of which I am the victim, and to which you have sacrificed the peace of my heart, the hope of my life. You begin to tremble? it needs not now, I have made it true to others—that lie, would you ask what it is?—your manhood."

Of aught that I said, or looked, or thought, in that dread hour, I have never been conscious. At these words, a cold and deathlike mist seemed to gather round me, and through it, as in a dream, I heard in ever varying tones, the wild chant of Ronald's passion.

"Yes, you are that lie, and I am your victim, but you can cancel the wrong, oh angel-fiend. You can change my torment to raptures of heaven. You shall be a man to all the world, if you will, but a woman, a sweet, warm, living woman to me—you must love me, Laurence."

Ronald was at my feet—the frown had passed from his brow, and still dimly, as in a dream, I heard his glowing accents, and felt, rather than saw, the light of his glowing eye. But I spake not—it was not a time for words.

"I am weary of seeing you thus encased, thus imprisoned—do off, do off these hated garments, which wrong your heavenly grace and beauty—float before me, swan-like, in loose, light robes—throw off the narrow bondage of that vest—let your heart beat freely, let your bosom heave high, heave wildly, till the very remembrance of my sorrow be buried beneath its white waves."

Still silence, as of death.

The Hermaphrodite

"Smile upon me, speak to me, do not look at me with those moonlight eyes. Why are you so cold and so still? do you take me for a spirit, as you once did, do you doubt again whether I am human? you need not speak, silence gives consent."

I know not by what miracle it was that I gathered strength, for a moment, to fling him from me, to rise from my chair, and creep trembling towards the shelf on which my pistols lay—not on him, God knows, would I have turned them, but upon my own blasted bosom. It was in vain—Ronald laughed as I snapped them, one after the other—the charges had been drawn.

"I saw you load them last night—I had the prudence to unload them."

I grew faint again—I leaned against the wall for support—I looked towards the windows, they were clearly barred—the door of the inner room was locked—even had it been otherwise, I could not have reached them, for the grasp of the demonized youth, strong with the strength of madness, was again upon me, and his voice, hushed to a stern and terrible whisper, sounded again in my ears.

"Do not curse, do not pray, do not struggle—it is all in vain. I fear no curse but that of losing you—God himself, if there be a God, will not come between me and my right. I bear in my bosom a wondrous fire, a strange alchemy, that can turn marble itself to molten flame. You are mine by fate, mine by the power of my will, and my first crime is also yours, for it is born of the union of your soul and of mine."

"Ronald!—you will blush for this tomorrow, but I shall weep for it all my life."

"Yes—women weep, and it does not cost them much, but I have bought you with tears of blood."

Still, other words of terrible import, half heard, and dimly comprehended; still that terrible grasp, straining me closer and closer to the heart which, once pure and peaceful, was now in its hour of volcanic might and ruin. On my part, a faint but rigid struggle, a sob, a mute and agonized appeal to heaven—that appeal was not answered. Suddenly, I felt Ronald shiver and tremble—gaining courage, I raised my eyes to his face, and saw the burning flush pass, in an instant, from his cheek—exhaustion was already subduing the fever of his wound, maddened by wine—a certain

The Hermaphrodite

confusion of thought was visible in his countenance. This was the critical moment—by the mercy of God, I took advantage of it.

"Ronald, you have been drinking, but I am faint, and cold, and ill. Let me get some wine—let us drink together."

"You seek to escape."

"How is that possible? the wine is in your room—the outer door is locked—you yourself have the key."

"I have it, and shall keep it—well, go, go—fetch me the wine; I have drunk, but not deeply enough."

So saying, though with a certain reluctance, Ronald released me from his grasp. Trembling and dizzy, I ran to the closet in which the wine was kept, and returned, in a few moments, bearing two well-filled goblets. Ronald snatched the glass I offered to him.

"Here is to love!" cried he, holding it high, "here is to love, a past without a reckoning—a present without a future!"

He drained it to the dregs, was silent for a moment, and then turned in wild fury upon me.

"Sorceress! murderess!" he cried, "I have drunk death, and no other hand than yours prepared the draught—but think not that I will die alone. You have made me pledge you in poison, you shall pledge me in blood."

With one hand he grasped me again—with the other, he sought his dagger. As he held it aloft, I smiled, and shrank not, but it was not destined to fulfill its errand of deliverance. Ere he could strike me, his arm was paralyzed, a tremor shook his whole frame, he stared around him for a moment as if in utter darkness and bewilderment, and then, as if felled by a mighty blow from some unseen hand, he sank upon the floor, heavy and senseless as a corpse.

The drugged wine had done its work. No marble could have been more unconscious than Ronald, as I laid him upon his couch, bound up his wounds afresh, and wrapped him in warm coverings. He heeded not my last farewell—he saw not the frantic haste with which I despoiled my head of the long, fair hair so dear to him, and flung it from me, as an unholy thing—he heard not the dull, sullen echo of the door as it closed for ever upon me.

But it was a merciful thing, the stupour of this seeming death—without it, he had scarce had the power or the courage to live. It was in pity that

The Hermaphrodite

the angel of Oblivion waved his flag of truce over the pale sleeper, and kept at bay for a few hours the bloody and merciless forces of memory and conscience. Disease and despair would be alike subdued by his gentle ministration.

But tomorrow? oh—tomorrow!

Away, away, in the deep, dark night—away, through unknown paths and untried difficulties! away to solitude, to freedom, to desolation! Why do these avenging Furies hang upon the footsteps of an innocent sufferer, and scourge him to the wildest flight? How has the curse of eternal wandering fallen upon one who never mocked at Jesus, or at the meanest of his brethren? Better that curse on him than his curse on others. Away, away at the maddest pace. Canst thou ever know fatigue again? will these rigid limbs ever relax in weariness, will that brain with its burning, wiry pulsations ever again be laid upon the gentle lap of sleep? It is very still, this night—no sounds, save those vague murmurs which may be spirit voices, or the whisperings of the stars. The sentry, in his lonely walk, cries out: "Who goes there?" One accursed of God—good brother, let me go in heaven's name, for the devil is behind me. "The devil?" well, if not he, it is an angel with a flaming sword—whether of the two were preferable? a strange embarras du choix, hurrah!

Morning dawns—the hand of God hath waked up the sun and sent him, flushed with sleep, on his day's errand. The world of sound wakes up also—thank God, that speaking stillness is over. But here come human forms from out their dwellings—men? let us shun them even as women. They too are full of evil and danger—the purest heart among them contains a criminal thought, a wish unblest

The Hermaphrodite

2

[This section of the manuscript is 121 pages, numbered 50–171. The first page is obviously not the beginning of this portion of the narrative; we can only speculate how Howe intended to bridge the space between. Laurence remains the narrator (and is clearly the same character), but he has been transplanted from a German university to Rome. Ronald is absent, although he exists as a memory for Laurence. Laurence has a new companion, Berto, a Roman nobleman who tutors him in a rich array of subjects using unorthodox modes of instruction. It emerges near the end of this portion of the narrative that Berto is in fact the nephew of the unnamed Count in whose hermitage Laurence lived during his ascetic retreat—the life from which Ronald rescued him.]

Chapter [17]

At length, stepping timidly along from word to word, like one who crosses a brook upon stones slippery and uneven, I began to parse and to construe. I mastered by turns verses, Psalms and Chapters. I became ambitious of surprising Berto by the rapidity of my progress. I determined that my knowledge should one day equal, if not surpass his own. How far I might have gone in my Rabbinical career, it were now not easy to determine; for, in the full tide of my enthusiasm, I was checked and thrown back by the perverse will of Berto. But for him, I should never have known the first letter of the Hebrew alphabet—but for him, I might have become the most learned Pundit of my day.

I had passed a month in severe study, and fully intended to devote many more to my new pursuits. I sate one evening in my quiet room, with my books and papers strewn about me—a weary frown was on my brow, for I was endeavouring, from my tired brain, to weave anew the broken tracery of the time worn language. Suddenly, a well known laugh interrupted my labours, a firm grasp was laid upon my shoulder, and Berto saluted me with these uncourteous words.

"Will you have done with all that?"

"What do you mean, Berto? I am committing the Decalogue to memory, in preparation for tomorrow's lecture."

"Take my advice, and leave it alone. A little of it is well enough—Moses was a man of genius in his way, but too much behind the present day to occupy our attention for any length of time. Come! our month of Eastern exile is over now, and I am glad of it. Long and tedious has it seemed to me—here, let us drink to our return to civilized life."

As he spoke, he uncorked a bottle of unquestionable Lachrymae Christi, and compelled me to join him in a pious libation to the shades of David, Solomon, Judas Maccabeus, et autres.

"Dear old barbarians!" he cried, holding up his glass to the light. "The study of you has been so dry that rivers of wine must flow to lay your learned dust. Here's to your endless health, and to a year's separation from you!"

"I suppose you will explain all this, Berto," I said, "but to me it seems the strangest of all your strange caprices, to have entered suddenly upon pursuits of such gravity, to relinquish them as suddenly, and before we can have derived any benefit from them. If it is thus that you propose to direct my studies, I can only regret that I ever consented to put myself under your guidance."

"Ingrate," replied Berto. "Thou fillest me with indignation, and I almost repent me that I have taken thee under my care. Hast thou learned nothing from this month of application? Hast thou not in the first place forgotten infinitely of nonsense which was working in thy brain before? Laurence, to forget is to learn something that many never know. Hast thou not, moreover, learned to study Hebrew? is that indeed a small lesson? Thank me at least for that."

"I am not disposed to trifle with holy things, Berto," I remarked in that tone of concentrated irritation which a man especially reserves for a quarrel with his best friend. "These mystic letters are grown dear to me. In the depths of this ancient language, my soul has found new springs of life. I worship the God of Abram, Isaak, & Jacob. I feel myself the child of Adam and Eve, the subject of David, the pupil of Solomon—"

"And the brother of Cain," adroitly suggested Berto. He continued, "What you say is partially true, and entirely commonplace, but I am able notwithstanding to answer you, and a thousand like unto you.

"It is good, it is refreshing now and then to dive into the very depths of the past, but not to get oneself drowned in its waters, especially while the young, blooming future stands upon the shore, waiting to be wedded

The Hermaphrodite

to us by the hand of destiny. The past, like the poor, we have always with us—the present, the Christ of love and of life is with us for a time only. I am credibly informed that Hebrew is the language of the upper heaven—if so, you will soon have an opportunity of learning it not as a dead, but as a living language. For the present, dear fellow pedant, let me persuade you to open your ears to the melodious Roman tongue, and your eyes to the Roman world around you."

"Explain to me, Berto, your plan of study."

"Willingly, my dear friend. Know that I abhor onesidedness, fixed idea, and all the insanities of the learned. For them, the earth should stand still, for me, it turns round, and shews me a new face every day. Moreover, as for the mere material of knowledge, I hold it to be of small moment—the fact is ever trivial—its grandeur and importance are simply relative. The development of the capacity in us is the only real and permanent result of our mental labours. In this view, I desire to do entire justice to every fibre of my brain, every nerve and muscle of my body, and I therefore give to each its appointed time of training and exercise. I would be wise rather than erudite, can think upon most subjects, wish to profess none. I have therefore marked out twelve studies for the twelve months of the year, twelve apostles for the Gospel of my life. I devote annually a month to the study of ancient languages, one to that of the modern, theology has its appointed month, so have Mathematics, so political economy, antiquities, men and manners. Since I have completed this arrangement of my time, men have invented a new physiological psychology, phrenologismus by name, and this has grieved and puzzled me not a little, as my number was already full, and I cannot possibly make a year with thirteen months."

"What is to be our occupation for the next month?" I asked.

"The consideration of existing civil and social relations and institutions. As the time of Carnival is approaching, we may prolong our investigations somewhat beyond the lunar limits assigned to them. The month following shall find us naturalists—the greater the change of occupation, the greater the relief, capisci?"

Our conversation prolonged itself far beyond the usual duration of studious or convivial tête à têtes. The theme was congenial to us, and the Lachrymae Christi was not otherwise. Finding the room at last rather narrow for minds of so expansive a character, we walked out into the streets of

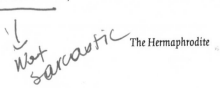

Rome, which, in the rapidly waning moonlight, were growing as dark and treacherous as a Jesuit's countenance, when the cold, keen smile is passing away from it. Even here, however, Berto felt himself cramped and confined.

"Fie on these streets!" he cried. "The houses almost kiss each other—like parted lovers, they threaten destruction to the wretch that comes between them. Give me air, air! an open space that does not, like these blind alleys, exhale charnel-like corruption!"

"The top of the Capitol is airy," I remarked, "but there are inconvenient angles in the staircase."

"The Coliseum will suffice for tonight—lead me thither, if you can find the way—I knew it once, but these cursed English have so bewitched the city with their bribes, that the very streets will not guide you aright, unless you promise them a Buona mano."

But once within the walls of the Coliseum, Berto became still more ungovernable than before. As he entered, he knelt and kissed the ground. "Oh! my Roman mother!" cried he. "I thank thee for my Roman birth." He arose and looked around him silently for some moments. At length he laid his finger upon my arm, and said:

"Shall this noble monument any longer lie in ruins? shall we not at least rescue it from further decay?"

"Scarcely, with our small fortunes."

"I will restore it to entireness," said Berto with tragicomic dignity. "I have hands to labour, but better still, I have a head to contrive. I have this moment conceived the idea of a giant subscription of millions, to be obtained for the purpose from every crowned head in Europe. I myself will stand before them even as Moses and Aaron stood before Pharaoh. I will say: Rome, the mother of you all, has never asked an alms of you, but she will deign to accept from you some small payment towards the immense debt you owe her; forget not that she made you that you are, and taught you all that you know."

"The thought is grandiose," I replied, "mendacity like larceny becomes heroic when performed upon a large scale."

"Am I a man to be refused by kings?" continued Berto. "Shall I not move the heart of a Gasconading French monarch? Shall a brute of a Russian autocrat defy my eloquence, or shall the little Soubrette that rides the lion of England awe me into shameful silence?"

The Hermaphrodite

"Austria has a peculiar policy," I suggested.

"So have I, and Austria will do well to respect it. Berto is Berto!" Here he struck his breast forcibly. "He is an universalist, and no specialist, an integral man, not a fractional manifestation of humanity. Am I a peacock, sir, or do I tell the truth?"

"The moon is a peacock," I said, "and the stars are the eyes in her train. See, she is fast closing her wings; in another minute she will fly down into the sea."

"See there! see there!" suddenly cried Berto, wildly pointing to the east.

"What do you see?"

"Why, that horrible conflagration on our right, to be sure. See how quickly it spreads—it will devour yonder church, yonder palace, the whole suburb. Help, help! alarm the watch! call the night police!"

I had some difficulty in convincing Berto that the luminous appearance in the East was occasioned by the rising sun, and very much more in persuading, guiding and compelling him through the tortuous streets back to his own dwelling.

When next I saw Berto, he was entirely himself, and seriously laid before me his plan of occupation for the ensuing month. He promised to make me acquainted with the schools, colleges, prisons, and eleemosynary institutions of Rome, but he especially insisted moreover that I should lay aside somewhat of my native shyness, that I should go more into the great world of little things, and make myself better acquainted with the minds and manners of living men.

"Why, how now, Berto? I thought we were to be students."

"This also is a study, and not the least among them," said Berto. "You are greatly mistaken if you suppose that I have the smallest intention of ministering to your anchoritic tastes—if I deemed your madness upon that point contagious, much as I esteem you, I should instantly forswear your company. Every man should be a savage once in his life, because every individual, to be a genuine man, should go through all the phases through which necessity has led the race. Man is born naked to the intent that he should begin life as a naked barbarian. To be sure, mothers will thwart the benevolent purpose of nature, but they cannot change it. The period of rude contest and of cruel conquest, the dawning of civilization, the first discovery of the superiority of cooked meat over raw fruit, the religious period, the

The Hermaphrodite

doubting, reasoning period, all these should succeed each other in the life of every man. But when the individual has reached the point of Christian civilization, when the wings of his mind and the tails of his coat are fully grown, and he has become rounded, polished, and educated into a fitness for the society of like rounded, polished and educated men, then it were a pity that he should creep back to his first state of barbarism, and forget all that he has acquired?"

"Oh Berto! the most of men do learn such evil in the world, such sophistical self-deception, self-worship, envy, cunning, superficiality of thought, flippancy of speech—were it not better that they could forget it all?—What else was meant by that divine injunction to become as little children?"

"And they can forget it all," said Berto, "if they will truly learn one lesson of the world. A new birth of innocence, a childlike freshness of heart and will are given to man in the very moment in which he comes to life as children to a school, not as debauchees to a feast with which, be it plenteous or stinted, he is never content, in which, though the wine and the jest flow freely, intoxication and disgust must wearily succeed each other, until they become merged in each other, one and indistinguishable. I tell you that they do not learn. The seeds of true and noble knowledge are not sown in their hearts, and the soil is left to bring forth such rank weeds of wickedness as it may."

The voice of the good Berto trembled, and tears stood in his strangely variable eyes. We were both of us silent for a moment, but I durst not remain so, for I knew that my friend would turn angrily upon me, as he always did when he had betrayed any emotion incompatible with his usually affected cynicism.

"Berto," said I, "your tears and your simile alike remind me of the Lachrymae Christi."

Berto laughed, and said: "I get drunk regularly once a year, and always on the same day—if I did more, I could not respect myself, if less, I could not know myself."

Our conversation now turned upon Roman society, into which Berto now proposed to introduce me.

"I approve of the discipline of society for men," said he, "but if I loved a woman, I should scarcely dare to expose her to its temptations and corruptions."

The Hermaphrodite

"Women are then more prone to evil than men."

"Not so, but they are educated rather to triviality and routine than to strength and virtue—they are taught to appeal to our indulgence, not to command our esteem. All things run easily to extremes, in their excitable natures, and as one sees their piety become superstition, and their learning, pedantry, so in society their love of approbation becomes outrageous vanity, and their coquetry something for which I can scarce find a name which would be at once true and decent."

"Why then should one make them a study?"

"To learn their high capacities, and to appreciate the wrong done them by education and position."

"If society be divided, as you say, into the injurious and the injured, for God's sake, let me keep out of it!"

A sudden remembrance came over me. "Berto," I said, "it occurs to me that I have never seen you with a woman but once—what has become of that beautiful, dark eyed fellow pilgrim of yours?"

As I spoke, Berto fixed his eyes upon mine with a questioning glance.

"What know you of her?"

"Nothing, save a moment's view of her face."

Berto seemed to ponder well my words. "It is strange," he at length remarked, "it is very strange that you should have thought of her today. I have myself known nothing of her since her arrival here, and this very day, I have received a billet inviting me to witness her profession, which takes place tomorrow. If you will come to me at this hour on the morrow, I will shew you a ceremony which some people call the bridal of the Lord— unhappily, one cannot always be sure that the bridegroom is present."

Berto now sought among the contents of his portfolio a copy of verses, which he handed to me.

"Read these foolish jingles," said he abruptly. "I once could rhyme."
The verses ran thus:

> What seek'st thou in the Convent aisle,
> The gloomy Convent aisle, ladye?
> Thou'rt full of young and lovely life,
> So is the world God made for thee.

The Hermaphrodite

It is my lofty, pious mood
Which makes the earth so worthless seem,
I fly, lest some dark shade of sin
Should sully o'er my heavenly dream.

Ah! sin may pass the Convent grate,
The guilt that haunts us is our own,
True life might plough and root it out,
I fear me, it will thrive alone.

If sin be not a fitting cause
Sorrow has made my calling sure.
My bosom hides a deadly wound
And God alone can work its cure.

God hangs on every forest tree
Some balsam for a fevered mind;
Who enters here with breaking heart
Leaves not his breaking heart behind.

In life I seek the peace of Death,
To God, my being I resign;
Be all the erring human His,
The perfect, the immortal, mine.

Blight not the holy germ of life,
The man must give the angel birth,
Know, none from earth ascend to heaven,
Who made not first a heaven on earth.

"Did you read your verses to the girl?" I asked.

"Yes, and many more, some more wise, and some more foolish. In desperate need, we all hit upon desperate expedients—you can imagine that none would be more so to me than the matching of words and the clipping of thoughts, usually termed poetry."

"What effect did yours have upon her?"

"It brought tears to her eyes sometimes—sometimes it seemed to convey to her no idea. She once said to me, 'you are a heretic, and what is worse yet, a philosopher—for such there is little hope, but I will pray the Virgin for you.' "

"Had you tried the effect of earnest reasoning upon her?"

"Most thoroughly and unsuccessfully—it was even a folly to try it. Who ever by reason convinced a woman, much less a girl? Born to feel, and not taught to think, they are ever the slaves of their own impulses, until they become the slaves of men, nor do they give up one caprice, until it is trampled under foot by its successor."

Berto was silent for some minutes—at length, he began unasked the story of Eleonora.

"It was in the Canton of ———— that I first saw her, with her moonlight hair, and her eyes of night—there is nought of the garish day about her, neither sparkle, nor bloom, nor noise—she was silent as darkness, innocent as slumber, fervent as midnight prayer. The niece, of the Parveeo, and the daughter of a saint, she was conceived in piety, and born in visions, and her destiny was decided before she had drawn her first breath. Her dying mother vowed her to the Virgin, and in early childhood, she embraced with ardour the idea of a religious vocation. Her father is a farmer whose easy circumstances have enabled him to afford his children an education more ambitious than wise—"

"How so?" said I, interrupting Berto, "because they are poor, would you cut them off from the advantages of scholarship and a liberal education?"

"No, fool that you are!" cried he; "have you been so long with me, and have not known me better? I would only say that in education, one should begin at the beginning. The children of well-educated parents are well-educated from their birth—in them, the eye is formed to beauty, the mind to order, and the heart to reverence, before they are at all capable of individual thought and exertion. An illiterate peasant is content that his children, in childhood, should be as illiterate as himself. Later in life, he sends them to school, and often to the University, to learn, he scarce knows what, or why—he will value most in them the acquirements which will shew most. Such a child, on the other hand, finds himself suddenly projected into a world of ideas, all of which are utterly new and strange to him—unfit to guide himself, and perhaps unwilling to be guided, he is at best at the mercy of his professors, who are not likely to consider either the peculiarities of his nature, or the necessities of his ignorance. He learns what he can, as

The Hermaphrodite

best he may, and comes out from the chaotic process certain at least that he is wiser than his father."

"Yet great men often come up from the mass of the people."

"Yes—thanks to themselves and God, who is more the Father of some men than of others."

"Will you finish your story?"

"Will you leave off your cursed interruptions?) *rapport*

"The clerical uncle adopted Eleonora at her birth, and assumed the charge of her as soon as she emerged from babyhood—she cut her teeth upon a rosary, and played at dolls with an Agnus Dei. She was taught to pray before she was taught to think; in consequence, she has never thought or prayed aright. She was a quiet and gentle child, and her earnest, reverential nature was easily moulded by her uncle to devotion and pietism, while her imagination took a solemn cast from the legends of saints and martyrs which constituted her only literature. The consciousness of her vocation, and of her educational advantages gave her a certain feeling of superiority over the young girls of the village, and though not haughty, she was reserved and cold with them. In my last year's travels in Switzerland, I fell by chance upon the chalet in which she dwelt, and became the guest of her uncle, over whose little household she presided, with scrupulous exactness. I was at once struck by the peculiarity of her aspect, and by the beauty which she attempted to disguise rather than to display. She did not wear the tight bodice, short petticoat, and coquettish cap of the canton, but in its place a twilight coloured robe long, loose, and half conventual in its form, in which she glided noiselessly about; more like an apparition, than a reality. I must say that she was no idle saint, but that her industrious fingers provided for the necessities of the good Curate. Still, she found time to indulge herself with mass and vespers daily, and varied the monotony of her occupations by singing her Ave Maria, or reciting the penitential Psalms. I was surprised, one day, to find her in the garden, engaged in plaiting a wreath of flowers. Encouraged by the secular nature of her employment, I ventured for the first time, to address a few words to her.

"Is this a fête day, pretty Eleonora?"

Her pale cheek reddened, but not with pleasure, as she replied in the affirmative. "And you are weaving that garland to wear to the dance, this afternoon?"

The Hermaphrodite

Half resentful, half reproachful was the look she gave me in return, as she said: "God forbid—it is a chaplet for the blessed Virgin."

"Can you guess what the Virgin would say if she could speak?"—"I cannot tell."—"I think she might say: 'thank you kindly, my dear child, but I would rather see the roses blooming on your brow than withering on my altar.'"

The girl was too much shocked or displeased to make me any answer— she bent her eyes upon her work, and murmured to herself, "avertite oculos meus, nec videant vanitatum." I sat down by her on the grass, and aided her to select the flowers for her chaplet. As I handed them to her I mentioned their Botanical names—she looked up with an expression of pleasure.

"Should you like to understand Botany, Eleonora?" I said.

"I do not care about it," she replied, "but I should like to know the Latin name of every thing—it is the sacred language, the language of the saints and of the church."

Oh! ye unhappy urchins, whose difficult Latinity is inseparable from the remembrance of aching heads and smarting backs, do ye not rather incline to think it the Devil's language?

"After various efforts, I entered into conversation with Eleonora, and by degrees was able to win her confidence. I found her almost hopelessly entangled in a network of dogma & superstition. Nature and reason had no voice in her heart—it was utterly under the dominion of a glowing supernaturalism. The deepest, most intimate wish of her heart was a pilgrimage to Rome, which her mother had vowed to accomplish, but from which death had hindered her. For the peace of her mother's soul, and the weal of her own, she was curious to take this pilgrimage upon herself, and even to take the veil in the holy City. She had dreamed, she said, that a stranger should guide her thither, and when I offered to be her guide, she thanked me with a look of eloquent delight."

"Was not this the maddest of all thy mad freaks? thou a pilgrim!"

"Perhaps so—it was for the good of another that I undertook the journey, and that is always a mad motive. At any rate, the matter was speedily arranged between the father and the uncle of Eleonora—it was decided that the former, with one or two devout friends should be of the party. Ere long, we assumed the staff and shell, and set out on our travels—I had hopes that they might have reached a happier eventuation."

The Hermaphrodite

"To what, oh most insidious Berto, didst thou endeavour to convert Eleonora—to thine own Platonic Mohammedan creed?"

"Not to irreligion, not to worldliness, did I strive to convert her, but to life and its truths. Had her years numbered twenty two, instead of seventeen, her captive reason might have been aided and incited to an effort, or her awakened woman's instincts might have been made to speak to her with terrible, resistless eloquence. But her Northern nature was not precocious—the innocence of her early age, the spiritual fervour of her young heart protected alike from the arguments of reason, and the allurements of sense. Her whole journey was one prayer against temptation and conviction. If I persuaded her to visit a gallery of paintings, she would look at no pictures save those of Madonnas, saints and martyrs. At every Cathedral, shrine or chapel, she paused to perform long and oft-repeated acts of devotion. If I led her to monuments of historical interest, and explained to her their origin, she listened with patience, but soon began to recite to herself her Ave and Credo. She had in her all the woman's strength of will, and devotedness of purpose, whether these be destined to absorb all else that is woman in her, I cannot tell. I seemed to see her pure soul sleeping in its transparent coffin, but I had no power over her or it. Pray God that since the coffin is irrevocably sealed, she may awake only in heaven."

Berto paused for a moment, but the only evidence of emotion distinguishable in him was the tone of assumed surliness in which he said:

"I wish you would not interrupt me with your endless questions."

"I am dumb," I replied, understanding well the meaning of his feigned displeasure. A moment more, and he proceeded to the end of his narrative.

"Well—Eleonora arrived in Rome as pure and passionless as she had left her chalet. I accompanied her to the convent to whose hospitality she was recommended. As we approached this goal of her desires, she stood still for a moment, and looked up at the young moon, then just rising in the heavens. "There is my Swiss moon," she said. "Eleonora," I said, "there is scarce a maiden in Switzerland to whom this moon does not bring either the thought or the presence of her lover. It shines upon the valleys in which they are roaming in innocent freedom, in a happiness you will never know. They love, they are loved—they will marry, and will rear up blooming families, while you are withering in your lonely cloister. They are following their true

The Hermaphrodite

vocation, derived from Nature and from God, while yours dates only from your own imagination and the wrongly exerted influence of others. Have you ever thought of these things? This world, you are about to renounce it for ever, without having known it or yourself—God grant that you may not dream longingly of it in your cell, and beat your poor head in vain against its wires."

"Oh Virgin mother!" fervently sighed the young girl.

"Yes—Eleonora—she whom you worship was herself a mother!"

The girl had listened silently to my words, but at this moment she broke abruptly from me, and sprang up the steps of the Convent, of which she rang the bell with a hurried and trembling hand.

"Do not fear," I cried, "I woo not for myself." But the door had already opened, and I could only follow her into the presence of the Superior, to whose care I reluctantly resigned her. As the moment came for our last parting, I took her unwilling hand in mine, and said: "Here ends our intercourse, Eleonora. I have tried to be a true and disinterested friend to you—should you ever have need of one, I pray you to remember me."

The girl fixed her dark eyes solemnly upon mine: "Signor Berto," she said, "you have been my soul's worst enemy." With these strange words of which the language at least was unintelligible to the Superior, and the meaning to me, she took endless leave of me—as she glided from the room I said: "God be with you, Eleonora,"—"and with you," she responded, in a softened tone. But the look that accompanied her words was not easy of comprehension—it was half friendly, half resentful, nor could I read in it whether my departure was matter of regret, or of relief to her."

Thus ended Berto's story.

At the church of —— on the morrow, there were garlands and choral songs, priests, prayers and incense. A long procession of nuns ushered in the heroine of the hour, the pale girl robed in white. They had availed themselves of her beauty to heighten the splendour of the sacrifice, and had attired her admirably well. Her satin dress displayed all the grace of her falling shoulders, all the slender roundness of her youthful form. Jewels hung glittering upon her white arms, and clasped her delicate throat. Upon her brow was the mockery of a bridal wreath. She wore it half meekly, half proudly, as if she had been glad that it adorned her for the first and last time. I stood near enough to see the expression of her countenance, as kneeling before the altar, she pronounced her vows. As I looked upon her, it occurred to me for the first time that a girl of eighteen is a Sphynx, an unsolvable riddle for which destiny alone knows the mot d'énigme. The pale visage before me was beautiful and soulful, but it was a chrysalid—what its metamorphosis should be, it had not been easy to imagine—no past was written on it, no future could be read in it—it was a glowing, earnest, beautiful present—God only knew what it should be. Was the pure soul fated to awake in its crystal coffin, or did the hand of the Highest himself hold it in enchanted slumber, in dreams of heaven? Oh girl! the day might come in which thou wouldst curse the mother that bore thee, and vowed thee to a false, ungenial life. Or one may see thee sitting in worn out, idiotic patience, wondering why death is so slow in coming, and why one cannot hear his footsteps. Or do they not say that love sometimes creeps into the cloister, in priestly garb? ah! some guilty, monstrous passion, cheated of its true ends and instincts, deplored as a crime, hidden as a disgrace, the bastard of necessity, not the honoured child of choice and freedom. God shield thee from such love, unless indeed the worst should prove better than none—but even then, thine innocent life must become a lie, and thy pure spirit must endure the hideous leprous garment of hypocrisy to be its clothing in life, its cerement in death. Oh! ye hapless souls whom adverse circumstance and native weakness compel to live a lie, whose lips confess a faith rejected by the sickening heart, who cannot, dare not speak out the truth before high heaven and die! what curse, what torment is like unto yours? In what Purgatorial waters will ye find again the integrity that crumbled away from you, piece by piece? Oh ye fallen ones, whether ye lie careless upon the earth, or bite the dust in the fierce agonies of your remorse, who shall lift you from it? who shall teach you to stand upright once more?

But let us return to the present, since the present alone was there. The preliminary ceremonies being over, Eleonora pronounced her vows in a voice clear and even firm. We saw her buried beneath the pall which betokened her living death—we heard her dirge chanted by the ghost-like choir, and rung out by the tolling bell—we saw her shorn of her fair locks, crowned with thorns, and dressed in the dark garb of the cloister. Soon the

The Hermaphrodite

rite was over, and we had taken our last look of her. A crowned bride, she had come to us—a veiled nun, she disappeared behind the convent grate, and we should never see her more.

We stood together in that great assemblage, a little group of the few who would remember Eleonora. The old father from whose quiet and bounded being she had sprung up, like a fountain, heavenward—the young brother who had lost in her a part of his own life, these gazed at the scene in mute sorrow, more dazzled than gratified by the splendour of the ceremonial which had set its seal of office upon Eleonora's piety. Beside them, Berto looked on with a cold intensity. Would she not look back at us? was she not young enough to grace with a tear the triumph of enthusiasm over nature? would she not break from her new bonds this once, and fall at her father's feet, to invoke with sobs his last blessing? Not so—the maiden's mind was otherwise possessed. One last view of her face we had, as she reached the grate which separated the church from the convent. She stood there for a moment, surrounded by the brilliant procession that accompanied her, but she saw us not. The dark eyes were raised, and upon her lips played a smile of impassioned inspiration. The heavens were opened to her view, and saints and angels in shining robes stretched out their arms to clasp her within the spirit world. At this moment there came, from the distant choir within the convent, a strain of almost unearthly music. It was too much—the inner, sublimer self had taxed the flesh beyond its utmost power of endurance, and with that wondrous smile fixed in her face, as in marble, she swooned in the arms of the Lady Abbess, as the latter advanced to receive her, and died a momentary death, under the too keen sword of the spirit. Thus aptly the veil of night closed between us and her, and we had seen, as in a mirage, the sensible expression of her spiritual destiny. I looked at Berto, but even in this critical moment, the current of his blood brought no message from his heart to his cheek. He looked on quietly, as one who studies deeply the meaning of the scene before him—only, as we turned to depart, he stooped to take up a rose which the Sposa had dropped, and placed it in his bosom, without uttering a word. I could not rouse him, that day, to wit or even to anger.

Had not Berto told me a lie about his indifference to women?
Still, an extinct volcano may be as cold as a snow mountain—why not?

The Hermaphrodite

Chapter [18]

In the pit of the theatre behold me next, awaiting, with the Mephistophelic Berto the début of a young Ballerina, already famous in expectancy, and of whose grace and beauty report spoke wonders. The house was crowded to suffocation, and the impatient public early began to express, by the usual noises, their zeal for punctuality. As is usual, when the opera does not form the principal attraction of the evening, no very special care had been bestowed upon the selection of it, and the audience endured the first act with a very desultory attention. This being once at an end, a great tumult commenced in the house, which was not easily appeased even by the watering of the boards, or the first notes of the symphony introducing the ballet. The latter was entitled L'eremito degli Alpi, and I could have mused strangely enough over the purport of these words, had not Berto growled out in my ear:

"They will of course have common sense enough to make the hermit dance, and the Ballerina pray—otherwise, the exhibition were a very tame one."

Before I could reply, the curtain rose, and the stage displayed as much of Swiss scenery as could be supplied by the scene-painter's canvass and pencil. In the back ground were crags, snow mountains, and torrents which seemed as well able to run up hill, as to run down. On the left appeared a very bold group of rocks, in black and white lead, and from behind them peeped out the semblance of a hut, not altogether unlike my sometime Alpine residence. Soon came forth the corps de ballet, in the holiday costume of the very canton of ———, in which I had so long made my abode. A dance now commenced, followed by a pantomime which seemed to have some bearing upon the tenant of the mysterious hut. One of the peasants commences a narration, which obviously paints the unseen hermit in the gloomiest colours. He points upward to the sky, and then downward to show that he is in league with the elements, and holds them in obedience to his will—but the mimic conversation is interrupted by the gay measure of the waltz, and in its giddy whirlings, the narrator and his audience forget their terrors. Suddenly, in the very height of their gaiety, a clap of thunder is heard—the sky grows dark—a storm-cloud gathers around them, and as they stand, petrified, in mute terror, the door of the hut opens, and a dark form issues from within, wearing on its face a black mask. In one hand the stranger bears a huge volume, and in the other a hazel wand, which he waves with a stern and threatening gesture, as he points to them the path by which they must depart. Some of them turn to fly, the more courageous determine to remain—they come forward in turn, to deprecate his anger, and to explain to him the innocence of their intentions, but all in vain. He is inexorable in his anger, and as he waves his wand again, the threatened tempest bursts, in all its fury, upon them. They all retreat in desperate confusion, and crowd upon each other in their haste to leave the scene. They are almost out of sight, when suddenly a soft strain of distant music is heard—the hermit turns in wonder—it sounds again—the thunder is stilled, and as he stands passive, transfixed, a light lithe form bounds in starry circlings to his feet, and hangs quivering before him, like a butterfly poised upon a flower. A loud roar of satisfaction greeted the heroine of the evening, as if the Roman lion were prepared to devour, with his eyes at least, the delicate morsel now flung to him. She was a magnificent blonde, a perfect vision of bloom and sunlight, and with the veil of early maidenhood still softening the vague outlines of her form, the tender traits of her transparent face. As she pled for her companions, every look, every motion of her pantomime was a treasure of art, worthy the sculptor's marble, and the painter's canvas, and when approaching the front of the stage, she commenced the adagio of her pas seul, the whole house hung breathless upon her movements, and was as silent as if the beautiful performance had appealed to every sense in one. This once over, the theatre fairly shook with frantic applause, which subsided only when the swift measure that followed held them spell-bound in a new delight. As I witnessed this, my vague recollections gathered to certain remembrance. Those wavy circles, those brilliant leaps, those tiny fluttering steps which fell like the leaves of a rose, when the first autumn wind shakes it—those cloud-like, wave-like, breeze-like movements of hers, I have already described them—I saw them not now for the first time. It was Rösli who danced before the magician-hermit, and who wooed him as she had won me. Nor did she woo in vain. The dark man looked on carelessly at first, then stealthily, then intently. The wand trembled in his hand—his head drooped, and the outlines of his shrouded form softened from their attitude of stern defiance, to one of rapt attention. The Rösli had half triumphed over his evil mood, yet as her dance was ended, he turned abruptly to leave the scene. With one bound, she overtook him, with another, she laid her hand upon his shoulder, and quick as thought pulled the black vizard from his face—he gazed at her one moment in astonishment, but in another, a touch of the magic wand had laid her senseless on the ground—the hermit strode gloomily to his cell—the villagers carried off the inanimate Rösli in mournful procession, the public roared, stamped, and shrieked applause, and so ended the first act of the ballet.

The first scene of second act presents the interior of a Swiss cottage. Upon a rustic couch lies the graceful form of Rösli, wearing still her white robes, and her crown of flowers. She seems at first half inanimate, but as her mother approaches her, she half rises from her couch, and languidly leans her head against her mother's breast. The latter interrogates her as to the cause of her illness, but she sadly shakes her head, and presses her hand upon her eyes and upon her heart, to express the sorrow which oppresses her. At this moment a post horn is heard, then a knock at the door, and a lady enters, in travelling costume, but half concealed by a mourning veil. Rösli's mother hastens to offer her every humble attention, but the lady seats herself in an attitude of deep dejection, and draws from her bosom a portrait, upon which she gazes with tears. Rösli approaches the lady Dorothea, and by signs inquires of her the cause of her distress. Dorothea explains to her that the portrait is that of her only son, who has been taken from her by an evil spell, and in search of whom she has long wandered hither and thither. She has sought information from every wizard far and wide, and has at last learned that her son inhabits an enchanted dwelling, and that a maiden who loves him is destined to deliver him from the spell. As Dorothea relates in pantomime the story of her griefs, Rösli asks to see the portrait—she starts back in astonishment—it is the face from which she has torn the mask. She now explains to Dorothea the circumstances of her own adventure, and expresses her determination to seek the haunted spot again, and herself to destroy the evil charm. Dorothea clasps her in her arms, and is frantic with delight, but Rösli's mother frowns upon the undertaking, and tries to dissuade her from it. Rösli takes the cross from her bosom, and swears upon it to accomplish her object, even at the risk of her life. She kneels to implore her mother's blessing, makes a sign of encouragement to Dorothea, and bounds eagerly from the cottage.

The Hermaphrodite

The scene changes, and presents to view once more the hermitage, darkly visible in the moonlight. A strain of softest music sounds, as in the distance, and as if responding to its call, a shrouded figure steals forth from a thicket of bushes, and glides furtively across the stage. It is Rösli who peeps timidly in at the hermit's window, and starts back, frightened at the lurid light which glares from within. She takes courage, however, and knocks at the door—she is answered by the savage barking of a dog within—she runs to hide herself, returns, knocks again, is again driven back by the same cruel greeting. She stands for a moment in utter dejection—she expresses in pantomime her disappointment, her sorrow, finally her strange love for the strange being within. Raising her eyes and hands towards Heaven, she implores the aid of higher powers to accomplish the purpose so dear to her. In answer to her prayer appears a kind fairy who bestows upon her a golden reed, and a coil of silken cords. As she stands still perplexed by so strange a gift, the fairy seizes one end of the silken ladder, and flies with it to the roof of the hermitage, beckoning to Rösli to follow her. It were not easy to describe in words the airy grace with which Rösli made this difficult ascent—as well might one attempt to tell how the moonlight walks abroad at night, leaping fantastically the dizziest heights, lying down to sleep in the bosom of dark waters, madly flinging its golden frolics in the very face of the black, sullen midnight. She mounted, however, and stood beautifully poised upon the apex of the crazy roof tree. Here, the fairy was decently dragged out of sight by invisible ropes and pulleys, and Rösli, drawing after her the silken ladder, and folding her hands upon her breast, sank within the dark chimney, followed first by a moment of silence, and then by a loud peal of applause. As she disappeared, we heard faintly the music of the golden reed, destined like the lyre of Orpheus to lull to sleep the dark powers that kept guard over the inmate of the enchanted hermitage. *thank you!*

But let me resume the present tense, as the scene is yet present to my mind. The next call of the scene-shifter's whistle brought to view the interior of this magical abode, lighted by unholy fires, and guarded by fiends in various shapes. The hermit sits in the midst, surrounded by books, parchments, and various implements of the black art—at his feet crouches a fierce hound, who starts, and growls angrily, as at the approach of some unwelcome visitor—the strange shapes too all turn towards the chimney, in attitudes of defiance and distrust. But from within it sounds the enchanted music, and all the demon household is spell bound by its holy power. The master, veiled again by his black vizard, feels the gentle influence—he listens first in wonder, then in sadness, he bends his head and weeps. His fierce hound sleeps at his feet, and he sits motionless as in a dream, while the fair form of Rösli emerges from the hearth, and glides towards him. They gaze long and earnestly at each other, and as he seeks to rise, the Rösli begins the soft incantation of her dance, and weaves around him the magic circle of her graces. She had reserved for this scene all the richest treasures of her art. Attention was utterly absorbed by the expression of her countenance, with its alternations of passionate entreaty, and suddenly returning timidity, by the thrilling motions of her arms, the bendings of her sweet head, the infinitely varied windings of her form, which made her mortality appear most like a transparent garment, folded this way and that, shaken lightly out, gathered softly in, by the slightest volition of the soul that wore it. The dark man is out-enchanted—he kneels at her feet, he clasps her knees, he yields him, rescue or no rescue—then follows an impassioned love-scene, then a rhapsodic measure of joy and triumph. Finally, Rösli demands from him as a pledge of his love the surrender of his hazel wand. He refuses—she points to the mark left by the blow he gave her—at last, he reluctantly gives it up to her. She waves it over her head, and the witch flame burns up high on the hearth—she waves it again, and the fiends, waking, glare upon her, and the dog growls angrily. She waves it a third time, a clap of thunder is heard, and the building falls, with a tremendous crash—the dark shapes pass away in flame—the dog springs at Rösli, and dies with a horrible howl. The black mask drops from the face of the hermit—Dorothea rushes in, and falls in raptures upon the neck of her rescued son, who leads her to Rösli as to his deliverer. But lo! the fair child turns pale and droops—she sickens, faints, falls—the angry demon has smitten her with death—her own life must pay for the rescue of her lover. He bends over her, he raises her in his arms—but all aid is in vain, and Rösli must die as Sylphides die, and as angels lie down to sleep. Like a white rose, full blown, which instead of withering, folds itself back into its bud again, so the Rösli subsided, from her brilliant and airy life, to a cold and statue-like stillness. In her last agony, her arms flung over her head, her lips met those of her lover in one fervent kiss—the attitude was precisely

The Hermaphrodite

that of Canova's exquisite Cupid & Psyche—another moment, and she lay in marble repose, the fairest of the Niobides.

I was silent, and more deeply moved than I should care to confess. An ambitious little critic behind me neatly delivered himself of the following little speech.

"Till I saw her move, I thought it the greatest of pleasures to see her in repose. Till I again saw her in repose, I thought it the greatest of pleasures to see her move."

"It is ill talking of such things," said Berto, gruffly. "I feel them grimly and tragically, with that rage of the soul which Beauty gives to those who cannot possess it."

I took advantage of Berto's rage of the soul to steal away unobserved, in search of the histrionic boudoir of the metamorphosed Swiss maiden. I might almost have been guided to it by the fragrance of the flowers with which it was strewn. The door stood ajar, and permitted me to hear her agitated respiration as she stood, panting for breath, like a noble steed who has been urged to his utmost swiftness. Around her lay the garlands and bouquets which had crowned her brilliant success. She had adorned herself with the fairest of these, and was surveying herself in a cheval-glass, with a smile on her lips, and all the joy of triumph in her eye. As I paused, still unseen, at the threshold, a young Abbé, a handsome and dissolute man of noble family, stole up behind her, and endeavoured to imprint a kiss upon the white shoulder, left all too bare by her half unlaced bodice. I should have smitten him to the ground—it needed not. Rösli's innocence was still her best defense, and she turned upon the intruder a flashing glance of indignation, before which he shrank back, abashed and repulsed. In another moment, recovering himself, he said:

"Pardon me, fair Ballerina, but you are beautiful, and must be worshipped."

"Yes, Signor Abbate, but I am pure, and must be respected."

For the guardian of the children had not forsaken Rösli. Methought I saw him at that moment, grown with her growth, grand in his austere anger, scourge forth from her presence him who would have left the first mark of desecration upon the temple of the living God.

This incident had changed the current of Rösli's thoughts, had marred the beauty of her triumph. She had been warned often of the evil in the world, but must it creep so near her, forcing her to spurn it with her own foot, to smite it with her own hand? Could it be that she should some day blush for her own graces, be ashamed of her own beauty? She looked again in the mirror, but as if she had sought there something other than herself. Tears gathered in her cloudless eyes, and as she threw herself upon the sofa near at hand, I heard her murmur:

"Oh, mother!"

"I bring you tidings of her," said I, abruptly entering. Rösli's countenance grew pale as death—she looked wildly around, and then fixed her eyes upon me.

"You have seen my mother? Is it well with her?" I answered in the affirmative.

"My poor father is not dead? oh! thank God—he will live to bless me when I return. Do they grieve for my absence—are they tired of waiting for me—have the little ones forgotten me?"

These, and a thousand other enquiries rapidly succeeded each other, and were as rapidly answered. Rösli's tears flowed with her words, and her long compressed emotion seemed to rise with the expression that gave it vent. Though I sat near her, she had taken but little note of me. Her heart was in her far off home, with all its purest and best affections, nor was it until she had quite wearied herself with talking, and with weeping that a sudden remembrance seemed to strike her. She looked in my face, she paused and changed colour. "Who are you?" she said, abruptly, "and where have we met before?"

"Have you so soon forgotten the hermit?" I asked, with a certain malicious emphasis.

Rösli sprang from her sofa, seized my arm, and drew me close to the hanging lamp—she looked at me earnestly for a moment, and then said:

"Yes—you are he. I remember you."

But at this moment the call-boy came to announce her carriage. She turned away from me, and looked once more in the glass, with a smile and a sigh. She shook off, as a garment, the melancholy which had gathered around her, and made a last pirouette ere she suffered me to envelope her in her cloak. This being accomplished, she took leave of me with a gracious wave of the hand, and glided, like a phantom, from my presence.

The Hermaphrodite

"Truly, it was a very moral action, your visit to the lovely Ballerina," said Berto, on hearing of my adventure. "I am happy to see that, in spite of all your scruples, you are at length fairly launched on the turbulent waters of dissipation. After turning your back upon all the high bred women of Rome, you are at last caught in the silken leash of a dame de l'Opéra."

"Berto, for shame! what motive but one of the purest benevolence could have led me—"

"To the feet of the prettiest woman in Rome," said Berto, mocking me: "Oh! your motives may have been well enough. I do not question them—I am talking of your actions. The Abbé too went in charity, no doubt, and came away in love. Your glimpse of him was but a prophetic vision of that which you will yourself one day attempt, only with better fortune."

"Even if it were possible for me to put myself upon an equality with the Abbé, (and you know, unkind Berto, that it is not) I can imagine no greater torture than the remorse he should feel, who should in the smallest degree pervert so pure a creature as that young girl."

"Do you think so?" asked Berto, "you speak in great ignorance of the poverty of life in emotions, and of man's boundless appetite for them. Know that remorse, like despair, is a luxury, and that the prospect of a grand, bitter, heroic repentance is often among the inducements to sin."

Chapter [19]

Again I saw and welcomed Rösli upon the boards. Again I saw the waving of her white robe, the magical play of her features, and all the graceful witchery of her plastic limbs—so floats the snow-drift, upon the winter-wind which, like an angel, bears it up, lest it should fall, and be polluted by the contact of earth.

Deep sadness came over me as I looked on this young creature, and pondered doubtfully her future fate. How often would she be led here, arrayed in these milk-white robes, a doomed victim at the altar of the world's pleasures? Pure, lovely, and defenseless as a newly opened flower, how long would it be before some rude or cunning hand should pierce the gentle defences of Nature, and ravish from her breast the dear treasure of her innocence? Yes—swift of foot and light of heart as thou art, Swiss maiden, a dark shadow is pursuing thee—if he overtake thee, thou wilt fall, and a fallen woman rises not again.

Why not?

Because the whole world rises up to hold her down, and her own sex will be first to lay the tightening grasp upon her throat, to mock at her repentance, to deride her tears, last to rehabilitate her with the whitened garments of redemption. True, the providence of God might have hidden for her precious lessons and renovating truths in the very depths of sin and shame—the golden hair of the Bacchante might wipe the feet of the highest and holiest one, and he might say to her, "Thy sins are forgiven thee." But he is one whom the world knoweth not.

"At whose funeral do you imagine yourself to be?" suddenly cried Berto, interrupting my sober train of thought: "from your countenance I should infer that you are studying the part of chief mourner."

In reply, I ventured to communicate to him my sad forebodings of Rösli's fate.

"Nonsense," answered Berto: "I would not share your power of extracting bitterness from the sweets of Life, for all the wealth of Torlonia. Still, if you will amuse yourself with that poisonous alchymy, let me urge you to pursue it on a wider scale, and in a more philosophical spirit."

"By extracting more bitters from more sweets?"

"Certainly. Your pity for the Ballerina is an insult to the misery of the whole human race—it is a libel on the Providence which makes all men, au bout du compte, wretched alike. Think of the wide difference between the actual fate of each one of us, and the gay aspect and emotions of an hour like this. Those fair women who seem the very stars of the evening—for them, darkness waits without. Beside the footman who undoes the carriage door stands for some a Fate, for some a scowling Fury. Some of those bright eyes will not be closed tonight, until they have wept out half their light. Some of those graceful heads will be laid on pillows made thorny by guilt or anguish. I see yonder one of the most beautiful women in Rome, married to a man whom she detests, and who has a horrible sort of love for her. Think of the drive home with him, the unwelcome conversation, the scarcely endured caress, the door locked like a tomb, upon that struggling heart, and its most dreaded enemy, the twelve hours of the night, each with a new horror of its own—think of this, and tell me, do you pity the Ballerina?"

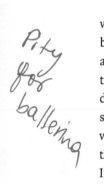
Pity
for
ballerina

The Hermaphrodite

"But I remember her simple and blameless childhood, her early surroundings, her honest parents—"

"Remember also the squalor, the poverty, the monotony of the life she has abandoned. Remember the little, close cottage, redolent of tobacco and of goat's flesh—think too of the hardened hands, the withered face, the stocking knitting, the baby-tending, the empty brain, and often the empty stomach—would you, if you could, restore her to all these enjoyments? she would scarcely thank you for your good wishes!"

Rösli herself seemed, that night, to give the lie to my melancholy forebodings. Never before had her dance been so magnetic, her pantomime so poignant, her movements so thrilling with joyous life. Her opaline eyes flashed forth that inmost light which usually slept calmly in their transparent depths—her smile was electric. The enthusiasm of the public rose to its highest pitch—loud plaudits followed her at every step, and her path was, for that night at least, strewn with flowers. Among the garlands which were flung upon the stage, I saw something thrown from the box of the —— family, (of which our Abbate was a younger scion)—a circlet that glittered as it passed through the air, and sounded heavily as it fell upon the stage. I saw Rösli start and change colour as she perceived it. I was glad that she did not herself raise it from the ground, or make the giver of it happy by one gesture of pleasure and surprise. She received it coldly from the hand of one of the comparses—our eyes met for a moment, before she disappeared behind the scenes.

Less bewildered by her grace & beauty than startled by the intense feeling her dancing had displayed, I deemed that some danger might be near her, and resolved at once to go to her. If that serpent priest should find her alone, and unprotected, it might be well for her to have a friend at hand, and so, under pretence of making a *giro* among the boxes, I contrived to escape from the tutelary care of Berto, and to bend my steps, unseen, towards the little tiring room in which the Rösli rested from her labours. I approached softly, for the door was half open, and I listened for a moment to assure myself that Rösli was alone.

She was not alone—from the room within I heard her voice and that of another, in earnest conversation. But that other was not the ribald Abbé—a fresher and purer organ it was that made with hers such gentle music. Why did I stand there listening to words which were never meant for my ear?

The Hermaphrodite

why did I not at once enter, or depart? I could not tell, that youthful voice had a peculiar charm for me—it held me, rooted to the spot; and I resolved, every moment, to pass on, and still I stood there.

"Leave me, I pray you, and come hither no more," said Rösli, with sudden energy and determination of manner.

"Not until you have given me permission to return, and take you hence forever."

"What is it that you propose to me?" asked Rösli, half angrily.

"Marriage," answered the unseen, with much earnestness.

"That cannot be," said Rösli, with firmness. "You were born to rank and fortune, and I am a peasant's child."

"If rank and fortune were aught to me," replied her companion, "I should rest satisfied in them, I should not be here, at your feet, but you well know how lightly I value them."

"You are very young," continued Rösli, "and I should deserve ill of you if I could take advantage of your inexperience. I have learned moreover that you are the only son and heir of your father—you have surely no right to marry without his approbation, and I need not tell you that in this instance, you could not meet it."

"The right to love, and to choose whom I love, is one which I derive from God himself," said the youth, with passion. "But since you are disposed to attach so much importance to these circumstances, let me inform you, in confidence, that I am not the heir to my father's estate." Here the speaker lowered his voice, but my attention was so riveted upon his words that I should have heard his slightest whisper.

"I have a brother," said he, "a brother dearly loved, sadly lost, but who is still alive. Where or how he dwells, I know not. I fear me, he must be a sad and solitary man, but I am ever in pursuit of him, and shall continue to seek until I find him. When that day shall come, and it will be a happy day for me, I shall proudly reinstate him in his rights. His shall be the ancestral home, his the fair fields, the retainers, the pomp and wealth. But when I shall have given all this up to him, there yet remains a rural lodge for me, in the loveliest nook of the whole estate, beside a silver lake—there will we dwell in happiness. Unless my brother be much changed in heart, we shall find him a gentle landlord."

The Hermaphrodite

And I heard this—my ears drank in those welcome words of love, love for the exile, the outcast, the repudiated of God and man. As I listened, all the strength which the world's cold unkindness had given me suddenly gave way—I reeled, gasped for breath, sobbed, struggling in the agony of an emotion utterly new.

Reader, hast thou never been unmanned by a similar discovery? hast thou never borne injustice and contumely with a sorrow which becomes scorn, a scorn which becomes patience, until some unlooked for word of sympathy has suddenly overcome thee, wringing from thy stern eyes the tears which unkindness had but frozen there? If not, read on, and thank God that the world has not fed thee with poisons until the real food of human affections has grown deadly to thee.

It was my brother, the boy brother I had left, now grown to generous & noble manhood—my heart told me that it was he—none else could have stirred its pulses so fearfully. For a moment, I thought that I must rush in, and clasp him in my arms, and gain at least a remembrance of his fair face as it now was.

But no! I had sworn to see him and his no more. Why should I tear his heart with new struggles, disappoint his noble designs, and give to the old, time-blunted sorrow the poignancy of a new grief? It was kinder as well as wiser to spare him the pain of meeting as we should have met, of parting as we should have parted. I paused but for a moment, and passed on. The outer darkness of the night received me—I was alone, I had no brother.

As I walked away, some one followed and soon passed me with a light and bounding step—it was the form of a youth, with a short cloak gracefully wrapped about him. I did not see his face, but I doubted not that it was the brother who had been so near to me, a moment before, but from whom I was now separated by all the length of my mortal life. Should I not yet overtake him? Should I not lay my hand upon his arm, and say: "behold and bless this once, only this once, the wanderer whom thou seekest." No, no, in God's name, no! Still I followed with my eyes intently fixed upon his receding form, hoping, oh so earnestly, that he might at least look back, and that the light of some passing carriage might reveal to me his countenance. But it was not so. The projecting angle of a house hid him for a moment from my view, and ere I had passed it, the darkness of the Roman labyrinth had swallowed him up. He was gone, and I walked back to rejoin Berto.

The Hermaphrodite

"What has agitated you so oddly?" asked my friend, as I sank into the first seat that offered itself. "Your pulse is dancing a most eccentric measure, and your face is utterly colourless. Has Rösli then been unkind, or untrue?"

I was in no mood to bear jesting, neither had I at that moment any power to conceal the trouble of my mind. I narrated the story to Berto, as soon as I was sufficiently composed to speak. He listened with the kindest and most serious attention, but was quite incredulous of my supposititious relationship with Rösli's unseen suitor. He argued long in the endeavour to convince me that the conversation I had overheard would apply quite as well to a thousand others, as to me. Had Philip been many days in Rome, as his intimacy with Rösli seemed to imply, I must have met and recognized him, or if he were still in the city I should yet see him, so Berto averred.

"It has always been a mania of yours, caro ti, to imagine that every thing befalling you is quite peculiar and individual to yourself—you will not perhaps believe that there are a hundred families in Rome, each of which has some one member at least in the same relative position as yourself. You do not even know whether the individual whom you overheard, rejoices in the cognomen of Philip."

To satisfy me yet further, Berto made inquiries at every hotel in Rome, but without any result. He succeeded at length in convincing my reason that it was quite against all probability that Philip and I should have met upon that spot, at that moment, and without seeing each other. Still, I only half disbelieved it, and my heart still cherished those gentle words which had fallen upon it like the passing benediction of a loving angel.

§

The days of Carnival were come at last, and the gloomy streets rang with songs and shouts of merriment. The palaces that line the Corso hung gaily out their crimson banners, and their balconies were crowded with pretty women, in holiday attire, while the street below swarmed with a multitude in which every quarter of the globe had its representatives. Passing strange was it to see the dead Rome rise from its tomb, and come forth to hold such wild carousal in the grave yard in which it had so long slept with its children gathered around it. It was as if the monks of some great convent had suddenly thrown off the bonds of ecclesiastical discipline, and discarded the cowl and scapular for the buskin and garland of the comedian; as if

The Hermaphrodite

they had made themselves drunken with the wine of the sacrament, and having seized the sacred torches of the altar to light their frantic revellings, were dancing madly to the music of the mass. Berto compared it to the ancient Oracle that spake but once in a year, or to the annual eruption of a Volcano, whose glowing, burning stream of Life rolled on, and bore all things, even my dead ashes, along with it. Little as I had in me of the masquer or reveller, I yet deemed it too precious an opportunity of study to be lost—and so I ventured forth into the crowd of squeaking and grinning buffoons, protected by the sober disguise of a domino, and accompanied by Berto.

Berto's influence

Berto, of wider nature than I, had in his heart some chords which responded to the wild gaiety about us. He averred that it was important to his peace of mind to assure himself annually that the folly of the race had not decreased, and that the dangerous and deadly gift of wisdom was still withheld from it. It was a pleasure to him to lose himself in this frantic sea of mirth, and he assured me that he had often gathered in it pearls of experience. There were many, he said, who wore disguises that they might act the truth, and who hid their faces that they might dare to show their hearts. Their whimsical madness was, he said, truer to their natures than their decent deportment of every day, and the man in the mask far less disguised than the man one meets every day face to face. And this, methought, was true—true also in a wider and a sadder sense. So intolerant, so incomprehensive is society become, that fervent hearts must borrow the disguise of art, if they would win the right to express, in any outward form, the internal fire that consumes them. There is scarcely one great passion of the soul which would not, if revealed, offend the narrow sense and breeding of the respectable world, and the few who are capable of these powerful emotions, and who must express them, must speak as with the voices of others.

But we did not proceed far in the grave argument from which I have quoted, for it became impossible to hear or to think any thing. I was tumbled hither and thither in the crowd of revellers, myself mute and impassive, without a jest to offer, or even the power at laughing at those of others. From the windows was rained upon me a fitful shower of sugar and plaster, but I shook the dust from my head as I had so often shaken it from my feet, and struggled on. Women, wondrous bold in their disguises, laid their

The Hermaphrodite

fascinating touch upon me, but went no further, the touch was enough—chilled and mortified, they turned away, and felt that virtue (if indifference be virtue) was gone in to them. Now we were waylaid by a party of pretended Nobles decked in tinsel bravery, now a troop of devils, with horns and tails danced and yelled around us, and would have condemned us to the mild hell of their company.

"Are ye then not ashamed, oh Romans, to be at once so abject, and so merry? do you forget the days of your heroic deeds? the stern warriors, your fathers, the she-wolf that suckled you? Roman liberty was a grand thing—so was Roman virtue—"

"Angi, ed è il maccarroni anchessa una gran bella cosa!" shouted one near at hand, who offered it to me from a vessel of the basest form and use. Berto plucked me impatiently by the sleeve.

"Are you mad?" quoth he, "that you preach to these people? You might as well talk to a swarm of butterflies, only let me warn you that some of them are hornets in disguise."

"What mean you, spies?"

"Aye, what else? does not every street in Rome lead to the Castle of St Angelo? I don't approve of your moral reflections either—is it not a sacred and imprescriptible right of the human animal to be a fool as often as he pleases, which is upon the whole, as often as he can?"

But the carriages now drove the crowd from the middle of the street. They bore along a strange medley of nobles and citizens, of natives and foreigners—among the latter predominated the Gothic English, so blasphemed by Berto. One would have said that every region of the world had sent its ambassadors to this court of misrule. Berto stood beside me to point out the most marked personages in the brilliant crowd.

"There," said he, "is the lovely Colonna who adorns the newly conferred nobility of the Prince Torlonia. He bought her and his title at the same time, and I can venture to assure you, from what I know of him, that he must have had them at a bargain."

"She is beautiful, at least. What a lovely oval countenance! what eyes! what a touching expression! it is a vision to haunt one—"

"Yes—she shews beside him, with her fair melancholy face, like a lily blooming on a cypress bough, or a young moon hanging upon the edge of a thundercloud. Behold in the noble outline of her countenance the proudest,

The Hermaphrodite

oldest blood of Rome. See in his the narrow, sordid look of his merchant fathers. He inherited nothing but their thrift, and I doubt whether he enjoys his enormous fortune half as much as the extortions by the aid of which he amassed it—and she, bought like a piece of merchandize, and guarded only as something fragile and costly, is pining away in her childless and joyless wifehood as sadly as she could have done in the convent to which she had else been doomed. I have seen her at a ball drop fainting beneath the weight of her diamonds, but heavier, deadlier still does the weight of her dear-bought splendour hang upon her young heart."

"Does he love her?"

"Love?" repeated Berto, with infinite scorn—"we do not desecrate that word by applying it to such men. He is fond of shewing her, and is at the same time watchfully jealous of her, as becomes a gray beard to be—But see, there is one Lady S. gifted with a tiny foot, in which I verily believe that her whole soul resides, and has room enough and to spare. Do you observe how gracefully she has arranged it upon the cushion of the front seat, with scarves and flowers, to challenge the admiration of the crowd? I would lay any wager that it will be a mark for missiles as well as for eyes."

As Berto spoke, the carriage in question passed beneath a balcony occupied by a noisy troop of artists, from which fortress the insolent garrison fired a sharp volley upon the little foot. The owner of it sustained the charge at first with self possession enough, but soon a sharp pointed lime was thrown, which hit with such force as to stain the satin slipper with blood—the little foot was now fairly dethroned, the lady hastily withdrew it from the public gaze, and as in the suddenness of the movement, the mask dropped from her face, I saw angry tears in her eyes.

"Here is a party of Russians, who are, I have no doubt, exceedingly splendid and filthy in their private habits—here again is a Polish princess, richly endowed with diamonds and scrofula. Yonder carriage contains an Englishwoman of handsome fortune, who married her courier. But look up at the balcony opposite: that stout man carries in his veins the lees of the rich Buonaparte blood. He has some reputation as an author and a naturalist, but is chiefly remarked in society for his rude manners and dirty hands."

"Fie, Berto! have you not enjoyed his hospitality?"

The Hermaphrodite

"No," said Berto, "it is not a thing to be enjoyed. On the whole, however, I am somewhat his debtor, for if I have been entertained at his house, it has been greatly at his expense. I have seen there a distinguished artist and his beautiful wife pushed without notice into a corner, and left to the companionship of a silent piano, and I have seen at the same time a filthy devil of a Jew banker elevated to the post of honour, and receiving the tenderest homage of the prince, whose note he had probably discounted."

And so on, and so on, until the confusion so thickened that Berto and I lost ourselves and each other in the crowd.

§

After these days was announced a horse race on the Campagna, and thither, whether I would or no, Berto carried me. The race ground was marked off on one side of the beautiful aquaeduct which bears the name of the emperor Nero. We found a large multitude assembled on the spot, and among them all the liveries and notabilities of Rome. A large area was occupied by the carriages of the Roman and English nobility, and within, on the very bounds of the course, were erected temporary scaffoldings, commanding the best view of a sport so unusual in Italy. Here Berto and I soon took our places. We had hardly done so, before I recognized, at a little distance, the graceful vision of Rösli, attired as a lady of fashion, and wearing her honours with a mingling of naiveté and self-possession. She seemed scarcely conscious of being almost as much a subject of attention here, as on the boards of the theatre, and bore the fire of an hundred lorgnons with entire equanimity. I was struck with the dignity and simplicity of her toilette. No superfluous ornament, no glaring contrast of colour marked in her the tawdry tastes and habits of the stage. She wore a dress of green silk, of that vague and vanishing shade which belongs neither to grass, nor cloud, nor wave, but which appears and disappears in all of them. Her white bonnet was adorned without by a single drooping feather, within, a wreath of green leaves surrounded her delicate face, and seemed the most appropriate foliage for so fresh a flower. In her hand she held a bouquet formed of green leaves and white flowers. She returned my greeting with a smile, but her attention was obviously engrossed by the scene below, where had just appeared the equine heroes of the day, and their riders. They were four magnificent English horses, and the purity of their race shewed itself in their swelling

The Hermaphrodite

veins, delicate limbs, and fiery eyes. The riders shewed blood too, in their way—they were all young, and of noble families, and wore, of course, the jockey costume. Each had chosen, however, for his jacket and cap, the colour that suited him best. One was attired in scarlet, one in blue, one in buff, and a fourth in green and white. I soon perceived that Rösli's eyes were fixed upon the latter, and as I detected a mute interchange of looks and signs between them, it occurred to me that the correspondance in the colours which each wore could scarcely have been accidental. It was for him that she had adorned herself with those snowy plumes, those bouquets of green leaves—the fairy-like dress which became her so well was perhaps his gift, and no other hand than hers had embroidered the green and silver scarf which was tied across his shoulder. In an instant, I had coupled these observations with the remembrance of Rösli's unseen lover, and weaving between these isolated facts a whole tissue of imaginings, I felt that some mysterious sympathy linked me to the youth before me, and sought eagerly to obtain a view of his face. But this was turned towards Rösli, until the groom led up the fine animal he was about to mount—he stooped a moment to examine the reins, stirrups, and saddle girths. At length, all being in readiness, he laid his hand upon the horse's mane, and with a joyous leap sprang into the saddle. Having mounted, he took off his cap, and bowed to the company. I had a full view of his countenance—my heart leaped to my throat. Did I know him? that rich blonde hair, those laughing eyes seemed familiar to me, yet there was a wide gap between the child I had left, and the young man whom I now saw. Not that the beauty of the child was gone—no, it had deepened, expanded, intensified—it was like, and yet so unlike, and my yearning heart might so easily lead my eyes astray. As I hurriedly scanned each feature of his gracious countenance, and doubtingly compared it with those which my remembrance still treasured, a joyous smile passed over it, and like an angel's torch, threw its radiant light upon the half-effaced record—in that light, I read at once and unmistakably the secret of Nature. At the same moment I heard a bystander say, in reply to a question of Berto's:

"He in the green jacket is Philip, Viscount —— and son of——."

It needed not those words to tell me that I had seen my brother.

In the darkness, I had allowed him to pass me, but now that I had looked upon him, I could no longer refrain myself. "I must make myself known

The Hermaphrodite

to him," said I, springing forward, and struggling, as in a nightmare, to scream out his name; but Berto laid his iron grasp upon me, and exchanged with me a look of solemn intelligence:

"This is not the moment," said he, and as he spoke, the trumpet gave the first signal, and the four riders ranged themselves abreast. Another blast sounded, and they rose in their stirrups, and stooped, ready for the start. A third, and they gave their impatient steeds the rein, and dashed bravely into the distance. With breathless anxiety I followed them in their long sweep. So true and even was the motion of the horses that it scarcely seemed rapid, until you measured it by the ground they had passed over—now they were out of sight, and I marked the Rösli straining her eyes after them in vain—now they reappeared, and all seemed nearly abreast—I saw Philip shoot past the others, he kept ahead—with whip and spur they could not distance him—proudly, beautifully he rode, fearless as an Apollo bestriding his winged steed—he was near, another moment, and he would have passed the winning post. "He has won!" I shouted, looking at Rösli—to my astonishment, the colour suddenly left her cheek, she tottered, and leaned against the railing for support. I looked below—the brave steed was riderless, and a crowd gathered with a faint noise around a prostrate form. Philip had been thrown from his saddle—with one leap, I found myself beside him—they had raised him from the ground, but I heard them say that he had ceased to breathe. The cap fell from his brow, and shewed the seal of death already there.

"No! there is yet life in him! he is not dead! Philip, my mother's son, the only one of my blood that ever loved me!" I cried, struggling to throw myself upon his body, to hold him in one last embrace. But at that moment, I saw a vision that paralyzed the pulses of my heart. It was the face of an old man, bloodless, tearless, stony, riven with despair as by lightning, frozen with sad astonishment, piteous yet dreadful. I sprang to my feet—our eyes met—a horrible convulsion passed over his features—I pointed to the dead boy, and smiled.

I saw the old man drop senseless to the ground. A servant's hand chafed his brow, the arms of servants carried him away—I did not overtake him with words of pity or of comfort, did not even follow him with my eyes—it was not my fault that he was sonless.

The Hermaphrodite

But he was gone, and there was now no spectre to fright me from the side of him whom death had restored to me. His mortal spoil seemed to me an alms of nature, a fragment flung to me from the feasts of fuller hearts. I carried him like a babe to my room. I laid him on my bed, smoothed his ruffled limbs, and sat for hours holding his frozen hand, looking in his face, talking mutely with his spirit. I have some remembrances too of a fair girl with dishevelled hair and disordered attire, who rushed into the darkened chamber, weeping frantically. She soon grew as still as I, and sate silently beside me, watching the dead. But that might have been a dream, as indeed all the rest seemed to be. I only thought of it when I heard that the manager of the Theatre had forced Rösli to dance, and that she had fallen in convulsions upon the stage. I interfered so far as to pay the necessary penalty of her forfeiture, and at an expense of several thousand sendi, procured for the poor girl the right of a week or two of decent seclusion.

But dead as Philip was, they took him from me. They tore him from out my arms to wrap him in costly cerements, to lay him in a scutcheoned coffin. For me, too, a messenger was dispatched. The tutor of other days, weeping for the loss of his beloved pupil, came to me, and announced with some hesitation that my father wished to see me, and hoped that I would at least attend the funeral, which was announced for the day following.

"My father?"

"Yes, your Grace."

"How does he call himself?"

The tutor here repeated the name and title of my father.

"I know no such person," answered I.

The poor tutor stared at me for a moment in great embarrassment, and timidly murmured something about Christian charity, ties of blood, painful estrangement, happy reconciliation, etc, the which I hastened to interrupt.

"Yes—all these words may mean something to you—for my part, I comprehend them not. There was a man, a hard and haughty man, who bestowed Cain's curse of wandering upon his unoffending child. If that man has sent you to me, return and tell him that I know him not. Bid him enjoy his revenues, improve his acres, plant his trees far and wide. Let him gather the gold into his coffers, the wine into his vaults—he does it for the children of another—he will be the last of his name."

"Oh no! you will relent—time will bring you better thoughts."

The Hermaphrodite

"No, I have sworn it by the living God!"

"Vengeance is mine, saith the Lord."

"Yes, and He has measured it out, this time."

§

It must have been some days later than this, that I found myself at the gate of the lovely burial ground without the walls of Rome, in which, as in perpetual exile, the dust of the Protestant stranger is allowed to repose. Yet the Pontiff who granted them this ungracious hospitality was not altogether churlish in heart, for he has allotted them a spot of rare beauty. Near it stands the triangular monument of Caius Sextus. The ilex and the cypress give it their grateful shade, and birds and flowers congregate there, but with a more chastened melody, a tenderer bloom, as if fed and watered by the spirits of the gentle dead. There lie the ashes of Shelley—there wanders the pensive shade of him whose name was writ indeed in water, but in that water of heaven in which God writes his own rainbow promises.

Many a family has there left its tenderest and most cherished flower— many a loving soul has sown there the golden seed of its dearest love, and turned patiently away, to bide God's time for the harvest. Many a mother has there laid her babe, hushed by angels to its last sleep, and even in her anguish has thanked Him who had provided for it so sweet a resting place. There might we read of many, as we do of one

> fenne a Roma,
> Ando nel Cielo

In the day when the Lord shall make up his jewels, He will not forget his Roman etui, nor the pearls which lie treasured in it.

It was a delicious evening, and my faded eyes were bathed in a sea of softest, golden, velvet light, and my weary soul was wrapped in its wedding garment of undying hope, as I approached the spot where Philip slept. Tranquil, deeply penetrated with solemn thought, I knelt beside my brother's grave, and gave God thanks for the love which was wisdom, the wisdom which was power.

"Oh! my brother!" I said, "it is well with thee. Not for a thousand kisses, not for a thousand words of love would I exchange the perfect communion my spirit may now hold with thine, the heavenly messages which thou shalt

The Hermaphrodite

whisper to me in the still night. Oh brother! thy life would have been a blessing, but thy death is a blessedness." As I mused thus, I sank upon the ground, and laid my head upon the newly made grave, as on a pillow. I thought that Philip talked with me, and told me that the gate which had seemed of ice, without, was within of shining crystal—that he had fallen asleep on the lap of a pale angel, and had awoke in the arms of the perfect and holy One, the beautiful Christ.

I know not how long it was before the sound of approaching footsteps recalled me to this lower world. I looked up, and saw before me, the stony face, the broken form of that hard old man. He leaned upon the arm of the tutor, and was followed at some distance by several servants. A shudder passed over my frame—I would have walked away without any interchange of greetings, but after a moment of painful silence, he held out his hand to me, and said:

father

"My son, I have wished to see you."

"There lies your son," I answered, pointing to the grave at our feet, "and he is yours no more."

The stony face quivered, and the hard eyes wavered for an instant, but he commanded himself. Beckoning to those who had followed him to draw near, he raised his hand, and said in a firm voice:

"I call you all to witness that this is Laurence Viscount ————, my eldest and only son, and heir to my titles and estates. In the presence of all of you, I invite him to return to his father's roof, and to give his filial support to my declining years."

A momentary pause followed these words—I wished to give to my reply all the force and meaning of deliberation. When I did speak, it was with a slow and determined accent.

"Old man," I said: "mark well my words, they are the last you will ever hear from me. There was a day in which, at your request, under cruel threats, I abandoned your succession to my brother. You cast me out without a cause, and I became to you and to him as though I had never been. I swore then before you, that I would never bear your name, nor wear your crest and title, nor stand in your place after you. I swore it in hot and angry blood—I repeat it in calm and cool determination. The event which has changed for you the exigencies of life, has in no respect altered our relations towards each other.

The Hermaphrodite

The past

"Eternal necessities sometimes hang on the decision of a moment. Omnipotence itself cannot undo a deed, nor avert its consequences. The past, my Lord, is beyond control—it has made you what you are, made me what I am, and has made neither of us for the other."

We stood there, looking fixedly at each other—the tyrant and the outcast, the aggressor and the aggressed had changed places. I had not sought, had not hastened this vengeance—it had come to me in the slow but certain progression of Providence—it must have been, it was to be. The old man turned away. He had no word to say—there were no tender recollections to which he could appeal, no acts of paternal love of which to remind me. I saluted him coldly, as he departed. In the faces of those who witnessed this strange scene, I saw the expression of mingled pity, horror, and wonder. Arrived at the gate of the cemetery, he looked back at me once more. I met him with the same bow of formal courtesy, and he pressed his hands upon his eyes, and uttered a faint cry as they led him to the carriage that waited for him without. I stood there, in the soft golden light, and watched him until he disappeared from my sight and from my life forever.

The night gathered like a curtain around me, and the stars were my consecrated candles, and Philip's grave the altar at which I bowed my head.

Chapter [20]

Those who have followed my vagabond fortunes thus far with some brief interest and goodwill will be now compelled to greet me in a new guise. What will you say to me, fair reader, if I present myself before you in feminine masquerade, stockaded with buckram and cotton, hanging out the veil, that feminine banner of deceit, upon a tower (in Solomonic phrase) some six feet in height, and with a wide moat of emptiness between the outer curtain of my entrenchments, and the inner, inexpungable fortress of myself. Will you recognize me with an astonished smile, and a "who would have thought it?" or will you treat me as men and women are apt to treat an old friend in an equivocal position, and pass me staring at nothing, or at me as if I were nothing? Let it be as you please, quite as you please. If you know me not now, you never knew me, and so, questioned or unquestioned, let me pass.

There is another masquerade the reverse of this, which is common and natural enough. Women, the adored of all, but trusted of none; women, the

The Hermaphrodite

golden treasures, too easily lost or stolen, and therefore to be kept under lock and key, women, who cannot stay at home without surveillance, who cannot walk abroad without being interrogated at every turn by the sentinel of public opinion; women, I say, are very naturally glad now and then to throw off their chains with their petticoats, and to assume for a time the right to go where they please, and the power of doing as they please.

What a new world does this open to a woman! what a delightful, dangerous abyss of novelty! It is a world of reality in exchange for a world of dreams—it is dealing with facts instead of forms, with flesh and blood, instead of satins and laces. She can hear the conversation of the camp, the cabinet, the café, the gaming table. She can learn how men talk and act when they are drunk, and angry, and sincere. She will marvel to find so much or so little in them. If she be so minded, she may learn to drink, game, and swear with the best of them. According to her own powers of feeling and perception, she may find a keen pleasure in new investigations of men and things, a mischievous delight in the usurpation of rights not her own, or a philosophical satisfaction in intellectual relations divested of the dangerous attraction and repulsion of sex. Tell her to go home and make her papa's tea, or mend her children's stockings—how her eyes will flash, and if she be English, how she will crush you with the Shakespearean line about fools and small beer, to both of which, in other forms, she may nevertheless be addicted. And this masculine mania may last long, and go far, but it will not last forever. However strong, or depraved, or metaphysical the emancipated woman may be, she will in the end feel the want of some one to bully and protect her, the necessity of being cherished and admired, or kicked and cuffed. And so some day she will ignominiously strike her flag of defiance, and creep back to her woman's trappings, and to her woman's life as best she may, happy after all her wanderings if she can [find] some kind brute to play the Beast to her Beauty, some one who though he may outrage her best feelings, laugh at her convictions, and offend her taste, will yet praise her eyebrows, and pay her bills.

But it is not so easy to account for my appearance in petticoats. It would certainly seem odd enough that I, who had roamed the world so wildly, and with such a luxury of freedom, should consent to take upon myself the bondage of this narrow life (the true meaning of the term "petticoat government" being that the petticoat governs her who wears it). How could

The Hermaphrodite

I bear the endless tedium of its trivial details, or mimic a sympathy with its microscopic interests? How could I risk myself among these fair, frail creatures, at the incessant peril of shattering their delicate sensibilities by my brusqueries, and of jarring their irritable nerves by a thousand breaches of feminine discipline?

That I did so, I must confess—I consented, for a time, to womanhood, but conquered its scandals. But in making this acknowledgement, I am anticipating the statement I am bound to make, of the reasons which led me in this new direction.

"I shall introduce you to my sisters, this evening," said Berto abruptly to me one day.

"To your sisters? have you really any such relations?"

"Have I not told you so? have you not often seen me return from visits paid to them?"

"Yes, but had you professed to have come from your grandmothers, it would have conveyed the same impression to me. I always supposed you were a Phoenix, solitary of your kind, begotten without father or mother, a creation of divine caprice, an experiment never before made, and not likely to be repeated."

"It is almost so with both of us," said Berto, his face darkened by a momentary gloom. "Still, I have these sisters, and am fond of them, though my relation to them is but a partial one. They are the children of my mother, but they are good girls, and there is one amongst them whose story cannot fail to interest you."

"You know, Berto, that I am vowed against the society of women, and you know my reasons therefore. I even treat with poor Rösli by proxy, and you cannot be surprised if I respectfully decline all intimacy with your sisters."

"May I be cursed if I know why you should not frequent the society of intelligent and well-bred women, even as others."

"You forget then, Berto, that I have been dangerous to them?"

Berto laughed wickedly, a sly, inward laugh, which he seemed avariciously to keep in for the delectation of his own diaphragm, as if it had been too precious to be wasted in noise and grin. I did not like that laugh—it almost aroused my ire.

"Come, my dear Ambign-tragigne," said he at length, "let me assure you upon my own authority that you are no longer so fatal to women as you

The Hermaphrodite

deem yourself. It is true that you were a pretty boy, a very pretty boy, but now look at yourself in the glass—you have grown careless in dress, indifferent in manner, and absent of mind, these are sins that women rarely overlook. However, to veil still further your perilous beauties from their eyes, I have hit upon an ingenious device. I have informed them that an English lady of distinction wishes to pass some weeks in the seclusion of their house, and it is as a woman that you will be seen and known of them."

"As a woman? that is a poor jest for one so witty as you, Berto."

"I do not jest," said Berto, "and if you will but listen to me, I shall soon convince you that I have important reasons for the proposition I have made to you."

After a brief display of incredulity, mingled with ill-humour, I allowed Berto to explain himself.

"You may remember," said he, "that the month which begins tomorrow has been destined beforehand to the pursuit of the study of men and of manners. This is a subject which we can scarcely pursue together, since we have not both arrived at the same degree of illumination. In this science, I am in advance of you."

"Yes, but a month later, we shall be naturalists, and then I will take my revenge."

"Well, we shall see," answered Berto. "In the meantime, I am going to Naples, in pursuance of a favorite plan, to pass a little time among my friends, the Lazzaroni. Theirs is a very genuine form of human nature, and deserves profound study. I wish that you should pass the time of my absence with my sisters, and this would be impossible without the disguise I propose. It is important that you should see men as women see them, and no less so that you should see women as they appear to each other, divested of the moral corset de précaution in which they always shew themselves to men. My plan will afford you an excellent opportunity of accomplishing these objects, and you owe it to me and to yourself to improve it."

"No, no, Berto, if you are in earnest about this absurd scheme, and I can scarce believe it, you must shew me some more cogent reason, before I can consent to become a party to it. Petticoats! a corset, ugh! ruffs, and cuffs, and muffs! good Lord! no, thank you, Berto. I am not quite such a fool."

Berto walked up and down the room uneasily, looking at me, and muttering between his teeth. At length he stopped, and abruptly cried out:

disguise

"Well then, there are other reasons, fool that you are to wish to know them. It is well sometimes to have faith in other people, as well as in oneself, but since you cannot trust me, listen to me:

"Your father has left you unmolested for a time, but he has not given you up—baffled in his first attempts, he is crouching like a tiger, to spring upon you more vigourously than ever. Since the day he was made aware of your presence in Rome, he has not ceased to dog your steps—his spies follow you, wherever you go. I have known this for some time, but today has brought me a more important revelation of his intentions."

"What mean you?"

"Briefly this. I chanced to pass the Bureau of the British Consulate this morning, and it occurred to me to drop in and inquire for a promised letter. I did not find the Consul at his desk, but a clerk handed me the letter, and civilly asked me to walk into the inner room, and await the arrival of my friend. He must have entered unobserved by me, for I was startled by his voice, as I sat in the window, reading my letter, concealed by the heavy curtain. In this position it was that I overheard a conversation which was never meant for my ear. The subject of it was the urgent necessity of making out a writ of insanity against you, in your father's behalf. One of the parties was the Consul himself, the other was ———, the confidential agent of your father. The latter averred that you were subject to frequent aberrations of intellect—he gave a false and exaggerated account of some passages of your life which might indeed bear that interpretation to any but the few who really know you. He spoke of your unnatural hatred towards your father as one of the strongest symptoms of your mental malady, and cited your behavior in the cemetery and your refusal of the inheritance as facts which put the matter beyond all doubt. This last circumstance made a strong impression upon the Consul. He had known young men who voluntarily forsook the paternal roof, to run their own wild races with destiny elsewhere. He had known others who bore the same dislike to the Author of their days, here the Consul sighed, but for a young man to refuse such a fortune, and such a title! clearly, it was a case of mania, if not of downright madness.

"Make it downright madness, will you?" said your father's emissary, and I heard as he spoke, the jingling of golden coin.

The Hermaphrodite

"Should we not in the first place obtain a certificate of the fact from some respectable physician?

The other replied that the certificate of your father's travelling physician could easily be obtained. The Consul then suggested that to render this available, there must be some examination, etc etc.

"An Italian lawyer will settle it for us without these useless ceremonies," said your father's man, gruffly, and as he did so, he counted out the gold, put it back into the purse, and the purse into his pocket. The fee was large, the temptation mighty, and the poor Consul promised to execute My Lord's pleasure, with as little delay as possible."

Yes—it was all clear enough. My father thought that by consigning me to the hopeless and irksome captivity of some Maison de Santé, he should soon break my spirit, and compel me to accede to his terms—should this prove impossible, he would at least enjoy a horrible vengeance, and drag me down to destruction with him. Once in his hands, I might have languished forever in some dungeon of his own choosing, or if allowed at length the benefit of legal investigation, would it be easy for a man who has lived according to his own impulses to prove to men without impulse that he is not insane? It was a clever, well-devised scheme, and worthy of him who had invented it.

"Well, what say you to my tale?" said Berto, as I sat and pondered, without reply or comment. "Speak, man, let me know your mind."

I started from my seat, I shrieked out, "oh God! thou hast made me battle my kind!" and fell, convulsed, in Berto's arms.

§

As soon as I had recovered my senses, Berto renewed his entreaties, to the effect that I would forthwith adopt the disguise proposed by him. Flight, he said, and truly, was out of the question, for a time. I could not have my passports made out without my father's knowledge, and my course, were it southward or northward could easily be traced. By disappearing entirely from the scene, I should convey to them the impression of a sudden escape, and they would be more likely to seek me any where, than to remain in Rome, awaiting my reappearance. I saw clearly that his plan was the best that offered itself, and moreover the easiest of execution. Berto had provided me with a suit of feminine habiliments, but as I had never before worn them, it required all our combined skill to endue me with them. Our clumsy fingers were sadly at fault among the endless hooks and eyes, the lacings and eyelet holes. I pricked myself with the pins, and strangled myself with the ribbons. I looked so tall in my new clothes, that Berto clapped his hands and danced around me, exclaiming: "oh! la grandeur des Anglaises!"

Once equipped, my friend undertook to drill me, and tried to give me, in one hour, all the benefits of his long and accurate observations of women:

"Laurence, do not hold your head so stiffly erect. Let me see you sit down, slowly and softly. For heaven's sake, do not put back your hand to divide your skirts, it is not a feminine custom. Your legs are too far apart, your knees must touch each other. Let me see you rise, that is pretty well—now, walk—petticoats en avant, mince your steps, and undulate a little more in your movements. Let me hear you laugh—not so loud, if you please, and pray make a more gradual disclosure of your teeth. You will do exceedingly well, I think—upon my soul, you are a handsome creature!"

But to me the women's garments were like the fabled vest of Hercules, full of uneasiness and of torture. They reminded me of that mad revel at the Bier-kneib, and of ——— and of ———.

Berto guessed perhaps at this, for he immediately led the conversation to another channel, and began to prepare me for my introduction to his sisters.

(Kind reader, weary not of our endless conversations—must we not introduce you to them also?)

"Two of them," he said, "have arrived at the limits of their youth, and are neither married, nor likely to be so. My sisters are of natures at once too enlightened and too expansive to doom themselves to the narrow ropewalk of Conventual life. They are, on the other hand, too proud to present themselves as candidates for selection in the great woman market of society, and this pride grows upon them now that the bloom of their youth is passing away. Their tastes and habits are not those of common women. The elder is a student, and has some pretensions to authorship, the younger is an artist of real merit. The order of their household is simple and quiet. They have no lovers, and few intimates of their own sex. The most enlightened of the priesthood, a few artists, a few strangers, these compose the little circle

136

"tutor"

The Hermaphrodite

over which they preside, and these are glad to enjoy the society of women at once so intelligent and so genial."

"You speak of two of them—is there then a third?"

"Yes, there is a third," said Berto, with a sigh—"the youngest, the fairest, once the gayest, and even now, it may be, the happiest."

"I remember now that you once spoke of her history—what is it?"

"It is a strange mingling of sorrow, love, and madness. She was ever more womanly than her sisters, depended more than they, upon the affection of others for happiness. While her sisters devoted their days to art and literature, her more simple and sympathetic nature found for itself a very different occupation and destiny. Nina was not so clever or so ambitious as they, but she had what they had not time for, a lover. This was Gaetano di M ——, a young man of high promise, and who united in his person all the advantages of cultivation and intelligence, rank and wealth. He became betrothed to my sister, and they should soon have been joined in marriage. Unhappily however, a temporary political disturbance arose in Rome. A conspiracy, it was said, had been discovered, in which Gaetano appeared to be implicated. He had always been suspected of liberal opinions, and those in power were glad of a pretext for banishing him from Rome—America was his place of exile. Nina was most eager to accompany him thither— she wept, she prayed—I can still remember her on her knees before me, imploring me to allow her marriage to be celebrated at once, that she might share the fortunes of her beloved one. God forgive me that I said her nay, but the way was long, and the voyage rough and perilous for one so delicately nurtured. We had hopes too of a speedy pardon for him—his family is rich and influential, and we were told that his absence would not exceed a year or so. Nina at last became calm, and insisted no further upon making the journey with him, but when she parted from him, she said to him with great earnestness: "Gaetano, I shall follow you every step of the way—" "how so?" he asked, and she led him to her little boudoir, and showed him spread upon the table a provision of maps, charts, and books of travel. "These will be my guides," she said, "you will write me constantly of your movements, and I shall study so diligently that I shall soon have a clear idea of the countries in which you will dwell, of their aspect and climate. Do not then dare to be unfaithful to me, for my soul goes forth with your soul, and wherever you may be, I shall stand beside you." Gaetano departed, and Nina fulfilled her promise. With my assistance, she traced out the course of his ship across the ocean. All my Geographical knowledge was put in requisition, and the little enthusiast even conquered the difficulties of the English language, that she might read the best books descriptive of America. She passed her days in these studies, in writing to her lover, and in reading his letters a thousand times over. Gradually, she began to make to herself a story of his life, and from the data given, to trace for herself a more detailed outline of his daily movements.

"He is on the Mississippi today," she would say, or on another occasion: "something tells me that he is this moment looking on the Niagara." We were sometimes startled at the intensity of these impressions, but as all love is madness, I thought her no more crazy than any other lovelorn damsel. In the mean time, she had relinquished, one by one, every pursuit and interest of her former life. Her companions, her flowers, her music were all neglected. She sang no more, she talked no more, and when I led her perforce into some gay scene, her absent manner and inexpressive face made it painfully apparent that her thoughts changed not with the changing scene. Thus passed the first year of Gaetano's banishment, and during all this time, she had full and frequent letters from him. But these letters suddenly ceased—his family received no tidings of him, and all our inquiries availed not to discover if he were alive or dead. Nina, as you may imagine, was in a pitiable state. That she hoped when all others had ceased to hope, that she insisted upon going to seek him, that the impossibility of so doing brought on a dangerous illness, are all circumstances so natural that I do not pause to describe them. For the phenomena presented by her recovery, it is not so easy to account. Her illness was a fever, whose violence was succeeded by a deathlike stupor, in which she lay for many days. More than once did we gather round her bed, expecting to see her breathe her last, but hour after hour, day after day passed, and still she did not die, though one could hardly say, she lived. At length, to our surprise, the shattered forces of her nature seemed to rally. She began to take nourishment, and was able to leave her bed. Still, she continued strangely inanimate, she never spoke, and shewed no perception of external things. She would sit, day by day, in her armchair, with eyes cast down or closed, mechanically taking the food that was brought to her, and suffering herself to be dressed or undressed, laid upon her couch or led to her chair as passively as an

The Hermaphrodite

image of clay. At first, we spoke softly in her presence, fearful of irritating her weakened nerves. Soon we grew alarmed at her continued silence, and endeavoured by every threat and persuasion to induce her to speak. We found that we might converse before her upon any subject, without exciting her attention in any degree. I began to fear lest the fever had destroyed her hearing, if not her reason. We summoned to our aid the best medical advice that Rome could furnish, but it availed nothing. The disease was in the brain and nervous system, but it was not to be reached by physical agencies. I know not how it happened that it occurred to me, one day, to speak to her of her lover. I took her hand in mine, bent my lips to her ear, and said very distinctly: "Gaetano is in Louisiana." To my surprise, the long silent Nina at once replied: "he has long since left it, and is now on his way to the Sault Sainte Marie."

"How do you know it?" I asked.

"I have made the whole journey with him," she said: "do you not see our bark canoe, and the Canadian guides? at night, we draw the canoe on shore, light our fire, and sleep there—early in the morning, we rise and pursue our way. I have been on many streams, and in many forests, since I saw you, my good Berto."

"Why did you not give us news of your travels?" I inquired.

"I thought you were all dead," she replied, and relapsed into silence, nor could I make her speak again, that day.

From this time, I visited her sedulously, until my departure from Rome. I found her ever occupied with her imaginary journey, which she described with the most ingenuous simplicity. She never voluntarily entered into conversation, but she always answered my questions upon this one subject, and even with apparent pleasure. On one occasion, she threw her arms around me, and embraced me affectionately, saying: "Dear Berto, you [are] kind to feel this interest in our fate." As her arms fell back, after this effort, she muttered: "Somehow, they seem to be always empty."

On my return to the city, after a long absence, I found that Nina's physical condition had somewhat improved. She had been made to recognize her sisters, and had been induced to take a little exercise—still, her mind remained in the same abnormal condition, and so does to this day. On being addressed, she makes answer, but immediately relapses into silence.

The Hermaphrodite

She has, apparently, no knowledge of external facts, no thought beyond the dream life in which she dwells, with her phantom lover. All this is rendered somewhat marvellous by the fact that we have at last received some indistinct tidings of Gaetano. We have been assured that he is alive, and that he has probably, as she avers, passed the Sault Ste Marie, on his way to the hunting grounds of the North."

By this time, Berto's narrative had brought us to the dwelling of the three wondrous sisters. Like most Romans, they inhabited some portion of a dilapidated palace. I was glad to find that it stood somewhat aloof from the more frequented parts of the city, and was blessed with a garden shaded by lemon trees, and made musical by a silver voiced fountain. The young moon shown upon the ancient structure with a tender and charitable light that spared its ugliest scars and seams, and seemed for the time to win back the grimed arches and blackened pillars to something like their pristine purity; for in this sense also, reader, as in so many others, is moonlight akin to love. But am I a superannuated tourist, that I pause to describe an object so familiar as a Roman palace? or do I seek to infringe upon the patent rights of Murray's stereotyped logarythms for the calculation of all the charms and désagréments of the eternal city? Let us pass to the interior. Having ascended to the fourth floor, we knocked for admittance. A man who was rapidly dwindling to an old woman undid the door for us, and led us through the hall and antechamber into a large room, dimly lighted, and adorned chiefly by pictures and wellfilled bookshelves. Two women, of fine, though not youthful appearance, advanced to receive us. They greeted Berto with evident affection, and Cecilia (I was introduced as an Englishwoman) with polite curiosity. A third, young and very lovely, sate apart from the others, and neither spoke nor moved on our entrance. Had I not guessed her to be the heroine of Berto's tale, I should hardly have taken her for a living being. She was not only motionless, but to all appearance, bloodless. To look at her, one would have supposed the fluid in her veins to have been white, and not crimson. Instead of radiating animal heat, she seemed to impart an icy cold to the atmosphere around her. Her attitude was neither ungraceful nor uneasy, but most uncommon. Her head was bent forward, her hands were gathered in an exquisite knot upon her knee—her eyes were so nearly closed that the dark lashes alone seemed to

The Hermaphrodite

divide the marble cheek, from the marble lid. Having questioned his sisters concerning the state of her health, Berto approached her, laid his hand upon her head, and said with great distinctness: "Nina, Berto is come to ask how Gaetano and you have passed the day."

In a moment, her whole countenance was as it were, transfigured. It was as if a mask of death had suddenly fallen, shewing the face beneath lit with intensest life. The full eyes opened upon us with their deep yet dim beauty, the pale lips parted gracefully, though reluctantly, and a smile of rapture passed over the countenance, and permeated its every line, without disturbing any of its features.

In the smiles of grown people a certain struggle is, for the most part, distinctly visible. The play of the muscle-machinery is often painfully apparent, and one sees that it is not without difficulty that the soul, the ever-hoping compels the poor toil-worn body to forget for a moment its fatigues and sufferings, and to make in its own way its poor show, its farthing illumination of gladness. Nina's smile was more like an electric gleam of delight which the same soul, enfranchised and soaring free, might in passing cast upon its human prison. In a voice of strangely musical intonation, she uttered these words:

"Thanks, dear Berto—we are happy, but weary."

"What has fatigued you?" asked Berto.

"The pursuit of the grisly bear."

"Tell me about it," said the brother.

"The creature is strong, and swift, and cruel," answered Nina, "he has fearful claws, that can deal death with a single blow."

"Have you been successful?"

"Surely. Our horses are fleet and strong. Gaetano is skilful in the chase. He has overtaken and slain the bear. Now, he is resting beside the camp-fire, and I must sing him to sleep."

"Looks Gaetano as he used to look?'

"Oh no! he is attired like a savage, in skins and a blanket, with a hunting pouch, and bow, and spear. His carbine is slung at his saddle bow, and instead of a sword, he carries an axe. But he is beautiful in his wild attire, and the Indians call him the young fir-tree, so slender and erect is he."

"And you are his wife, Nina?"

The Hermaphrodite

A slight tremour passed over Nina's frame, and her utterance was broken and uneven, as she replied:

"Berto, I know not what that word means. We are wedded, oh yes! we have been wed for years, and I have no heart but to love him, no hands but to labour for him, and yet, and yet, look at these," and she held up her arms, "somehow, they are always empty."

What a depth of woe was in those words. It was the voice of murdered nature crying upwards from the ground. It was the sorrow that the poor girl had long ceased to know, but which she still felt and must feel till every fibre of her frame had quivered its last. Love was so built in with the structure of her whole life and being, that the one could only perish with the other.

"There spoke the *woman*," said Berto, turning to exchange with me a tearful glance.

Yes, there had spoken the woman, the wife and mother, the maiden bud, frost nipt and doomed to die, but bearing painfully in itself the germ and essence of the flower and fruit. The senses had ceased to feel the sharpness of their own privations. The brain, turned inward upon itself, was fed with pleasing dreams, and waited upon by the phantoms of friendly forms, but the poor flesh and blood would sometimes speak, impatient of dragging on alone its dumb agony. No angel messenger had brought to it God's blessing on Nature's law. The heart beat vaguely feeling for the responsive beatings of another heart—the gentle lips thought it strange to find themselves so long unkissed—the arms stretched themselves wonderingly out and fell back empty.

Are not the saddest Rachels those who weep for the children that are not, and have never been?

A joy that we have known remains ever a joy. Privation cannot destroy its reality. Inasmuch as it is the boundless desire of the soul made finite and tangible, the word become flesh, it has a certain immortality of its own, and having been, cannot altogether cease to be. But to bear lifelong in one's bosom a wild deep longing of Nature ungratified, that is perilous. For then the infinite towards which we tend casts its shadow all too darkly upon us. The sense of it may sink to Melancholy, rise to Inspiration, or wander to madness, but in either case its glories will be fantastic, fatal, and its revelations will be as unlike to truth, as is the shedding of blood to the flowing of water.

The Hermaphrodite

While more than one of those present perhaps indulged in the preceding reflections, a female attendant had advanced, and with Berto's assistance led the passive Nina from the room.

The spell of her presence once removed, the two remaining sisters entered into conversation with me, anxious as it seemed to divert my attention from the extraordinary scene I had just witnessed. They spoke of the pleasure which they promised themselves from my visit, and assured me that Berto's account of me had led them to form the highest idea of my talents and acquirements. But, these preliminary compliments once over, my thoughts so reverted to the beautiful clairvoyante, that I was fain to lead the conversation back to her.

"Have your sister's symptoms been investigated by any men of science?" I asked of her they called Briseida.

"Only in a medical point of view," she replied. "We have never known any who were learned in Somnambulism. Even if such an one had crossed our path, we should hardly have dared to permit any experiments to be made. Our poor sister has already been a scandal to the priesthood."

She then informed me that the family confessor had taken it upon himself, long since, to assure her that Nina was possessed of an evil spirit. Not content with this, he had one day taken advantage of Berto's absence to enter the house, followed by deacon, sub-deacon, and various neophytes, in solemn procession. In defiance of all remonstrance, they had forced their way into the sick room where Nina lay, hovering between life and death. Here, regardless of her perilous condition, they had burned incense, sprinkled holy water, and had repeated over her every form of exorcism, in tones which grew louder and more violent as the devil showed himself more and more stubborn.

At length the priest, irritated beyond measure, laid his hand upon Nina's shoulder, and shook it angrily, crying out: "in the name of Christ I adjure thee, that thou come out of her!" Nina had not then spoken for many days, but at these words she opened her eyes, shook off the ungentle grasp, and raised her right arm. Pointing with her finger towards heaven, with a deep and earnest voice she said: "touch me not, for I am not yet ascended unto my father and your father, unto your God and my God." The next moment, she fell back, as still and deathlike as she had been before, but they had

The Hermaphrodite

been awed by the majesty of her manner, and were silent. Our physician entered at this moment, and protected us from further molestation."

"When, after this, we gave the confessor his congé," said the Gigia, "and told him that we should transfer our confidence to the kind and liberal father Silvio, he shook the dust of our house from his feet, and went his way; muttering any thing but blessings upon us. For more than a week afterwards he sent daily to inquire whether the dumb devil had as yet manifested himself amongst us. Finally, I lost all patience, and sent him word that the devil had indeed appeared to us all, in the guise and garb of a priest, and that moreover, he was not dumb, but spake in very bad Latin. He received at the same time an admonition from Cardinal Lambertini, to whose authority we were forced to appeal, and we heard no more from him."

"Are your ecclesiastics in general so ignorant and superstitious?" I asked.

"What would you have?" said Gigia, "they are ecclesiastics. Their education is narrow and onesided. Their axioms are mere suppositions, and they teach as truth dogmas which would make all else that is, untrue."

"Yet," said Briseida, "even to those of us who esteem them most lightly, their companionship becomes a matter of habit and of necessity. I myself am not the devoutest of Catholics, and reck little of their power to bind and to loose, yet when my heart is oppressed by sorrow, I fly to the church, and hear my mass with effusion, with tears of consolation—it brings before me the emblems at least of things most holy and beautiful. I am not Philosopher enough to be consoled by a religion of thought alone."

"As for me," coolly remarked the Gigia, "I do not know that my heart is ever oppressed by sorrow; but my mind is sometimes empty, and my brain fantastic and gloomy. On these occasions, I too go to church, but it is to see Rafael's sybils, or Domenichini's frescos."

"Or Michael Angelo's Last Judgement, at the Sistine Chapel?" I suggested.

"No, that is not so agreeable a subject of contemplation to us poor sinners. When I contemplate that picture, I always see myself on the left, going down, down, down, and all the hypocrites I have despised in this world stand on the right, smiling triumphantly at me. Ah! per me è un disgusto!"

The Hermaphrodite

"Hush! you girls!" cried Berto, with a tremendous frown. "You are hea-
thens, atheists, infidels—know you not that I never allow treason or impiety
to be talked of in this house when I am in it?"

This interruption called forth an universal laugh, and Berto, having put
an end to our theological discussion, began to speak of his intended journey
to Naples. The Gigia had long since planned a pilgrimage thither for herself,
and she now exerted all her eloquence, to induce her brother to take her
with him. But Berto was not to be persuaded.

"At my age, not to have seen Naples!" exclaimed Gigia.

"That is an approach to candour which I never before knew you to make.
Let us know the age, that we may correctly estimate the greatness of the
misfortune."

"There is a picture in the Royal Museum which I am most anxious to
copy."

"I will have it copied for you at my own expense."

"You do not know, Berto, how fondly I have dreamed of the rich and
gorgeous redundancy of life in the South, of glowing seas and skies, of
Capri, Posilippo, the Chiaja, the Lazzari—Rome is gloomy and desolate as
a cemetery—Naples is brilliant and vivid as a flower garden."

"Ah!" said Berto, "I do not like to dispel people's illusions—they are as
much better than realities, as heaven is better than earth. The Naples you
imagine is so much finer than the actual Naples, that I cannot find it in my
heart to deprive you forever of the former, by shewing you the latter for a
moment."

"Well," rejoined Gigia, "I have sworn not to die without having seen
all these beautiful things, and most of all, the fiery dragon, Vesuvius, and
Herculaneum and Pompeii, the tombs of its victims."

"You are under oath not to die until you shall have seen them? then I
shall benevolently struggle to prolong your life, by keeping you away from
them as long as possible."

At these provoking words, the sisters assailed Berto with any number of
those little Roman vituperatives which are so much more explosive, and so
much less effective than one cutting phrase spoken in cold English. N.B.
When you wish to give the greatest possible relief to your own feelings, at
the smallest possible expense to the feelings of others, swear only in Italian.
For the Italian is furious, but not vengeful in his rage—he cannot degrade

his graceful language by a brutal epithet, and so he invents a thousand fantastic impossibilities to swear by, such as the blood of the moon, body of Bacchus, and others in the same sort. The Englishman, on the contrary, his ire once roused, instantly contemplates and invokes on the head of his adversary, the direst of calamities. Having emphatically God-damned to hell the soul of the offending party, his conscience is satisfied and his heart is at rest.

The kiss of peace having been at last interchanged, Berto gave in a few words, his parting instructions to his sisters and myself.

"Farewell Cecilia," said he, "I charge you that you prosecute your studies diligently. These ladies will indulge you with solitude, and intrude upon you only when your force of attraction becomes irresistible, and you draw them towards you as a lodestone attracts iron. You will see that Briseida does not serve you up a smoking proofsheet for your breakfast, nor pour out her midnight oil for your morning's coffee. Gigia is more a woman of the world, but she too has her moments of distraction, in which she might grind you up for paint, or try on your fair face the experiment of a new varnish.

"Girls, be discreet, be hospitable. Give Cecilia the freedom of your house and hearts. Unlock for her all the choice books, all the treasured papers. Especially, Briseida, do not fail to peruse with her that singular German manuscript left me by the good Count ———."

"The Count ———?" I repeated, with a cry of astonishment. "The illuminatist, the solitary? the proprietor of a hermitage . . ."

"In which you were once glad to take refuge from the world."

"And the uncle, moreover, of a graceless nephew—"

"Who has now the honour of taking leave of you," remarked Berto, with a profound bow, and instantly disappeared from the room, and from the house. I would have called him back, in the intent to pursue further the new vein of information which had so unexpectedly opened before me, but it was availed not. He was gone on his own crazy way, Providence and the moon alone knew whither. In his absence, I turned to Briseida, who in a few words confirmed and explained her brother's statement.

"The mother of us all," she said: "was a Roman woman, not nobly born, but distinguished by extraordinary beauty and rare talents. But she was twice married, and first to a German nobleman, who became the father of

The Hermaphrodite

Berto, and who died shortly after the birth of his son. By his will the child, born in Rome, was to be sent to Germany at ten years of age, there to receive his education under the care of his paternal Uncle. My mother subsequently married again, and we were born, but we knew not Berto until he was some eighteen years of age, and then, and ever since, he has been the delight and the torment of our lives."

I barred and bolted my door, that night, with unusual care, before I ventured to divest myself of my newly donned attire. Briseida followed me with offers of assistance, which I hastily declined, preferring to unravel alone the mysteries of stays and petticoats. As I stood before the glass, I bethought me for a moment of the reel and the bottle—I could not understand by what means I had got into the complete armour of silk and linen which encased me, nor how I should get out, save by some sudden burst of fury, strong enough to tear asunder eyelets, laces, buttons and all. But I soon felt that this would not avail me, and that my stays, like my destiny, were stronger than myself. They had been ordered for a hysterical young lady, and would bear any amount of wrenching and pulling. The scissors lay temptingly before me, but why should I by one cut betray my ignorance of female science, and destroy articles of toilette for which I should not care to be measured again? With a patience nearly allied to desperation, I began to untie little knots, and to follow little strings to their remote sources, repeating at the same time the tenses of an Hebrew verb. Getting somewhat provoked at the resistance of one of these, and finding myself at the same time aground in my verb, I gave the string a violent jerk. For once, I had done well to be angry. I felt the mighty fabric of the corset give way, my chest was free, my task accomplished. Berto, the considerate Berto, guided by I know not what kind genius, had procured me a pair of corsets à la parisienne.

"I, a woman?" I repeated to myself, and in shame sprang upon the bed, and hid my head beneath the clothes. And I dreamed, oh! I dreamed of one who had once almost made a woman of me.

Chapter [21]

The sisters of Berto were glad of an addition to their circle, though I am not convinced that it would have been less welcome to them in the shape of a handsome young man. Many and amusing were the comments I heard made upon my manners and appearance. They found me, if not awkward, at least shy and abrupt. My height also astonished them, as did the muscular strength displayed in my movements, and the depth of my voice. When one of them however was disposed to dwell upon these peculiarities of mine, the other replied: "ah! le donne Inglese sono cosi." They were too polite to trouble me with personalities of any kind, and so, things went on smoothly enough between us. There was no jarring, no friction, no jealousy. I had my occupations, and they were sufficiently engrossed with theirs. Gigia had her studio, and a boudoir adjoining—she was often at work in the Vatican, and often at play in the Corso or on the Monte Pincio. Briseida had her book room, which knew its own disorder, wherewith the stranger intermeddled not. Beyond was the sickroom of Nina, to which Berto had promised me free access. They had fitted up for me a coquette little apartment, which had sometimes been occupied by Berto during his mother's lifetime. The balcony on which I took my coffee commanded one of the finest views in Rome. The sun generally came to pass the afternoon in my room, and when he and his golden chariot took their nightly leave of the streets of Rome, mine was the last window at which he stopped to pay his parting compliments.

We sometimes met at meals, sometimes mine were served to me at my own hour, and in my own room. The manière d'être of the ménage was simple and quiet enough. There were but two evenings of dissipation in the week—one of these was the regular night at the Opera, which few Italians deny themselves; the other was a modest evening reception, at which I ventured to assist, having first assured myself that it brought to the house none who would have any possible interest in penetrating my incognito. At these receptions were present divers dignitaries of the church, a few men of letters, a stray artist or so; but the favoured guests of these and of every other evening were two young men of rank, of whom I shall hereafter have occasion to speak more fully. Briseida often entertained her guests with recitations of her own verses, and even with improvisations upon some given subject. Gigia sometimes arranged a tableau vivant, or more frequently exercised her talent in making piquant sketches of those present. For the most part, however, the evenings were passed in conversation, which, whatever else it might have lacked, was at least never wanting in vivacity and variety.

On one of these occasions, I was requested to bring into play my musical talent which, though not cultivated to artistic accuracy, was yet capable of enchaining a less indulgent audience than that of the Casa S——. Wearied as I was with a tedious tête à tête, I was not sorry to take my place at the piano. Having preluded slightly upon the keys, I fell into a musical reverie, and led my hearers through various fields of harmony, it must be confessed, with very little thought of them. And here let me ask, what true artist ever sings to the audience actually present before him? Do those frivolous women, those commonplace men inspire him with all the varied passions of his song? Is he really appealing to the sensibilities of those simpering maidens, or of their haughtier but equally trivial mothers, or is he determined by that daring burst of melody to take by storm the heart of the little critic who sits perched on a music stool in the foreground, sharply on the look out for a false note, and enjoying in the music only the conviction that he understands it better than did the maestro in whose labouring brain it had its spirit birth. The company listens, rather in dumbness than in intelligent silence—the critic administers his small criticism, now in a patronizing nod, now in knowing winks and frowns. The singer sees and knows little about it. His soul breathes for the time a wider, purer atmosphere than that of theatre or concert room. To somewhat infinitely above himself, yet also infinitely within himself he addresses those deeply breathed passages, those daring flights, those high notes which seem, like the song of the soaring lark, to drop, full of liquid light, from the empyrean. He could not sing thus for money—he could not sing thus for patronage. He may be needy and desirous of both, but for the moment he is not venal, not vulgar. He is lost in the impersonality of art. Not even if his dearest friend, his heart's fondest love were in the throng, could he sing to them. The artist who woos in song, is for the moment a wooer, but no artist. Even thus is it with one who makes a mournful melody a medium for whining out to those who hear him, some sorrow of his own. For though thy strain and thou be alike sad, yet hast thou no sorrow when thou singest, save the infinite melancholy of the universal human soul. For it cannot be that thy art shall be lost in thee, thou canst only lose it, or be lost in it.

The Hermaphrodite

But to return to myself. I had begun, as requested, by an air from a popular opera, but having performed this, I did not wait for the suggestions
of the company, but followed the songs as they suggested themselves. I
gave them my souvenirs of Malibran in *Otello* and *Cenerentola*, snatches from
Beethoven, von Weber, and Bellini—a melody of Schubert's, a barcarole of
Venice, a jodel of the Alps were each in turn woven into this odd mosaic,
which terminated in a magnificent strain that I had caught, that very morning, from the mass in the famous side chapel at St. Peter's. In this, my voice
and my soul rose and swelled together. At each note I discovered new depth
of significance in the music, new power in myself to render it—I was led
on to try that power to the utmost, abandoning myself to the momentary
passion that possessed me. My audience was breathlessly silent throughout
the performance; nor was it until some moments after I had ceased to sing,
that some one exclaimed:

150

"It is precisely the voice of Uberto."

And the others cried out in chorus: "Yes! it is indeed quite the voice of
Uberto."

"And who may Uberto be?" I asked of the person nearest me.

"He is the famous Contraltiste, distinguished by the Pope's especial
favour, and the best singer in the choir of the Sistine chapel."

Despite the hardening trials through which I had already passed, I could
not listen to these words without a discomposure which must have manifested itself by a sudden change of colour and expression, for Briseida cried
out: "You are ill, Cecilia!" and led me out to a balcony whither the thanks
and attentions of the company did not pursue me, and where the evening
star, my earliest and most constant friend, kept me company.

From that night, I sang no more in Rome.

But what manner of women were the sisters of my friend? not altogether
such as he had described and I imagined them. They were certainly fine
women, well-developed, well-accomplished, and tolerably well-principled,
yet Berto was not quite at the bottom of their secrets. Into these, I was soon
more or less initiated, and from my observations I learned the astounding
fact that Nina, so far from being the only one of the trio who had loved,
was the only one whose solitude was unconsoled by the bodily presence of
a lover.

The Hermaphrodite

The Gigia had from the first preserved towards me a tone of polite hospitality, which never [led] into more intimate intercourse. Briseida, on the contrary, met me at first with a certain reserve, which was gradually dispelled by our better acquaintance, until at length a warm regard sprang up between us, and I found myself taken into her confidence, whether I would or no.

I have said that these two ladies were each provided with a lover, at the period of my visit to them. Briseida, being the elder, naturally had for hers a youth some nineteen years of age, a simple hearted and studious child, whom she admonished and be-Mentored in a manner truly edifying, and who had the singular merit of thinking that he understood all that she thought she had explained.

Pepino was not a type of the pure Italian. He was well grown, graceful and pleasing, but his physical constitution gave evidence of that feebleness of organization which sometimes results from the intermingling of opposite races. The light complexion and blond chevelure which contrasted so well with his dark eyes, shewed that it was the German element which had tempered in him the fire of the Italian blood. His mental qualities were singularly in accordance with the indications of the external man. His was a nature all passive, all recipient, gifted with a quick appreciation of the good and beautiful, and yet suffering the things in which he delighted to slip from his grasp, for want of energy to retain them, or of courage to fight for them. He was a creature of sentiment and affection, not of will and passion, a man to weep over the ills of life, but in no wise to overcome them. Gentle, sensitive, ever anxious to please, ever seeking in others the purpose and the strength he should have sought in himself, he was the very man to become the sport and the victim of women, the very man to betray them by the same weakness and indecision which led him into their toils. Yet he might have fallen into far worse hands than those of Briseida, who at first had regarded him as a mere youth, to whose life she might impart an useful direction. Whether her love for him had been of gradual or spontaneous growth, I know not—certain it was that he had come to be the centre of all her thoughts, the inspiration of her life. Could Pepino have chosen for himself, at this moment, he would probably have become the husband of Briseida. But men like him rarely choose, and for Pepino it would have been eminently difficult to do so, his parents having long since chosen for him. He was the only son of an ancient Roman family, whose rank had always been of the noblest, but whose decayed fortunes needed to be propped up by wealthy marriages. His father, whose opulence was derived from his German wife, had always been on the look out for a profitable matrimonial investment for his son. Two years prior to Pepino's acquaintance with Briseida, he had been promised in marriage to a Polish Countess, of enormous fortune. His fiancée was a silly, sickly young girl, with a countenance darkly pallid, and an enormous black chevelure, remotely suggestive of Plica Polonica. En revanche, she was supposed to be endowed with untold wealth, and appeared on public occasions blazing with diamonds. Distasteful as she was to him, however, he was doomed to marry her, and he knew it. He might talk of the inalienable rights of the human heart, but he was not the man to make them good. Nor did they exist for him—for no man has a right to the thing he loves, unless he have the courage and devotion to die for it. Had Briseida been a worldly and designing woman, angling for the handsome young nobleman, and determined to win him at all hazards, she might possibly have succeeded. It would then have been the contest of two strong wills on the neutral ground of a timid, irresolute soul. But Briseida was incapable of forming such a purpose, and of accomplishing it by her own calculations. She loved her young pupil, and no woman who really loves can condescend to win the man she loves after this fashion. Despite the thirty five years which had given her experience without worldly wisdom, she was still almost childishly impressionable and impulsive, still trusting, as candid souls ever are.

It was not from his parents that Pepino had received the impulse of acquiring knowledge. In his childhood, they had only taught him to fear their displeasure, and obey their will, the very lessons least needed by the timid and passive child. Later in life, he had fallen more under the guidance of a learned uncle on the German side of the house, from whom he had derived the blessings of a tolerable education, a good library, and the desire to make use of it. He had found in those around him but little sympathy with the tastes thus acquired, nor is it surprising that the society of Briseida should, at this period, have had charms for him which that of younger and prettier women could not supply. The literary reputation of Briseida had first attracted him within the bounds of her exclusive circle, and the ostensible object of his visits to her was an attempt at mutual instruction in

Pickle

The Hermaphrodite

the German language. Pepino had acquired a partial knowledge of it from his Uncle, and Briseida in other days, had by much teasing persuaded Berto to give her some lessons in his father tongue. Pepino was almost daily at the Casa S——, though I did not always see him there. Briseida possessed the only copy of Goethe's Tasso to be found in Rome—it was borrowed from Berto's library, and Pepino and she used to pore over it by the hour. It so happened that I entered the study softly one day, and found them seated side by side, with their backs toward me. I observed that their heads were close to each other, but that was because they had one book between them. The dictionary lay upon Briseida's lap, and Pepino turned over the leaves, but that was on the principle of the division of labour. After various lowly uttered phrases, which seemed, as far as I could judge, to be a very free version of the text of Goethe, I heard Briseida exclaim:

"My dearest Tasso! it is nearly Ave Maria, we must leave off—indeed we must."

The arm of Tasso took a poetic license with her waist, as he replied:

"My charming Leonora! I cannot break off just yet, this is a very interesting scene!"

I thought so too, and stole away as I had crept in, unperceived.

After this, I ventured one day to ask Briseida if she had ever thought of matrimony, and if her single life was the result of fortuitous circumstances, or of choice and determination—her reply was too characteristic not to be recorded.

"Cara mia!" she said: "in this blessed country, love and marriage are, so to speak, in a state of divorce, one finds them in spite of, not in each other. Marriage is here completely an affair of reciprocal interests and convenience, in which the mere circumstance of womanhood makes it incumbent on us to require little, and to offer much. I can sing for you the whole matrimonial scale, from the highest note to the lowest. It runs thus: a woman young, beautiful and rich may obtain a husband who shall be either young, rich, or handsome, or even one who may combine these attributes, though such rarely marry until their dissipations have brought them to a premature decrepitude, and health and fortune alike require a nurse. A woman rich but not young may find a husband who shall be young, but not rich. A woman who has but her youth and beauty may get an old man, rich or otherwise. A woman simply of intelligence and of education, who shall be neither young, rich, nor handsome may choose between the three alternatives of a life like mine, a convent, or marriage with some decayed stump and remnant of a man, probably without fortune, certainly without attractions, or qualities that command a woman's love. Now, my dear Cecilia, I may be too vain, but I do esteem myself too highly to submit to such a fate. Many women in my position are glad to accept a husband, in order to give themselves the liberty to betray him with impunity, but I am not of those vile ones. I have had to choose more than once between marriage such as this, and my modest life, embellished only by literature and by friendship. I need not tell you that I have always chosen the latter, and that I have never had reason to regret my choice."

"And Pepino? he will doubtless make the same noble choice?" I asked, in a tone of subdued raillery.

"Pepino cannot choose," answered Briseida, with heightened colour. "He is already betrothed—even were it not so, he must still marry, and must never marry me. I have never allowed him to speak of any other connexions between us than those already existing. Nor is his intercourse with me of a nature to unfit him for the destiny that lies before him. I have sought on the contrary to strengthen him for it, and to help him to thoughts and pursuits which will give dignity to his life, and alleviate the cheerlessness of his uncongenial marriage."

I am sure that she spoke in entire good faith, and who shall say that there was not much of truth in her words. If they were not wholly true, she deceived herself, not me. She was silent for a moment, and when she spoke again, it was with a more agitated utterance.

"The day is coming," she said: "when even this must cease, when one who cannot hold his happiness dear as I do, will yet acquire the right to exclude me from the horizon of his life. To me, he has been a beautiful truth, to her he will be but a commonplace, inevitable fact. It will be a bitter day for both of us, but I do not think of myself, I only wish him happy."

"You should not wish him that degradation of taste which would make him happy with a woman who is your inferior, and his."

"Do not give me such thoughts," she said, and turned away, her eyes filled with tears.

As I left her, I said to myself: "women are like the vines that ripen on the sides of volcanos—it is only on the perilous brink of destruction that their

The Hermaphrodite

finest qualities are called out. Your saints of vines that grow in colder, safer regions, are apt to be thin, acid, and sadly wanting in body. No—it takes the generous volcanic soil to nurture rich blood in the heart of a woman, and the foot of a thankless lover to crush it out."

I speak not as a moralist, but as an aesthetic philosopher—kind reader, be not too severe upon this last doubtful sentence—tell me rather, art not thou, is not every man by turns the one and the other? ☆

Do not imagine, however, that I soberly approved of Briseida's conduct with regard to Pepino. It was certainly full of danger for both of them, perhaps even gravely and morally wrong. But Briseida seemed to me one of the few who know their own minds. There was nothing paltry, or trivial, or ungenerous in her composition, and I did not feel myself called upon either to anathematize her conduct to herself, or to betray it to Berto. I ventured indeed to suggest that she should ask her brother's advice in the matter, but she replied, with a shrug of the shoulders: "Berto è un originale!"

Thus answered, I thought it best to leave her to take her own way, hoping that it might not prove very remote from God's way—for even as we know not the afflictions which prepare us for happiness, so we know not the errors through which another must pass to his highest virtue.

The Gigia, with all her artistic power, with all her talent for life, interested me far less than her elder sister. As she had accomplished more visible results than Briseida, she had become the object of more general notice and commendation—it was perhaps in consequence of this that she had become warped and hardened to worldliness. For I soon observed that while Briseida valued chiefly the praise of those who were in sympathy with herself, and brought such honours as she received, as offerings to the altar of her love, the Gigia coldly counted up her gains, and calculated how each success should become the stepping stone to another.

I think I have said that she painted admirably in oils. Her copies were in great request, and her own compositions were sold before they left the easel. It was easier to judge of the merits of her paintings than to determine the value of Briseida's uncoined thoughts, and the world (reader, every body has a world) accorded to her the pre-eminence in point of talent. Thus is it that the mediocre fulfillment of a mediocre promise imposes more upon men than do those high and excelling capacities which can only promise in time that which they can fulfill only in eternity.

The Hermaphrodite

But what if the realization of these post mundane promises were to prove like unto the flowering of a centenary aloes—long waited for, beautiful and brilliant, but past with all its golden bloom, in a day or so, and nothing left for the soul but a brief remembrance, and another slow, weary century of growth?

The devil writes such notes as this on every pious work!

Gigia was inferior to Briseida in beauty of feature and expression—on the other hand, she was better made, and much better made up. She was always dressed with elegance, and the hands that wielded her skilful pencil were white, delicate, and irreproachably well-ordered, while those of poor Briseida generally bore the true literary stain. Her habits of mind too were better fitted for shining in society. Without possessing much valuable information upon any one subject (for even her skill in art was but tact, taste, and a certain faculty of arrangement and imitation) she had a readiness in conversation which people mistook for the overflowing of a full mind. She was au fait with the current news and events of every day—she knew enough about new books to have the air of knowing more, and had moreover a piratical talent for appropriating to herself many of the good things carelessly uttered by Briseida, and of reproducing them at a happy moment as her own.

Gigia too had a lover, I should say rather, a gallant, inferior to Pepino in youth and beauty, but no less superior to him in tournure and knowledge of the world. The Conte Flavio was one of those Italians, (not a very numerous class, by the by) who have travelled and have seen the world. He had been in England, and could drink tea. He had been in Scotland, and could drink whiskey. He had been in Paris, and could talk of its cafés, its theatres, its fascinating women and distinguished men—he might also have spoken from personal experience of its gaming houses, and of other resorts unmentionable to ears polite. He had been in Germany, could swear a German oath or so, and sing a student's song. He had attempted a voyage to the East, but had turned back, finding the sun of the desert injurious to his complexion, and the trot of the camel somewhat jeopardizing to his delicate diaphragm. He had ruined some women, and boasted of having ruined more, but would say, with a *fade* smile, laying his hand upon his heart, "that they had ruined him, that he had been all his life the victim of that dear, but treacherous sex." He was, emphatically, a worldly man of the world, and a professed coureur des femmes, but in attempting the conquest of the dexterous Gigia, he had gone somewhat beyond his depth. The affair was managed on both sides with consummate skill. I soon saw that the vanity of the two intrigants was more at stake than the heart of either—this was, because Nature had endowed them liberally with the one, and but sparingly with the other. It was a matter of piquant provocations, dexterous entanglements, equivocal words, wiles and glances. It was, in short, a continued effort on the part of each to sound the depth of the other's coquetry. Had this effort resulted in success, the game would have been dropped in disgust by both, for there is [no] heart, however vile, that is not repelled by vileness in others. There is no heart so false but that it may cherish the thought of inspiring in another a truer, purer affection than itself could feel, in the sad, faint hope of catching the good by contagion, and of being redeemed from its abasement by that ardent and disinterested affection, which is, as it were, the very lifeblood shed for another.

Thus, though neither Gigia nor the Conte Flavio was impassioned, each waited to be magnetized by the supposed passion of the other. The immediate impulse in each was the same, but their remoter aims were not alike. The ultimate purpose of Flavio was one of seduction, that of Gigia was marriage. Flavio would have gloried in showing to the world a fine woman, risking her reputation, and losing her heart for him—accordingly, every step that he took was calculated to compromise her, and to place her in the odious position of a woman who makes love. The Gigia managed however to checkmate him by preserving, in public, an implacable discretion. Having ascertained that his fortune and title were solid and indisputable, she formed the determination of sharing them with him. In this view, she forced him to take the initiative himself, and to pay for every favour of hers by attentions which almost pledged him in the eyes of the world as a man of serious intentions. I troubled myself but little about the progress of their coquetries, anticipating from them some cold catastrophe, or perhaps an angry separation which might leave both parties innocent according to human laws, but most culpable if judged by the truer standard of impulse and motive.

Gigia passed some hours of every morning at the Vatican, where she was copying the head of the Madonna di Foligno. I sometimes accompanied her thither, and soon observed that Flavio, who followed her in all her walks, and contrived to make twenty rendez-vous a day with her, never met her there. I could only account for this by supposing that he recognized and feared the mystic influence of the place. The divine presence of Rafael's saints would have too strongly rebuked the levity of the discourse which he was wont to hold with Gigia. Who would dare attempt an equivocal jest while standing before that austere, holy saint, on whose agony angels are waiting, and whose lips, absolved from all need of corporeal nourishment, are waiting to receive on earth the food of heaven. Or who that stands before the glory of the transfigured one, and is penetrated by the light of his love, will find it in his heart to devise a falsehood, or a flattery. Thus, these works of genius have an eternal presence.

Yet even to that sacred shrine of beauty and of holiness, I fear me that the Gigia carried profaning thoughts. The Roman youth who ground her colours and carried her easel was a perfect model of adolescent beauty— she seemed to carry on with him that condescending kind of flirtation with which even aristocratic women do not always disdain to amuse themselves. There was also an old Russian, whose wealth and barbarism dated from many ages back, who hovered around her, visibly attracted by the amenity of her manners—there were various others, of various shades of desirability, to whom I thought she gave more or less of encouragement. It was easy nevertheless to see that Flavio stood at the head of the list, and if she did not give up her heart exclusively to him, he was worldly-wise and wicked enough to look after his own interests.

But Nina, the blessed unfortunate, was my favorite study, in those days of my feminine seclusion—Nina, so deaf, dumb, and blind of body, so far-seeing and intelligent of soul. Dream-rapt, isolated from the actual world, half corpse, half angel, she still lived on in spirit with her absent lover, and enjoyed the happiness of a guardian angel, intently watching and protecting the fortunes of a mortal beloved. Whether she was cataleptic and insane, whether she was clairvoyante, and if so, whether the facts open to her knowledge had their place in the material or spiritual world, were all subjects of doubt and dissension among the more intelligent of Nina's friends. The more ignorant supposed her possessed of a dumb devil, like some of the demoniacs in the New Testament. Gigia briefly called her mad—Briseida considered her simply magnetic, while I became convinced of the presence in her of that abnormal illumination which is technically

The Hermaphrodite

termed clair-voyance. According to Berto's request, I had endeavoured to acquire the magnetic command over her. Others had failed to do so, to me it was given to succeed. Without abusing my power, I had yet some important interviews with her, the results of which I recorded in detail, for Berto's benefit. When I addressed her, she sometimes spoke in a rhapsodic manner, as if out of the fulness of her soul—sometimes she answered my questions with promptness, and with evident pleasure—sometimes, her replies were brief, languid, and unwilling. I find here at hand a fragment of one of her rhapsodies, transcribed by me at the time. I had asked her of Gaetano's success in the land of his exile. Her reply ran thus:

"Why does the corn that he has planted grow taller and greener than that of his fellows? Why is it that his horse is fleeter, his aim truer, his shot more deadly than theirs? Why do the trees of the forest keep for him their ripest fruit? Why does the wild vine reach to him her fullest clusters?

"It is because he loves, and is tenderly beloved. It is that my prayers have laid the powers of nature under contribution for him, and earth, sea, and sky can refuse him nothing. A feast is spread for him in the wilderness—he sleeps in the haunt of the serpent and the savage beast as on his mother's breast. For the man that, loving, is beloved of a woman stands in the garden of God, and is watered by dews of Paradise, but he who loves not and is not loved wanders in an arid desert, and the blessings of heaven know no road to his heart ————"

In the hope of awakening other faculties of her mind, I sometimes directed her attention to the mysteries of the unseen world, to the nature of God, the inner laws of being, the condition and relations of disembodied spirits, and other themes comprehended within the wide scope of the mystic-magnetic philosophy. She insisted that she had no knowledge of these things, and prayed me to relinquish the attempt to give a new direction to her powers.

"Why is it that I cannot make you look into heaven?" I one day asked of her.

"I have not been called there," she replied: "I have been called to follow Gaetano."

"But would you not gladly be there?"

"He is not there," she said, with much expression.

"No, but God is there, do you not love him?"

The Hermaphrodite

[The narrative breaks off at this point in Laurence's conversation with Nina. The last manuscript page in this section, numbered "171" even though it does not carry on the material from "170," follows.]

Chapter [22]

It was in a less gentle guise that my human brethren next came to me, and the tidings they bore to me were as a painful resurrection of evils whose remedy lay, not in reason, not in religion, but in that merciful gift of God, forgetfulness. Do I speak impiously in saying this? Methinks not. Kneel thou to pray, oh devout man, in the first agony of a wounded spirit—look up to heaven, will not thy tears mock thee? Lift up thine hands—ah! they seek but to grasp again that which thou has lost. Speak, speak to God, if thou canst—teach thy lips to say, "fiat voluntas tua," but thou art struggling with that will, even while thou sayest it. Thy heart speaks the truer language: "give back, give back, oh God! thou whose power to take away is infinite, be thy power also infinite to restore. If thou canst not help me, at least, destroy me. There is nought of good, nought of divine love in this anguish which oppresses me—it cannot be thy will, thou hast forsaken, forgotten me." But many years will pass, and every one of them will bring thee gentler thoughts. Nature will exercise a kind tyranny over thee, and will drive thee from the dreary ashes of thy joys. Wherever thou mayest wander, a thousand ministers will spring up to teach, to comfort thee, whether thou will or not. Thou canst not live and not be consoled. It needs not the teachings of another world to tell us that evil has its bounds, both in degree and in duration. It is true, oh man, that sorrow is absolute, but Life and Love are infinite, and nought but the Infinite can be Eternal.

3

[The final sequence of the narrative is composed of several much shorter manuscript fragments, only one of which is numbered and some of which are different drafts of the same scene. What follows is the editor's attempt to produce a readable text using all the manuscript material that logically fits into the narrative. A straightforward transcription of the manuscript pages involving multiple versions of the same scene can be found in appendix 2. Three asterisks indicate a gap in the story for which no manuscript exists. The narrative is clearly a continuation of the second sequence, though Laurence is occasionally referred to toward the end as "Laurent." Dressed as a woman, Laurence continues to reside with Briseida, Gigia, and Nina; Berto rejoins the family after his sojourn in Naples and reveals "Cecilia's" secret; and Berto refers (189) to Laurence's brother Philip's death, which occurs in section 2. (This reference is not quite consistent with the section 2 scenes involving Laurence's father and brother.) The major event in the first part of this sequence is the reading of the manuscript Berto has mentioned before taking his leave (146): the tale of Eva and Rafael, "Ashes of an Angel's Heart" (numbered in manuscript 1–27, plus two additional unnumbered pages). After a gap, the narrative brings the Ronald and Berto storylines together as Laurence sinks toward death. The manuscript ends as it begins—midsentence.]

Chapter [23]

At this very period, and while our minds were still occupied with the singular experiences of Nina, I recalled to mind the vague mention made by Berto of a certain manuscript, the legacy, possibly the composition of the dead Uncle whose posthumous hospitality had given me shelter in my evil days. I bethought myself of it upon a quiet evening whose deepening shades had found Briseida and her Pepino seated on the terrace, engaged in making the sunset beautiful to each other. A little further on I discerned the Conte Flavio, making love to Gigia very much after the fashion of a peacock, paying court to a tulip. For me there was no companion, and no companionship. The very twilight would not receive me into its friendly, intimate shades, but cast me out into the cold light of the rising moon, which began to cast here and there a streak of ungenial white. Even Gigia's tiny spaniel, forgetful of many kindnesses, and lumps of sugar, barked unkindly at my heels, and snapped at the hand I extended to caress him. It was obviously a matter of astonishment to every animate and inanimate thing there, that I durst venture into a lover's paradise, myself unloving and unloved. I was ashamed to be there, ashamed to display my loneliness before their eyes.

* * *

"You must not take it to your room," said Briseida. "The chief condition etc is that I shall on no account suffer it to go out of my safe keeping, even for the space of an hour."

"But Berto promised."

"I know it, and am in haste to perform—you shall read the manuscript to Pepino and myself in my study—he has never seen it, and I have read it but once, and with difficulty, given the nature of the characters, wh[ich] are not easy to decypher.

* * *

"What are you talking of doing in the library," asked the peacock, suddenly approaching the doves.

"Cecilia has promised to read to us the Count's manuscript. It has to us a painful interest," she said, addressing me, "from the supposition that it has had some part in the strange history of our poor Nina. Berto read it to her shortly before her separation from Gaetano, and when you have heard it, you will easily see that it may have had a certain influence in producing her sublime madness—from the coincidence of the leading sentiment of it with the idea of eternal and indivisible union of loving spirits which to our poor Nina became first a desire, then a conviction, then, a madness."

"And what a madness, weak, childish, unworthy!" exclaimed Gigia, with emphasis.

"Do not call it so!" answered Briseida: "it is childlike, but sublime."

"The sublime of folly," said Gigia: "to sacrifice youth, beauty, talents, health to the shade of one man. To die (for she is dying, poor thing!) for one poor wretch of a man, and he not the best or handsomest in the world, when there are so many fine men left in it!"

The Hermaphrodite

She smiled upon Flavio, as she spoke.

"So are the heavens full of stars," said Briseida, "but he is the one star revealed to her by the telescope of love."

"Brava!" cried Flavio—"Brava!" whispered Pepino.

"Bah!" exclaimed Gigia: "the comparison indeed may pass muster. You will excuse me, however, if I venture to remark that your long and diligent study of that telescope must have been rewarded ere this by the sight of many stars."

"That may be," answered Briseida, "but for every soul there is one pole-star, not many."

I could not forbear coming to Briseida's aid with a quotation from an unknown poet.

> "Through many passions, one great thought doth run;
> Through many seasons, one eternity."

"That is your English mysticism," said Gigia, tartly: "it means nothing. Constancy, in my opinion, should of right be numbered among the diseases of children, among those, too, which occur but once in a lifetime."

"Yet who ever vowed eternal love that did not wish above all else that he might keep the blessed vow? Who ever broke it, that did not either weep or rave over the weakness of heart, or the perversity of fate that compelled him to it? Nina's soul is stronger than fate, sister, I will not say the same of mine."

As we parted company, the conversation dropped into a couple of tête à tête murmurs, both of which I was skilful enough to overhear.

"And so the divine Gigia would not die for any man?" whispered Flavio, with an affected emphasis.

"For her husband, yes," answered Gigia, in like manner.

"Then you will acquire the distinction of being the first inconsolable widow on record."

"My ambition does not extend to widowhood," rejoined Gigia—I heard no more from her, for from the other side these words reached me, in the hearty and truthful utterance of her sister:

"Pepino! I cannot wish that my first love had been my last, but would God my last love had been my first!"

The Hermaphrodite

The eyes that looked into Pepino's eyes had so earnest and mournful a meaning that they awoke in my heart the ghost of a buried remembrance. Oh God! who was it that had looked even, even so upon me? I pressed my hands upon my forehead, and ill to faintness, sought the open air.

Thank God, I was not yet turned to stone! Thank God, I could still remember, and weep at the remembrance.

With these words she entered the house—as I followed her, I turned and saw the white robe of Gigia as it became lost in the shadow of the plane trees.

"And now for the manuscript," said Briseida, as she trimmed the picturesque brazen lamp on the study table, and arranged for me the cushions of her easy chair. "You must not read too rapidly, as I am not yet strong either in the German tongue, or in German mysticism."

The costly case enclosing the sacred relic was now produced—it was of precious wood, richly carved, and inlaid with gold and with precious stones. On the first leaf of the parchment within were written these words:

Ashes of an angel's heart.

The kindness of Berto enables me to subjoin an entire copy of what I then read.

Eva stood by the tomb of Rafael. She bent over it, and cried out: is our love dead, Rafael, and has the memory of it perished with thee? And the dead spake, and from his pale lips went forth a soft murmur, for the sun of love can give life and a voice even to pulseless marble. Not many could have understood the tongue in which he spake, for it was the language of another world. But God had given to this frail woman the aid of heavenly wisdom, and the blessed inspiration which men call madness was upon her.

And thus spake Rafael: blessed art thou among women, oh Eva, child of love—thou who hast taught me every human affection, thou who art the Alpha and Omega of my life. Blessed art thou for the love thou hast borne me, and for the faithful heart which turns into a blessing the curse of endless widowhood. Dear one who lovest sorrow for my sake, many spirits will come to thee, but listen thou to the angel of consolation.

Eva said, I cannot receive him.

The tomb of Rafael was in the loveliest spot that could be found—in a deep and beautiful dell, shaded by overhanging rocks and thickly interwoven trees—near it was a small quiet lake, softly sunken in the rocks, as in a vase. Eva called it her Lachrymatory, she had shed so many tears into it. A solitary dove, from whom death had taken her summer mate, kept guard over the grave, and made a gentle moaning, but she folded her wings and was silent when she heard the voice of Eva, for she recognized the presence of a sorrow higher than her own. The tomb was hewn out of transparent crystal, and through its clear purple sides Eva could easily distinguish the beautiful form of her beloved one, made angelic by death. Human skill had mercifully intervened to make its substance incorruptible. The face was lovely and calm, as in a dream of peace, but it was sealed, it could change no more. The dark locks lay lovingly upon the white forehead, but, had they been cast in bronze, they could not have been more immoveable. The eyes with their wondrous fringing of black, nature's masterpiece, closed by her that no one might miss the soul that once looked out of them, alas! poor Eva, they will look no more upon thee until thou too shalt be taken behind that dark curtain and let into the secrets of the world beyond. Here Eva came piously every day, to weep and pray—here angels came to weep with her and to comfort her, and here at times the voice of her agony moved even to pity the cold heart of death, and he permitted the spirit she loved to speak to her. I can write but few of Eva's words, but I love to remember them.

Oh Rafael! every thing changes save my love to thee—the sun rises and sets, the flowers bloom and die and bloom again—the year marches forward on the journey from which he never returns, and I am borne onward towards decay, death, and the grave, but my love is as deathless as my soul. The world of today is not the world of yesterday—these birds are strangers to the birds that sang to us last year, but my love is the same love that I felt when my heart was pressed to thine. Why do all things perish, except desire? why is the longing of my heart stronger and deeper than life itself? why has God made love immortal, and given to happiness the life of a day? oh Rafael, thy God is cruel.

No mortal being was near Eva, but as she stood by the tomb, she saw that one came to her, of a wild and withered aspect, of a wondrous beauty,

The Hermaphrodite

wondrously blighted. Its brow was crowned with faded roses, and pierced by pointed thorns—its white garments were stained with blood—it bore a ghastly wound in its heart, and in its hand was a cup of wine mingled with gall, which it held to Eva's lips, so that she could not but drink thereof, and as she drank, the spirit sang thus to her.

Drink deeply to sorrow
To glorious sorrow,
The truest thing thy heart can know.
Joy is a seeming
Love is but a dream,
The promise of thine eye
Is a lie in thy hand,
But the dead are dead, and the lost is lost.

That thou hast, thou know'st it not,
It may be more or less;
For the sunlight of pleasure so dazzles thine eyes
That thou canst not count aright thy treasure.
But by the void within thine arms,
By the silence in thine heart,
By the empty hands thou liftest to God
Which fall as empty back on thee
By dumbness and the blindness of thy soul
Light-deprived, love-bereaved,
Thou knowst what thou hast lost.

Grasp it, measure it,
Waken yet more to it,
Turn it around and around,
And see how entire
How hopeless is thy loss.

Thou as a mortal
Lovedst a mortal,
God chose him for thee,
Gave thee none other.
He has left thee forever.

The Hermaphrodite

Where wilt thou seek him
Or one like unto him?
There is no resurrection for thy love,
And the blessing of the past is the doom of the future.

A long, dull day
Without sunshine, without storm
Life shall seem to thee;
With infinite longing,
And only the finite to fill it,
Tis a burthen for two,
And thou bearest it alone.
Seek thee another mate, if thou wilt,
Piece out the ragged garment as thou mayst,
For thou art human, and will live humanly,
But for the blindness that thou hast known
Thou hopest and prayest vainly.

The arms of thy cross
Reach wherever thou turnest,
Northward and southward,
Eastward and westward;
Thou'rt bound on it, nailed to it,
Born to it, wedded to it.
Persuade the wood to tenderness,
Caress the iron to softness,
Then only shall fate take pity on thee,
And the grave give thee back the dead thou mournest.

And Eva said: "give me again thy bitter cup, thou terrible angel, let me drink it all, if I may only find death at the bottom."

But the angel cried: "I am Despair, and thine heart is not great enough to contain me." As she looked, he spread into a gigantic phantom, reaching from the earth to the clouds, but a thunderbolt struck him, and with a shriek, he vanished from her sight.

A fairer and gentler spirit stood beside Eva, and reasoned with her. She was called the Angel of the living world, and after this manner spake she:

The Hermaphrodite

"Daughter of sorrow, dry thy tears. Death comes not to thee as yet, and yet art thou buried in thine affliction, as in a tomb. I pray thee, raise those heavy eyes, and look upon my earth. See, how beautifully it is adorned of God for the delight of man. It is no valley of the shadow of death—it is the vestibule of Paradise—nay, so fair is it that many linger within its walls, and even when summoned to take a higher seat in their Father's house, are reluctant to go."

Eva made answer: "The spot on which I stand is all of earth that I ask of thee. Where Rafael lies, there is the house of God, there is the gate of heaven."

And the angel said: "I also wept when Rafael died, for he was pure to love, and beautiful to look upon. But I have many other sons. Beauty and love are not dead with him. Seek them, and thou shalt find them in other forms. Barren widowhood is not for thee, thou fairest one, for thou art a woman, and woman belongs to man, as man to God."

But Eva answered thus: "Thou knowest not then, oh angel, that it is appointed to the heart often to seek, but only once to find? knowest not, that for souls once wedded there is no widowhood? Rafael has departed on a far journey, and I am to follow him. Shall I then take to myself another husband, that I may be unworthy and ashamed to look upon him, when we shall meet? He is not dead, but liveth. Oh angel! wherefore persuade me not to forsake him, for I have appealed thus unto his God and mine: 'Thou wilt not leave my soul in the hell of loneliness, neither wilt thou suffer thy consecrated one to look upon the world's corruption.' "

Then the angel wept with her, and tenderly embracing her, said: "I will at least make his grave green and beautiful for thee—white blossoms and fragrant airs shall make it like to a bridal couch, and the frost and the sun shall not harm thee nor him, for I am the mother of you both, even as God is the father of us all."

And Eva smiled and said: "yes, mother, but it is written that a man shall forsake his father and his mother, and shall cleave unto the soul that is chosen for him."

Again, there came to Eva one of a stern and austere aspect, who reproved her with harsh words for the abandonment of her grief, and for her ingratitude to God. There was no music in his voice, no love in his eye—in his hand he bare a book, in which he had noted down every imperfection of

The Hermaphrodite

imperfection

her love and life—against these, he had recorded the many mercies she had received from God. Having summed up to her the two sides of his account, he exhorted her to waste no more time in weeping and lamentation, but to arise and go forth into the world, and labour for the good of others. And these are some of their words:

Spirit

So thou seest, Eva, thy love and life have been alike sinful.

Eva

Alas! they were alike given me of God.

Spirit

But God has removed thine idol, that thou mayest worship Him.

Eva

Had I not loved Rafael, I had never learned adoration.

Spirit

Be it so—God gave him, and God hath taken him away.

Eva

Not so. In that God gave him, God cannot take him away. Divine gifts are eternal—he is mine forever.

Spirit

Woman, leave these thy sophisms, and arise and weep no more. Or, if thou wilt weep, be it for thy sins and not for thy sorrows. Thy love was partly sensual, and partly selfish, and God will judge both thee and it. Thy sorrow is at the present useless and unreasonable, wherefore I bid thee go forth and do good works. Labour with thine hands, and declare with thy tongue the praises of the Most High, that thou mayst find acceptance in His sight.

Eva

I cannot understand thy words, oh spirit! Thou comest not from the heaven where my Rafael is, and the God of whom thou speakest is nearer to me than thou. Leave me then, I pray thee, to the dead and to Him.

The Hermaphrodite

Spirit

I will leave thee to the darkness of thine own heart, and to
them that sent me I will say—

Eva

That my soul doth wait in hope for the angel of consolation,
and that I have said unto God: Fiat voluntas tua.

But this unkind spirit would not depart without afflicting Eva once more
by his words, and as he was about to take leave, he said to her:

"Remember that he whom thou so madly lovest is not bound to thee
in any sense. If, as thou supposest, he be in heaven, he is free to choose
from those around him an angel higher in grace, and fairer in the beauty of
holiness than thou."

At these cruel words, a cloud came over poor Eva's sight, and her breath
failed her, so deadly was the thought that Rafael might forget her. She had
a woman's pride too, and at the thought of being scorned and rejected by
one so loved, her lip curled, and tears of passionate anguish burst from
her eyes. This was but for a moment—better thoughts came to her aid. As
she looked up, she saw the dove hovering near her—she remembered the
blessed Jesus, and she made answer after the following manner.

Jesus was despised,
Jesus was rejected,
Jesus was despised and rejected of men;
But he forgave them,
Ever, ever loved them,
Laboured, suffered, died for them,
And, dying, blessed them.

The love they rejected,
The prayers they despised
Were light to their darkness, and life to their death;
The blood that was shed for them
Crying to heaven
Brought them the blessing he died to secure.

Spirit of Jesus
Rest thou upon me!

The Hermaphrodite

As thou for the many, so I for the one
    Will pour out my heart's blood,
    In prayer and in passion,
For one ever worshipped, though loving no more.

    Oh! pour thou upon him
    Thy holiest blessing,
Give him thy love till he need mine no more,
    Let Rafael be happy,
    Let Eva be faithful,
And the will of the Highest forever be done.

As Eva sang, her fainting heart was strengthened. When her song was ended, she heard a sound more melodious than the first breath of the soft south wind, that promises summer and fruitfulness to the virgin earth. She looked, the dark spirit was gone, and an indescribably beautiful appearance was present to her entranced sight. She knew that she beheld the promised angel of consolation. He put forth his hand and touched her, and the fever of her wounds was calmed.

"I bear thee a message from Rafael," he said, "and Rafael is happy. He bade me tell thee that in his bosom is planted a golden seed, and that thou shouldst watch to see it ripen, and shoot up, and become a plant. It will grow and grow until it shall burst the tomb, and then will the days of thine earthly life be numbered. But woe to thee should another than thou be here and gather the flower that shall bloom from it, for then wilt thou be placed in a heaven where Rafael is not."

Eva repeated the angel's words: "and Rafael is happy." She wept: "I thank God," she said, "and yet the thought seems to rive my heart in twain. But sayest thou indeed that I am destined to Rafael and heaven?"

"Dost thou then prize the one above the other?" replied the angel.

Eva answered: "Yes, kind angel—for me the one cannot exist without the other. God hath made me so, and I cannot be otherwise. He knows and forgives that Rafael is nearest to my heart. For, did I know him to be in hell, I would pray that it might be permitted me to seek him there, and to change his curse into a blessing, by bearing it with him."

The Hermaphrodite

"Wilt thou ever love him as thou dost at this moment?" asked the angel, doubtingly—"there are many left as thou art who forget their love in heaven, and seek to themselves other mates on earth."

"And how do they meet the forgotten one?" enquired Eva.

"For such there is much of sorrow and perplexity," said the angel—"they are condemned to long and solitary wanderings, and whether they be ever permitted to renew their broken faith or not, I have never known."

"And wherefore didst thou not come to me before? thou gracious angel!" cried Eva. "Thy presence and thy words would have taken away the sting of my sorrow, and I should have given thanks to God, instead of accusing him of cruelty and injustice."

"My brethren are always sent before me to those that mourn," said the angel, "it is theirs to awaken the dormant soul—they force it to arise from its lethargy, and persuade or scourge it towards the gate of heaven, which is near the tomb of love. If the fugitive turn upon its pursuers and force its way back to the world, that gate remains shut upon him, the demon of indifference ministers to him, and pours for him a draught which deadens sorrow, and destroys the heavenly memory of the soul itself. But if the mourner recognize in those who afflict him, the messengers of God, he walks gently before them in the path of submission, and it is mine to lead him through life and through death to his loved one—But tell me, dost thou accept the care and guardianship of the golden seed in the bosom of the dead?"

Eva

I accept it thankfully.

Angel

It has need of music, prayer, and love.

Eva

To sing, to pray, to love were ever my delight, and shall henceforth be my duty.

The angel touched her eyes, and she saw him no more, but the transparent tomb was there, with its beautiful lifeless inhabitant. She looked, and saw that the golden seed had already burst its prison, and was putting forth its first tender leaves. Her heart was filled with joy, and she said:

The Hermaphrodite

"I will never leave thee for one moment, divine plant. Thy growth may be slow or rapid—it is all one. I can watch, I can wait for ages, but I cannot for one moment endure the fear of losing the blessed flower!"

So Eva watched all day, and sang, and prayed, and spake sweet words to her dead Rafael. When the night came, she essayed to watch until the morning. The moon looked lovingly upon her, and the stars held their little torches in her eyes. At midnight, she tuned her harp, and sang to it a mass for the soul of Rafael. As she sang, she heard spirit-voices blending with her own, and soon she saw no more the moon, the stars, or the grave—her eyes were filled with a brighter light, her ears with heavenly harmonies, and of herself she knew nothing until the first rays of the sun recalled her to herself.

Eva started up in affright, and looked anxiously towards the grave, but she saw that the widowed dove had watched while she had slept, for she was perched just above the tomb, and kept her eyes fixed upon it. Eva called the bird, and took her fondly to her bosom, but she spread her wings, and flew away—presently she returned, bringing with her a wild honey comb, wherewith she would have fed Eva, who weeping refused it, saying: "My tears shall be my meat day and night." But the dove flew back to her again and again, until at length she consented to receive the honey, and was refreshed thereby.

Eva kneeling began her morning's task, prepared to watch, and sing, and pray through another day. Her eyes were fixed upon the form of Rafael, her soul was rapt in heavenly meditation. She had not proceeded far in her orisons, before she heard, in the distance, the sound of hunting horns, and the baying of hounds, with which approached nearer and nearer the trampling of horses. She knew that it was the royal chase, and much she feared that the horsemen might invade her beautiful dell. They did not however break through its magical bounds, but as the noise began already to grow faint and indistinct, she heard a light footstep upon the fallen leaves behind her. It was the king's son, who had caught through the trees one glimpse of a fair woman, as he followed his stray falcon.

He came near to Eva, and spake courteously to her. He marvelled at her beauty, and at the unearthly light of her countenance. Gladly would he have won a word or a look from her, but it was in vain that he questioned her. She did not turn her eyes one moment from the tomb which was her garden

The Hermaphrodite

of hope, she changed not her posture, nor interrupted the tenour of her prayers. The widowed dove flew to him, and spread her wings as a screen before his eyes, that he should not look upon Eva, wherefore he, in great amazement, and with reverence, took his departure. But for the remainder of that day, he spake no word, nor smiled, nor ate a morsel of food. Only to them that questioned him, he replied that he had seen a spirit—more, he would not impart to them, but in his own mind he determined that he would seek again the strange place, and the strange woman.

Eva prayed, and sang, and wept through the next day, and through many days. Every night in like manner she watched until her eyes closed in spite of herself, and the dove took her place until the morning.

A pious train of palmers came to the dell, one day, and found the blessed one upon her knees, with her eyes fixed upon the crystal tomb—they chaunted for her the songs of their pilgrimage, they offered her precious and holy gifts which they had brought from a distant shrine, but no word could she speak to them, no look could she give them. Then they also went silently away, not knowing what to think of the matter.

Spirits also gathered around her, drawn from the stars by the music of her sweet singing—they prayed her to come with them, and offered to bear her on high, on their wings, but she spake not, looked not, but ever sang, and prayed, and poured out her soul to Rafael and to God.

The king's son returned to the grove, and as he came near he saw that she sate with her harp in her hand, and he heard her singing in ever varying tones of sadness and sweetness. Creeping softly near her, he knelt beside her feet, and listened with silent tears to the strain which was sometimes mournful, and sometimes extatic.

She sang of the days in which she had first seen Rafael, of the perfection of his beauty, the suddenness and earnestness of his love for her. She reminded God of the moment in which their souls became known to each other, and of Him who had betrothed them, she demanded the dead in marriage. She blessed the memory of that hour, and prayed Rafael not to forget it among all the joys of heaven. She told of their long and blessed communion, of the many days which had passed and had found them ever together, and ever one. She told of their bitter parting hour, and of the

The Hermaphrodite

unspeakable tenderness with which she had received the last word, the last breath of her chosen one. She sang sometimes with passionate energy and expression, some times slowly and mournfully, but never with the tone and accent of despair. Long and wondrously varied was the chant, and when it was ended the harp fell from her hand, she sank on her knees and prayed again.

Eva's time passed ever after this manner. The king's son came daily to her retreat, and looked on her in pious reverence. Her beauty sank deeply into his soul, and he would gladly have fallen down and worshipped her, but she looked not upon him, and scarce knew what manner of man he was. He, however, had forgotten his father's kingdom, and the crown which should, one day, be his. He had forsaken the feast, the dance, the court of Love, the prowess of arms. He had put on a garb of mourning for sweet Eva's sake, and had chosen the cypress for his crest. The king was informed of these things, and in great wrath caused his son to be summoned to his presence. He rebuked him for his idle and dreaming habits, which were fitter, he said, for a monk than for the heir of a kingdom. He commanded him moreover, on pain of his displeasure, to frequent no more the grove in which he seemed to find such delight.

The young man replied: "father, you shall sooner exile me from the world."

After this, people began to say that Eva was a witch, that her prayers were evil incantations, and her friendly dove, a bird of darkness and ill-omen. And the king sent priests to reason with her, but she heard them not, and soldiers to threaten her, but she heeded them not, and they themselves, when they saw her gentle countenance, and heard how she prayed, were fain to love and pity her, and returned to them that had sent them, with tears in their eyes.

In the meantime the wondrous plant was nourished by the tears, and prayers, and melody of true love, and its leaves were fresh and green. Eva watched its growth with untiring solicitude, and her heart told her that the day of release would soon come. But the time grew long, and sorrow began to scatter white hairs among her fair locks. She had learned to be grateful for the kindness of the king's son, and was glad that the dove flew at him no more, but nestled on his shoulder, and brought him honey in her beak.

The Hermaphrodite

At length came the king in person, with his horsemen, determined either to tear Eva from the tomb, or his son from Eva's presence. Eva was singing, as he drew near, and the hearts of the stern men were made to thrill by the wild, seraphic melody of her voice. She sang the glory of love, and its deathlessness, the heavenly beauty of sorrow, and its divine mission. At the last, she raised her voice, and appealed to the God of heaven for freedom:

> Giver of my happiness, friend of my suffering,
> Father of my spirit, and the spirit I love,
> Long have I waited in dimness and darkness,
> Long have I eaten the exile's bitter bread;
> Heavenly master, compassionate jailor,
> Release thou, release thou the prisoner of Hope!
> Blest was my burthen, if Rafael had shared it,
> Kindly, to the captive, thy good angels came;
> But what is life, save the presence of Rafael?
> And what is faith, but my trust in his love?
> Heavenly master, compassionate jailor,
> Release, in thy mercy, the prisoner of Hope!

And Eva knelt upon her knees, and wondrously she prayed. The king listened to her words, and his wrath was, for a time swallowed up in astonishment. The sight of his son, sunk in hopeless suffering, rekindled his anger, and he approached to seize Eva. Rudely he shouted at her, rudely would he have laid his hands upon her, but a strange sight arrested him. For the hour that was to consummate her long and fearful martyrdom was come at last. While Eva knelt, she saw her beloved plant suddenly agitated as if by some subtle wind,—another moment, and it had burst the crystal surface of the tomb, while on its highest branch appeared a starlike purple flower, that seemed to diffuse light and fragrance like rain.

"It is mine!" cried Eva, as she approached, trembling with delight, to break the stem of the wondrous flower. But even as she touched it, the plant received a new and vigorous impulse, and shot up to heaven, bearing with it a bright appearance of Eva transfigured, as it were, in light, while the lifeless form that had been Eva, sank upon the ground.

And Eva met her Rafael, and was forever united to him. And while she still gazed upon him in the fullness of her joy, he said: "dost thou forget

The Hermaphrodite

thy sorrowing friends?" Then Eva looked below, and saw the king's son fainting upon her dead body, and heard the dove moaning piteously. Then she said: "let us go and minister unto him," and it was permitted unto her to do so. She poured water upon him from the lake of tears, and he was baptized into newness of life. His eyes, moreover, were opened spiritually, and he saw Eva and Rafael in the splendour of immortal joy—at this, his soul revived within him, and he smiled and wept at once. When the vision of them had passed away, he took the dove to his bosom, and the harp on his shoulder, and proceeded on his way, a prince no more, but a pilgrim. Oft times when he was weary to faintness, he heard the echo of Eva's prayers and songs, and was comforted. And often, in his hours of anguish, he felt that his bitterest tears were wiped away by the hands of his angel friends. And when his last hour came, he heard gentle voices repeating these words: "Release thou, release thou the prisoner of hope." And the dove mourned for him.

Eva perceived a scar upon the transparent brow of Rafael, and she inquired of him, saying: "dearest one, what is that scar? who has thus wounded thee?" Rafael replied: "it is a deadly sin which I did once commit, and of which my soul still bears the mark." Then said she: "do the angels despise thee there-for?" And he answered: "not so—they compassionate and sympathise with me. Many of them have also scars from the like cause, and some of them are even mutilated to the extent of a limb or an eye."

"Did the Lord upbraid thee," asked Eva, "when he saw this mark of evil upon thee?"

"He did not," said Rafael—"he spake pityingly unto me, and pouring oil and wine into the wound, healed it. Tears stood moreover in his eyes, and it was told me that he wept thus when aught occurred to remind him of the sufferings of man upon earth, for that he had borne them in his own body. He hath also promised me that the disfigurement of the scar shall fade and be changed, until it become an ornament upon my brow."

Again Eva said: "Wherefore was it necessary that I should give myself up to the one thought and idea of thee, and abandon all that others deem good and beautiful on earth? I felt that it must be so, but I understood it not."

And Rafael said: "I will shew thee somewhat." Accordingly he led her before a picture (and I saw that pictures in heaven are living things). In this she saw a woman of a prudent and industrious character who went to many people with her wares. And she bought and sold, and received in return cumbrous coin which was a weight upon her steps, and which would not pass current in heaven. Her face was also careworn and troubled. Rafael now led her to another picture, and said: "look now on this."

And she looked and saw one who sat at the feet of her master, a man noble and beautiful to behold. And her eyes waited upon his look, her ear upon his bidding, her heart upon his love; and he poured into her lap her wages, which were of pure gold, and of the coinage of heaven. As he did so, she heard his voice, saying: "one thing only is needful."

And Rafael said: "one love only is possible, and in that I was that love to thee, thou couldst only, in seeking other things, have lost it. Thank God, therefore that thine eye was *single*."

Eva said unto Rafael: "what gracious power held me fast to thee, and gave me power to love thee unto death?"

And Rafael shewed her a ship upon a troubled sea, that seemed to be given up to the winds and waves, to be blown about and buffeted of them; yet the ship remained steady in its place, and could not be driven upon the shoals and quicksands that threatened it. Eva wondered when she saw this, and said: "why is it that this ship does not flee before the winds, and why does she not follow the current of the waves?" But even while she looked, the water became transparent to her sight, and she perceived that the ship was bound by a strong cord to an anchor sunken in the sand, and was thus held in its place.

"To thee too, God gave an anchor of the soul, both sure and steadfast," said Rafael.

Thus was Eva led from one truth to another. She had been blind until she again found her Rafael, but now all things became clear to her in the light of his presence. The problems of life solved themselves before her eyes—the instincts of her heart explained themselves to her, and she saw that within her breast had been planted a teacher higher and holier than the wisest among the sons of men. From this teacher, she had learned love—love had taught her constancy, constancy had taught her undying hope, and hope for the future had taught her renunciation in the present. Living for one in heaven, she had died to the world—seeking a spiritual and immaterial good, she had learned to sacrifice, with less and less of pain, every material and sensual enjoyment. Then she felt that she had been

The Hermaphrodite

as a child, that is led of a loving parent, whose weakness is disciplined to strength, and whose innocent ignorance is made the surest foundation for true knowledge and wisdom. Turning to Rafael, she said: "where is my master, that I may fall at his feet, and worship him for having made me capable of so great happiness?"

Rafael replied: "He is seen of them that love him, and is never far from any one of us."

Eva said: "I have not then seen him, for I have loved thee more, far more than him, but now I desire to adore him for the goodness that has made us one forever, for I perceive that He is thy father and my father."

At these words, the face of Rafael became illumined with a new and transcendant joy—he took Eva by the hand, and said: "now, truly, are we wedded and inseparable, for those who are one in him are one forever, wherefore open thine eyes, and perceive that he is with us."

Then I beheld the two forms locked in one fervent embrace, so that they seemed to be no longer two, but one. In like manner were the sounds of their two voices blent, in one harmonious strain. I heard a voice that spake, saying: "one God, one faith, one baptism." Then, a brighter and more celestial light encompassed them, and I saw them no more.

Funeral chorus—sung by the dead,
when Eva buried Rafael

 The majesty of death!
The kingly majesty of death!
  Life is a wretched courtier
  Seeking place and preferment,
Paying extorted homage
To a thousand wilful tyrants,
  Cringing to the elements
That threaten and defy him,
But death is a monarch crowned.

 The majesty of death!
The silent majesty of death!
Life talketh, striveth ever.
Death [hath] no need to speak.

The Hermaphrodite

His word is writ upon his brow,
His lightest touch fulfills his will;
Life prates of all his shallow secrets,
Death holds his in his heart!

The majesty of death!
The mighty majesty of death!
None reads his hidden meaning,
None questions of his mandate.
If, to the soul's Siberia
Or, to Hope's dear Elysium
He sendeth forth his captive
None knows, and none dare ask him?
Un-witting, and un-willing do his subjects
            Work his mysterious will.

The majesty of death!
The gentle majesty of death!
        Life giveth fever,
Death giveth sleep.
        Life wounds to madness,
Death heals to rest.
Oh man! thou hast many masters,
Death is the noblest and the kindest.

[*A draft version of the following scene is transcribed as fragment 4 in appendix 2.*]

un made

Chapter [24]

A silence of some minutes succeeded the reading of the closing paragraph. We were all, for the moment, unrealized. The vision of Eva was present to us, and the mind to whose health or sickness this vision had been revealed, held us powerfully in its spell. The very atmosphere of the room seemed dark and mystic, for the oil of the lamp had wasted away unnoticed, even as the evening had waned, and the fantastic shadows cast by its flickering light seemed like dim revelations of the forms that people darkness—Some one at length spoke—it was Pepino.

The Hermaphrodite

"What is it, how shall we name it?" asked he.

"It is a dream," murmured Briseida, "but a dream of heavenly truth."

"It is a mystery," I rejoined, "but one of those which light, and not darkness, veils from us."

As I spoke, a long, vivid tongue of flame darted upwards from the dying lamp.

"See!" I cried: "it is like the parting aspiration of a pure soul."

The next moment, we were left in utter darkness, and ere we could grope our way out of it, a note of wondrous melody filled the air, and thrilled upon our excited nerves, as if it had dropped from another world. It was followed by a wild, but solemn strain of melody, that seemed to be at once prayer, hymn, and dirge.

"In the name of God, what is that?" cried Pepino, startled at the unexpected sound. "Is it the spirit of Eva?"

"It is our own Nina," said Briseida, "but I have not heard her sing thus in years!"

As she spoke, she found her way to the door, and hastily threw it open. Light now streamed in upon us from the opposite side of the corridor. It came from an apartment which, though called from old habit, Nina's music-room, had been unoccupied for many a day. Briseida bade us follow her thither, and as I paused a moment on the threshold, I clearly distinguished the words and cadence of the swan-song of Eva.

Release thou, release thou
The prisoner of hope!

I entered, and saw Nina seated at her harp, her cheek flushed, her eye wild with the delirium of song. A loose white robe draped her lovely shoulders, and its open sleeves displayed the classic beauty of her arms. Her long locks too, were adorned with flowers. A hasty glance assured me that the long deserted salon had been newly swept and garnished, as if for the reception of guests. The coverings had been withdrawn from the brocaded chairs, and the branches were filled with wax lights. In an alcove stood a small table, upon which were tastefully arranged fruits and wines, with other materials for a light supper.

Nina did not allow our entrance to interrupt her song, but when it was at an end, she arose and came towards us, with words and smiles of welcome.

The Hermaphrodite

"What surprise is this that you have prepared for us, my poor Nina?" asked Briseida, in some anxiety. "Why are you thus attired? for whom are these lights, these flowers, this repast?"

"It is my fête," answered Nina, with a childish waywardness of expression. "Because it has not been kept in many years, shall it never more be celebrated? because none of you has brought me a flower and a good wish, may I not gather for myself some roses and jasmines? It was too ungracious in you all to neglect poor Nina thus, but Nina forgives you, for she is happy tonight."

"And why are you so happy, Nina?" inquired her sister.

"I will tell you," answered Nina, in a more subdued tone. "Today was my birthday, and my mother remembered it in heaven, and came to speak to me. Very beautiful were her words—I cannot repeat them, save that she said to me, more than once: 'what thou hast sought, that shall thou find, what thou hast loved, that shalt thou have.' She told me nothing more precisely, but she left me such peace and blessedness, that I could not but array myself in white, and come here to celebrate the heavenly vision with music and flowers."

"And you shall so celebrate it, Nina mia!" cried Briseida, "and we will keep it with you, but do not fatigue too much your delicate nerves. Remember that you are bound now to live, and to get well."

"Yes—the bridegroom comes. I hear his footsteps in the distance, and the darkness becomes light before me." She stood for a moment, as if lost in thought, and then seated herself again at the harp. Again her rapt soul spread its wings of melody, and we were borne with it to unseen realms, to unexplored depths of feeling and of foreboding. I was astonished at the power, richness, and variety of her voice. She seemed inclined to task its powers to the utmost, for her song, or rather the various snatches of song which succeeded each other in her strain, varied with strange caprice from the highest to the lowest notes, from light and gay to slow and solemn measures. It was difficult to determine whether of the two feelings predominated in her breast, their light and shade were so strangely mingled—there was a rapture in her anguish, and an anguish in her rapture. Perhaps the two are ever thus indistinguishably blent, in the intense moods of intense minds. At length her song ceased—she released the harp from the gentle captivity of her white arms, walked to the supper-table, and

The Hermaphrodite

poured out for herself a goblet of rich and rare ancestral wine. With a certain solemnity of manner she raised the cup to her lips, but ere she had tasted it, she turned to us and exclaimed:

> "Evviva! evviva!
> I pledge thee in wine of eternity,
> And I *leave the cup, but half drained*, for thee!"

In this last strophe, Nina's voice and manner had risen to the highest point of extatic inspiration. It was too much for her, and the concluding words had not died upon her lips, before the reaction was visible. The unwonted colour vanished from her cheek—the strange light of her eyes was quenched. Pale, and with tottering steps, she crept up to Briseida, and laid her cheek upon her sister's shoulder.

"Sister!" said she, "I charge thee, I charge ye all, that ye keep this wine cup sacredly for one who shall come to drink of it." She spoke these words in a low but distinct tone, and then, with a slight bend of her head, glided from the apartment.

Briseida remained behind to lock up with care the half emptied goblet in a cabinet of which she alone kept the key. As she did so, I questioned her concerning this new and extraordinary phase of Nina's malady.

"It is the passion of her suffering," said Briseida, "the end cannot now be far off."

"Is it her own death, or the arrival of her lover that she now anticipates?" I asked.

"It may be neither, and yet a mingled presentiment of both. Were it marriage, death, or madness, it were a relief that it should come."

Pepino having taken leave, Briseida retired to Nina's sleeping-chamber, and I betook myself to mine. But the words and notes of the Brindisi rang in my ears all the night.

* * *

As I sat alone, one evening, pondering upon times and scenes far distant, I heard a snatch of the Neapolitan Tarantella sung by some one in the corridor. The voice was not unfamiliar to me, but before I could remember to whom it belonged, the song was succeeded by the whine of a beggar at my door, who implored after the usual Southern fashion, in the name

The Hermaphrodite

of God and the Virgin, one single grano for an unfortunate with fourteen children, who all enjoyed remarkable appetites, with very limited means of gratifying them.[1] "Enter," I cried, and the beggar approached me with a slouching step, and coming nearer, held out his arms to embrace me.

"Rascal, what insolence!" I cried, starting from my seat.

"Oh thou worse than a dog, dost thou not know me?" exclaimed Berto.

It was indeed the old identical Berto, but in a madder guise than ever before. I must premise that the spring was, by this time, nearer to summer than to winter, and the genial Sicilian sun seemed to have had its full sway over the glowing countenance of Berto. Face, hands, and feet, for all were alike bare, were of the most brilliant copper colour. His shirt was neither fine nor clean—his breeches were fully open to the charge of incontinence—his lip and chin had long since been absolved from the allegiance of the razor—his coat and vest were, probably, upon the road— the fragment of a brimless and crownless straw hat enwreathed his brows, while his shoulders supported a dirty fishnet, and equally dirty bundle slung on the edge of a stout cudgel. I stared at him in astonishment—dirty and ragged as he was, he threw himself into the first chair that offered itself, which happened to be a beautiful fauteuil of painted velvet, the work of the fair Gigia, for the delectation of her Count.

"Well," said Berto, "am I not disgusting, am I not an unclean beast? would you like that kiss I promised you just now?"

"I cannot say that I am ambitious of any contact with your face—it looks as if it might burn one."

"Yes, I'm like all other *iron* men—when cool, I'm black, when heated, I'm red, when exasperated, I'm white."

"But why do you come to us so newly adorned and accoutred? Why Berto, what hands, what nails!"

"Look at my feet," was Berto's emphatic reply—he continued in his usual strain.

"I assure you, I have long suspected the popular prejudice in favour of cleanliness to be founded in error. There is no such thing as cleanliness, I

1. [*The Italian words for the "beggar's whine" appear at the bottom of the manuscript sheet:*] Per amor di Dio e della tanta Madonna, un grano per povero padre con quattrodici figlioli—molto appetito, molto appetito, Signore, e nulla da maniar.

will demonstrate it. Is not cold a negative quality? cold is, philosophically speaking, nothing but the absence of heat—cleanliness is, philosophically speaking, nothing but the absence of dirt. There is no such thing as cold, say the naturalists, there is no such thing as cleanliness, says Berto. Dirt is the law of nature, cleanliness that of civilization. I have now made acquaintance with dirt, and esteem it highly conducive to health."

"But how does that agree with your faith in cold water, and your love of bathing?"

"The one need not prevent the other—the fishermen of Naples pass much of their time in the water, but it does not interfere with the dirt which is essential to them. Many days, when I was in Naples, I dove for shell-fish, which I brought up, and sold in the market, with my brother-fishermen— the water made me cool, but I swear it did not make me clean."

"And so you have really been a Lazzaro among the Lazzari?"

"Of course, that was my especial object in visiting Naples. They are a peculiar race, and I was anxious to study them—I find them the most virtuous people in Italy."

"How so?" I asked.   ✶ ✶ ✶

It was now quite time that I should be released from the ignominious bondage of petticoats, that my legs should be disencumbered of a mass of articles utterly foreign to their use and purpose, and that my diaphragm should be allowed to expand in freedom broader than the lacings of a woman's bodice. Berto triumphed in the entire success of the deception, and was above all satisfied with my investigations of Nina's symptoms, but he was impatient to have me in his company again. It was therefore concerted between us that I should leave the Casa ——— on the day after his arrival, and that I should do so without taking any leave of the sisters. At the time appointed, I wrapped myself in my scarf, drew my veil over my face, and hurried with somewhat unfeminine strides to the rooms formerly occupied by Berto and myself—here I stripped off the odious disguise, shook the curls back from my brow, and assumed my wonted attire. This being accomplished, Berto and I had a savage carnival over the deposed vestments—we danced and shouted around them, we tore and trampled them, we sang them their death song, and then, without pity, consigned them to the flames.

The Hermaphrodite

"Oh ye devilish little things!" cried Berto, pathetically addressing my hose, as he held them over the flame. "What fools do ye make of us! how impiously ye tempt us to steal profane glances at sacred mysteries!" Another moment, and the delicate web was as though it had never been.

"Toga of hypocrisy," said I, gravely addressing the mortal remains of my quondam gown, "what an odious imposture art thou! thou art the ally of weakness and deformity, the cruelest enemy of beauty—thou art a very tissue of lies, wherefore receive thou the doom of liars!" and it was soon reduced to ashes—but why should I record such follies?

The next thing was to prepare for a visit to my late hostesses. Berto could no longer contain within himself his delight at the trick we had so successfully played upon them, and was anxious to enjoy the confusion which the discovery was likely to occasion them. I made of course a very careful toilette, and started with Berto for the Casa ———. Once arrived there, Berto concealed me behind a curtain in the ante-room, leaving the door open that I might not lose a word of the conversation.

"Well girls," said Berto, "I am sorry to state that Madame Cecilia has been unexpectedly summoned from Rome, and will not have the pleasure of remaining longer with you."

"I regret it sincerely," said Briseida.

"It is quite the same thing to me," said Gigia.

"But tell me, how has she behaved herself?" continued Berto. "Has she had any coquettries, any conquests? has she brought any scandal into the house? tell me the truth, you know that I am severe upon that point."

"Surely not, brother," replied Briseida with eagerness. "She has lived with us the life of a cloistered nun—shunning the conversation, and almost the presence of all men. She has passed much of her time with Nina, much also in study."

"She is a ridiculous prude," added the gentle Gigia, "a woman without heart, or heart without blood."

"What injustice you do her!" cried Briseida, "her nature is deeply sympathetic, but she has at the same time that stern strength which one acquires only by wrestling with the angel of despair."

"Has she, at least, been amiable and courteous with you?"

"She has not interfered with me," said Gigia.

"She has helped me much," said Briseida.

The Hermaphrodite

Berto went up to Nina, and laid his hand on her forehead saying, "Nina, what has Cecilia done for you?"

"Mi ha molto consolata," answered Nina, in her sweet, monotonous voice.

"Is Cecilia a woman, Nina?"

"Not altogether."—"is she a man?"—"almost."—"How is that?"—"no man can feel as she feels, no woman can reason as she reasons," said Nina, relapsing into silence.

"I am glad that you have spoken with such admirable candour," rejoined Berto, "for though Cecilia has departed, Cecilia's brother is here to profit by your frankness. Come forth, Laurent!" and great was the astonishment of the sisters when I stepped from my hiding place, and presented myself before them.

"It is Cecilia herself! Cecilia is a man!"

"Yes, and I dare venture to call him a handsome and most accomplished man, and heir to a princely estate. Are you not sorry that you did not know it? but your game is up now."

Berto was in extasy at the painful confusion of his sisters, whom he continued to torment and assail with great ingenuity—finally, reconciliation took place, and we parted in friendship.

As Berto and I walked towards our home, I reproached him with having described me as heir to a large fortune.

"It is true," he replied, "your brother Philip has been suddenly killed by a fall from his horse, and your father has written impatient letters, imploring your forgiveness, and still more, your return. He is in feeble health, and but for you, the family will become extinct in his person."

Was it a thought of vengeance that prompted me to say: "let it become extinct, I will not go"?

All the night long, I wept for my beautiful young brother. Ere it was over, I understood wherefore he had died. His beautiful and simple nature had already reached the limits of its child-like maturity—for mine a wearisome pilgrimage yet remained. But I could not dress myself in the spoils of the beloved dead, nor rear for myself new fortunes upon his grave. And so I wrote to my father that I would not come.

★ ★ ★

The Hermaphrodite

[*In this final sequence, Ronald returns. He and Laurence have met in the Roman Forum; Ronald is speaking.*]

" . . . it fares with one deserted by his guardian angel. My grief at your departure brought on a dangerous fever, but though long and seriously ill, I felt myself too young and too strong to die. Scarce recovered, I escaped from the bounds of the University, with the ostensible object of travelling for my health. It was no lie—what health of soul or of body could I hope to attain without having seen you, without at least a farewell embrace and blessing from you?"

"Oh Ronald! I left my prayers, my blessing with you—well you know that, but for the most frightful peril, I could never have resigned to other hands the care of one so dear."

"Then you did love me, blessed one? oh, but those words are precious to my ear—pour them out upon me, those unuttered blessings! give it back to me, that holy love which your heart gave me, and of which your will defrauded me. Give it to me, as spirit to spirit, as angel to angel!" and Ronald embraced my knees, and covered my hands with tears.

"Ronald!"

"I kneel in worship, not in prayer," said Ronald, restraining his emotion; "I was overpowered for a moment by the remembrance of my madness, but you shall see that I am not mad."

Ronald now spoke to me of his wanderings in every land, among all manner of men, of his wearied spirit and wasted strength, of his long cherished hopes, of their slow and cruel death.

"Do you know what it is," said he, "to pursue ever one thing, with ever one result? to pass every day in the same fruitless search, in the same vain longing, and to lie down every night with the same leaden disappointment weighing upon your heart—to pursue the human crowd and look and look into its depths, till every face becomes disgustful to you, because in each you have hoped and vainly hoped to find the features of the only loved, the only remembered—do you know all this?"

"Would God, Ronald, I could have borne it for you!"

"Thank God, you did not," said Ronald, fervently—he paused a moment, and continued.

"I wandered long, oh so far, oh so wide! I braved the heat, the cold,

The Hermaphrodite

hunger, fatigue—alone, alone, I bore that dreary agony—there was none to soothe me. I called aloud, and none but the wild vulture answered me. I wept, and none heeded my tears save the rough wind that dried them on my cheek—gradually, my relations with the world became utterly changed, all things in it seemed to me unreal shifting phantoms, and my life, one restless dream. Spirits now seized hold upon me, and claimed me as their prey—they mocked at me, and made to themselves cruel sport with my sorrow. Devils have led me up into mountain tops, and have told me: 'she is there.' Strange whispers have urged me to endless wanderings in dark woods and in sandy deserts, saying: 'yet a few paces further, she is there'—voices have come to me across the waters, telling me to seek thee on the opposite shore, and I have plunged in stormy seas, and have swum desperately, but never to thee, and breathless messages have come to me at midnight, calling me from my bed to love and thee, and I have gone forth to find thee, and found but the still, senseless night—then the spirits laughed me to scorn, and I threw myself on the ground, and cursed hope and love, and the thought of thee!"

"Ronald, you will make me mad!" I shrieked aloud. Ronald had roused himself almost to phrenzy by these frightful recollections, but at my voice he ceased to speak—he raised my hand, which he still held, to his forehead, and pressing it upon his eyes, said in a low tone:

"Oh God! that the remembrance of it should still have such power over me!"

Some moments elapsed before either of us had power to speak—at length, hoping to change the current of his thoughts, I asked of him:

"Tell me how the spell was broken."

"It yielded to the divine right of nature and of blood," said Ronald, in an altered voice. "I was suddenly summoned to attend my dying father—still wild, still dreaming, I returned to him; but when I looked upon his altered face and form, the voice of filial love awoke in my heart, the shock recalled me to my senses. I fell on my knees before him, and with bitter tears implored his forgiveness for my undutiful neglect. 'oh my father!' I cried: "it would have been better for both of us, if we had been together."

"I could not come to you, my son," said he—it was needless to add any thing to the tacit reproach conveyed in these words—it was the only one I received.

The Hermaphrodite

"My father now made me feel, not the weight of his displeasure, but the power of his love. He entered into my feelings with warm and tender sympathy, and forgot his own sufferings in his anxiety to soothe and comfort me. His words and counsels were precious to me—why did I learn their value only the moment before they became lost to me? When he felt the last approach of death, he summoned me to his bedside, and conjured me in words touching and solemn to abandon the vain pursuit of a phantom, and to apply myself seriously to the real uses and doctrines of life. He urged me to learn to administer his fortune and estate with wisdom and justice. 'Father,' I said, 'I conjure you to disinherit me—a madman cannot assume the management of an estate—a madman has no need of lands and titles—leave the inheritance to some one more fit to possess it, and bequeath to me only a competence, and your blessing.'

"My father explained to me that I had no right to reject the duties of my birth and station: 'With my lands,' he said, 'I leave to your care men who are almost a part of them, men who are in some sort my children and your brothers—will you turn them over to strangers, who may oppress and injure them? Shall my loved home be no longer the seat of benevolence and hospitality? shall my peaceful hamlet be scourged by a tyrant, or desecrated by a profligate?' My father's reasonings prevailed with me—I promised obedience, scarce knowing how to fulfill it, and had the mournful pleasure of seeing him depart for his long journey with a smile on his countenance, and blessings on his lips."

"Is then the good man dead?"

"He is, but from the hour of his death I have lived only to fulfill his wishes—the hamlet is tranquil and prosperous as ever—the sick are cared for, the weak protected, schools, roads, cornfields, all flourish as well as his kind heart could have wished. On Sunday, the old Theologue still thunders from the pulpit, and in the afternoon the peasants dance on the green as gaily as of old. The poet still quotes Virgil to the farmers, and the antiquarian pulls down their stone fences to find inscriptions and architectural relics. Nothing has changed, except the gay boy who once sang, and shouted, and frolicked among woods and waters the livelong day—the country people say that an evil fairy came and stole him away in his boyhood, and sent back to them only this miserable substitute."

The Hermaphrodite

"But why, dear Ronald, did you still draw the dark vestments of grief around you? why did you not throw them off and trample on them?"

"The weak among men are crushed by sorrow—the trivial fling it from them—the strong *bear* it," answered Ronald.

"Oh Ronald! I have been the blight and curse of your young life! would God we had never met!"

Berto's "Study"

"Say not so, Laurent—you have taught me great though mournful lessons. Earth contains no reality which I would exchange for the holy remembrance of you which I shall now take away with me, and which is all of you that earth can ever give me."

"Do you feel then that we must part?"

Ronald paused ere he answered—he came up to me, raised my head on his hand, and looked long and earnestly in my face.

"Yes," he said: "it is still the same strange face—the eyes that discern but judge not, the lip that trembles while it commands, the austere brow, softened by the glorious, sunny hair, belied by the rounded chin and cheek. These are the features my bereaved heart has worshipped—here is written the blighted promise of my life—oh God! oh Heaven! see ye that eternity repays it." He stooped to kiss me on cheek, brow, and lip, and said musingly to himself: "by day perhaps again, but by night, never, never!"

contradiction

These words awoke in me a consciousness of shame, and I snatched myself abruptly from Ronald's grasp, but as he turned to leave me, shame was swallowed up in agony—I sprang to his side—I held him fast with all my strength—we looked again into each other's eyes. One long gaze of tearless anguish, one mute appeal to heaven, and Ronald was gone, and the beautiful monster sat as before on the heap of stones, in the ancient forum, himself as mute and dead as any thing there.

On the morrow, I should have arisen with the sun, to set forth once more alone on my pilgrimage, but the morrow came, and found me passive in the bonds of deathlike weakness. The laws that bind the will to its subjects seemed to be suddenly abrogated, and hand, foot, and tongue, and even the brain itself were all sullen, leaden, immoveable, and seemed to say to the poor prisoner who had once commanded them: "despair and die, for without us thou canst do nothing. Gradually, even the desire to make an effort subsided, and the last spark of life seemed frozen out of me. How long I lay, thus unconscious, I cannot tell—when I unclosed my eyes, a dim light was burning behind a screen in my room, and I distinguished near me the forms of a man and a woman. It was Berto, who had found me ill, and had brought the faithful Briseida to nurse me. It was by the aid of a powerful stimulant that I had for a moment recovered my senses. I tried to speak, but it was with great difficulty that I managed to utter a few words.

"Berto, how is Ronald?"

Berto looked at me in mute surprise.

"Berto, how fares it with the boy?"

"It is well with him," replied Berto, promptly, and as I received the favorable answer, Berto, Ronald, and all consciousness of aught in heaven or on earth vanished from my mind again.

"This is a very extraordinary case," said the confidential physician, closetted with Berto and Briseida: "I have already seen several instances of anomalous humanity remotely related to this, but those phenomena have always appeared in individuals of low organization, of feeble and uncertain impulse. Never before have I seen one presenting a beautiful physical development, and combining in the spiritual nature all that is most attractive in either sex."

"Laurent is indeed," said Berto, "the poetic dream of the ancient sculptor, more beautiful, though less human, than either man or woman. But tell us, learned Medicus, he cannot be an exact equation between the sexes, one or the other must predominate in his nature—tell us, does the patient seem to you most masculine or most feminine?"

"Tell me first," replied the Medicus, "how *you* have both been impressed by this vague personality, how have you already decided for yourselves?"

"I recognize nothing distinctly feminine in the intellectual nature of Laurent," answered Berto: "he is sometimes poetical and rhapsodical, but he reasons severely and logically, even as a man—he has moreover stern notions of duty which bend and fashion his life, instead of living fashioned by it, as is the case with women."

"Unjust Berto!" said Briseida—the Medicus laughed.

"The Doctor knows that I say truly. The best women are capable, though not without effort, of arriving at an idea of duty, but this point once gained, you will confess that they are somewhat arbitrary in their application of the rule. The thing which they are most especially fond of doing, be it never so mischievous, is always their duty." Briseida knew well the hopelessness of

The Hermaphrodite

disputing with Berto, but she had also her evidence to give upon the point in question.

"I recognize in Laurent much that is strictly feminine," said Briseida, "and in the name of the female sex, I claim her as one of us. Her modesty, her purity, her tenderness of heart belong only to woman. The blood of a man does not so rush so instantaneously to his cheek at the bold glance of another—the eye of a man does not flash so quickly and proudly at the slightest breath of aught unworthy or impure—the tears of no man flow as hers before the sublimity of nature, or the unhappiness of man. It is true that she can reason better than most women, yet is she most herself when she feels, when she follows that instinctive, undoubting sense of inner truths which is only given to women and to angels."

"Brava! old girl," cried Berto, "you make out a pretty good case for your worthless sex, under the cover of Laurent's virtues."

The Medicus did the safest thing to be done by one who does not wish to decide a given point against either of the disputing parties, he laughed.

"Has your friend an excessive sense of physical shame?" said he, addressing Briseida.

"So much so," replied the latter, "that even when she lived with us in the guise of a woman, I never dared enter her dressing room without permission, and it is only since her illness that I have discovered that her arms, neck & shoulders are the most beautiful in the world."

"That turns the case strongly against you," said Berto, "what woman can keep to herself the secret of her own attractions? beauty undisplayed and unadmired seems to a woman as fatal as a plague or small-pox struck in."

"If I could think that Laurent is a man, I should leave him to his fate," said Briseida, a little provoked at her brother's impertinence.

"If Laurent be a woman, she may die without opposition from me," rejoined Berto, furiously, "the world already contains too many of those vain venal creatures!"

"I cannot pronounce Laurent either man or woman," said the Medicus, gravely, "but I shall speak most justly if I say that he is rather both than neither."

"Ah!" said Briseida, who had read something of Swedenborg, "a heavenly superhuman mystery, one undivided, integral soul, needing not to seek

increasing
max here pronounced
where it is when
gets Born narrator
is absent

on earth its other moiety, needing only to adore the God above it, and to labour for its brethren around it."

"But at least tell us," said Berto, "if this wonderful creature is likely to recover."

The grave answer of the physician was such as to send the brother and sister weeping to the bedside of their friend, one in their sorrow, one in their determination to aid the poor sufferer to the utmost, in his struggle for life.

In my long, dull night of pain, came to me a lovely vision, that seemed to bring me a moment's peace. The feverish clang of my pulses was softened for a moment, and my tightened brain was released from the iron band that seemed to press upon it. A sound of gentle music breathed upon my ear, and lo, a white dove descended to me as from the skies, and fanned my forehead with its silvery wings—the bird hovered long around me, and looked with its soft dark eyes into mine—it expanded and changed to the form of a maiden robed in purest white, with ever the same dark melting eyes, then it seemed glorified with angelic brightness, and with a gentle benediction, it soared slowly up to heaven. As I lost sight of it, I called aloud, "Nina, Nina!" and I heard beside me the sound of weeping, and the voice of one who said that Nina was dead.

Now strange and wondrous things were present to me, in brilliant and irregular succession—I seemed to wander through the wide space of the Universe, and to discern in the distance the brightness of heaven, and the flames of hell, then was I on earth again, but on earth as I had never seen it. The dead arose and spake with me, and with the living I communed also, and dead and living were so mingled and confused, that the one became to me as the other. I felt myself seized, and I turned and saw a pale woman, with long, loose hair, that strove and strove with might to bear me away in her arms, and she shrieked aloud in her frenzy, "he is mine, he is mine, I have died for him!" but one in the form of a young man came and tore me from her arms and from her breast, crying aloud, "give her up to me, she is mine alone, I have lived for her a life worse than a thousand deaths!" Then I lifted my hands to God, and cried: "take me, for I am thine!" for my bowels were utterly torn asunder by the love I bare to both of them, the woman and the man. Then I perceived that I was stretched upon a cross, and it was said in my ears: "a cross is not formed otherwise than of two loves or two

The Hermaphrodite

desires which cross each other or conflict." Then came night, and darkness as of death.

§

The visions of my fever slowly faded—the vivid glowing spectres vanished from before me—the tumultuous sea of imaginary life receded, and left once more visible the old landmarks of reality. I found myself lying upon my bed, in the old room whose walls were so familiar to me. One by one, pictures, books, my study table etc came out from the mist which had concealed them, and were present to me, at first by moments, then for a longer time. Berto passed before me, and I could see that his countenance was worn and pale. I heard too the voices of my attendants, and many words which would scarce have been uttered in my hearing, had not those around me supposed me alike insensible to sights or sounds. For I lay without breath or motion, a deadness and numbness had taken possession of my whole body, and my returning reason disclosed to me the fact that I could neither move nor speak. My eyes became rigidly fixed upon a single point of vision, and I saw but the objects which passed between me and it. The spell of a fearful trance was upon me, would my friends have the wisdom to distinguish between the appearance and the reality of death? a dreadful doubt, that soon grew to a more dreadful certainty from the words that reached my ear from those around me. I heard Briseida cry: "Berto, Berto, she is gone!" Berto came and looked at me, and ran to summon the physician. This latter arrived, and after a short examination, pronounced me dead. He wrote the customary order for my burial, and advised Berto to make the speediest preparation for the last rites of the church, as the season was far advanced, and the disease, though anomalous in its nature, might yet be fatally propagated by the presence of the dead body.

Berto and Briseida could not give up all hope, and continued, for some time, to rub and chafe my lifeless body, but with no visible result. My fate was now beyond their control, the funereal impresario had taken the instrument under their charge, and would bear me to my narrow vault, after a brief interval, in despite of a thousand Bertos. Though myself too dull and lethargic to take much heed of what was passing, I could still hear from time to time the sobs of Briseida, and now and then, a stern, sad word from Berto.

The Hermaphrodite

The last morning came—I was dressed in my grave-clothes, and laid in my coffin, with my passive hands crossed on my bosom. No stranger had been suffered to touch me—the faithful brother and sister had with their own hands ministered to my last necessities, and I knew by their voices that they still kept watch beside me. I heard the sound of many footsteps ascending the stairs, and silently entering the room. My brain was now excited to a vivid consciousness of the horror of my fate, and I longed earnestly for the power of averting it by giving some token of life. At this moment, I heard another step, oh how well known, and then the falling of one upon his knees beside me. Silence, dead silence from all—oh that he could have spoken, that I might but hear his voice once more! He knelt for

* * *

buried/
alive/
dead

Appendix 1

A diary or notebook that Julia Ward Howe began to keep in 1843, titled "Life is strange and full of change," includes a number of pasted-in jottings that seem to be associated with the Laurence materials. The notebook is housed in Houghton Library as bMS Am 2214 (321), Box 3. Below are reproduced the pertinent passages not already quoted in this volume's introduction. Ellipses indicate text missing due to frayed paper edges.

Page 21

Oh yes! ye have been steep . . . beauty of his eyes, ye have . . . him, ye can never again . . . but the heavenly. . . . ye have been consec . . . by the kisses of love . . . but Rafael . . . never utter an . . . and true.

Pages 22–23

Most men are afraid of madness—few will defy its dark power, or even attempt a struggle with its advanced guard—at the first look, we behold something mightier than we, and turning like frightened children scramble back to our strong hold crying to god to fight the demon for us.

Earnestly do I speak of the revelation of God to the solitary soul—it is the knight watching before the altar the arms he has not yet borne, it is the virgin waiting with fear and longing for the bridegroom—it is the heavenly wedding to which all are bidden, but to which men must be compelled to come. But that it does not exhaust the energies and necessities of man's nature is evident from the fact that unto all who have received the first a second one is necessary—the soul that ventures to the utmost bound of those unknown regions is at length scourged back by its own terrors, and warned to come thither alone no more. Having learned the extent of that which can be accomplished by a solitary mind, it remains for him to learn how much more can be effected by the conjunction of two that form one, and to see reflected in that other half of himself the other half of that truth which once his imperfection could but imperfectly receive.

The Hermaphrodite

Blessed lesson, what cost of blood, of meat, of tears is too great to pay for thee? Learned oftenest in momentary rapture, and lifelong desire and regret, but if learned, the key to the highest, holiest lesson, the lesson of the three-in-one of God, the soul, and the soul's . . .

" . . . member your brother Laurent." one more look, one more benediction, and I was treading my lonely way, through the solid darkness of the night, and knowing only that God would lead me.

let us consume the world ere its earth worms consume us

Page 24

though she loved me not. the creature breathes not, except yourself, who can say that he was happier than I.

Page 25

> Eva to Rafael
> Do not fear to let me see thee,
> Soul-enshrined as thou art,
> God said not that thou shoulds't flee me,
> But thine over anxious heart.
>
> Pluck for me a passing flower,
> Breathe to me a gentle word,
> I will ask no more, but thank thee
> For the token seen or heard.
>
> Many a rose tree stands before thee,
> Proud to show her conscious charms,
> Spreads her lucious beauty o'er thee,
> Clasps thee in her thorny arms.
>
> I am modest, I am mournful,
> Thou mayst crush me 'neath thy feet;
> I'll not even say: "tread lightly,"
> Death itself from thee were meet!

The Hermaphrodite

Yes! I have humbled me before thy wrath,
And thou canst rail at me, & so rail on.
But know, thou canst not paint me wholly vile
My sins may lie deeper than thy virtues.
So far as love is holier than hate
As resignation is than every [?]
Pour Contrition then self-righteousness
So far, found one, my virtues rival thine
Then plant me as you will, take yr small pleasure
For narrow souls lack room to bury grudges.

201

§

Shall the world lie between us like a tombstone
[?] then, nor I have strength to [?] it.

The Hermaphrodite

Appendix 2

This appendix provides direct transcriptions of unnumbered manuscript pages from which I have excerpted to create the more-or-less continuous narrative of the beginning of section 3 and following the reading of "Ashes of an Angel's Heart."

Fragment 1

At this very period, and while our minds were still occupied with the singular experiences of Nina, I recalled to mind the vague mention made by Berto of a certain manuscript, the legacy, possibly the composition of the dead Uncle whose posthumous hospitality had given me shelter in my evil days. I bethought myself of it upon a quiet evening whose deepening shades had found Briseida and her Pepino seated on the terrace, engaged in making the sunset beautiful to each other. A little further on I discerned the Conte Flavio, making love to Gigia very much after the fashion of a peacock, paying court to a tulip. For me there was no companion, and no companionship. The very twilight would not receive me into its friendly, intimate shades, but cast me out into the cold light of the rising moon, which began to cast here and there a streak of ungenial white. Even Gigia's tiny spaniel, forgetful of many kindnesses, and lumps of sugar, barked unkindly at my heels, and snapped at the hand I extended to caress him. It was obviously a matter of astonishment to every animate and inanimate thing there, that I durst venture into a lover's paradise, myself unloving and unloved. I was ashamed to be there, ashamed to display my loneliness before their eyes.

"You must not take it to your room, said Bda. The chief condition etc is that I shall on no account suffer it to go out of my safe keeping, even for the space of an hour."

"But Berto promised:"

"I know it, and am in haste to perform—you shall read the manuscript to Pepino and myself in my study—he has never seen it, and I have read it but once, and with difficulty, given the nature of the characters, wh are not easy to decypher.

The Hermaphrodite

"What are you talking of doing in the library: asked the peacocks, approaching the doors.

"Cecilia has promised to read to us the mystic manuscript wh Berto brought from Germany. It has to us a sad interest," she said, turning to me "from the supposition that it has had some part in the strange history of our poor Nina. Berto read it to her shortly before her separation from Gaetano, and when you have heard it, you will easily see that it may have had a certain influence in producing her sublime madness.

Sublime?" asked Gigia, contemptuously, "say rather childish, puerile, unworthy—to die for one man, one poor wretch of a man, and that not the best or handsomest in the world, when there are so many live men left in it And with these words, so characteristic of the two sisters, Bda & Pepino followed me into the house, and G & Flavio passed on, and were lost in the deepening shadows of the plane trees.

Fragment 2

by Berto. I know German enough to understand it, but I cannot decypher the German characters in which it is written."

"What are you talking of doing in the library?" asked the peacock, suddenly approaching the doves.

"Cecilia has promised to read to us the Count's manuscript. It has to us a painful interest," she said, addressing me, from the coincidence of the leading sentiment of it with the idea of eternal and indivisible union of loving spirits which to our poor Nina became first a desire, then a conviction, then, a madness."

"And what a madness, weak, childish, unworthy!" exclaimed Giga, with emphasis.

"Do not call it so!" answered Briseida: "it is childlike, but sublime."

"The sublime of folly," said Gigia: "to sacrifice youth, beauty, talents, health to the shade of one man. To die (for she is dying, poor thing!) for one poor wretch of a man, and he not the best or handsomest in the world, when there are so many fine men left in it!"

She smiled upon Flavio, as she spoke.

"So are the heavens full of stars," said Briseida, "but he is the one star revealed to her by the telescope of love."

"Brava!" cried Flavio—"Brava!" whispered Pepino.

"Bah!" exclaimed Gigia: "the comparison indeed may pass muster. You will excuse me, however, if I venture to remark that your long and diligent study of that telescope must have been rewarded ere this by the sight of many stars."

"That may be" answered Briseida, "but for every soul there is one pole-star, not many."

I could not forbear coming to Briseida's aid with a quotation from an unknown poet.

> "Through many passions, one great thought doth run;
> "Through many seasons, one eternity."

That is your English mysticism," said Gigia, tartly: "it means nothing. Constancy, in my opinion, should of right be numbered among the diseases of children, among those, too, which occur but once in a lifetime."

"Yet who ever vowed eternal love that did not wish above all else that he might keep the blessed vow? Who ever broke it, that did not either weep or rave over the weakness of heart, or the perversity of fate that compelled him to it? Nina's soul is stronger than fate, sister, I will not say the same of mine."

As we parted company, the conversation dropped into a couple of tête à tête murmurs, both of which I was skilful enough to overhear.

"And so the divine Gigia would not die for any man?" whispered Flavio, with an affected emphasis.

"For her husband, yes" answered Gigia, in like manner.

"Then you will acquire the distinction of being the first inconsolable widow on record."

"My ambition does not extend to widowhood," rejoined Gigia—I heard no more from her, for from the other side these words reached me, in the hearty and truthful utterance of her sister:

"Pepino! I cannot wish that my first love had been my last, but would God my last love had been my first!"

With these words she entered the house—as I followed her, I turned and saw the white robe of Gigia as it became lost in the shadow of the plane trees.

"And now for the manuscript," said Briseida, as she trimmed the picturesque brazen lamp on the study table, and arranged for me the cushions of her easy chair. "You must not read too rapidly, as I am not yet strong either in the German tongue, or in German mysticism."

The costly case enclosing the sacred relic was now produced—it was of precious wood, richly carved, and inlaid with gold and with precious stones. On the first leaf of the parchment within were written these words:

Ashes of an angel's heart.

The kindness of Berto enables me to subjoin an entire copy of what I then read.

Fragment 3

ness of heart or the perversity of fate that compelled him to break it? Nina's soul is stronger than fate, sister, I would I could say the same of mine!'

The conversation à quatre now dropped into a couple of tête à tête murmurs, both of which I was skilful enough to hear.

"And so," said Flavio, with a smile which betrayed very little of any thing within him save his teeth, "and so, the divine Gigia is incapable of dying for any man?"

"Yes, for any flirt of a lover. I might die for a husband," said Gigia, very emphatically.

"Oh yes, we all know that widows are inconsolable" was Flavio's reply. The vision of Eva

"Pepino" said Briseida in the other corner: "I cannot now wish that my first love had been my last, but would God that my last love had been my first!"

The eyes that looked into Pepino's eyes had so earnest and mournful a meaning that they awoke in my heart the ghost of a buried remembrance. Oh God! who was it that had looked even, even so upon me? I pressed my hands upon my forehead, and ill to faintness, sought the open air.

Thank God, I was not yet turned to stone! Thank God, I could still remember, and weep at the remembrance.

Fragment 4

Some one at length spoke—it was Pepino.

The Hermaphrodite

"What is it? what shall we call it?" sd he.

"It is a dream," murmured Bda, but a dream of heavenly truth."

"It is a mystery," I rejoined, "but one of those which light and not darkness, veils from us."

As I spoke, a long, vivid flame darted upwards from the dying lamp.

"See!" I cried, "it is like the parting prayer (aspiration) of a pure soul."

The next moment, we were left in darkness, and ere we could speak or exclaim a note of wondrous melody filled the air, and held us all entranced with its magic power. It was followed by a wild but solemn strain of melody, which seemed at once prayer, hymn and dirge.

"It is the spirit of Eva!" cried Pepino, half startled by the unexpected sound.

"It is Nina," said Briseida. "I have not heard her voice thus in years."

So saying, she hurriedly groped her way to the door and threw it open. Light streamed in upon us from the opposite side of the corridor. It came from an apartment usually unoccupied, and thither, with anxious haste, Briseida made her way. As we followed her in the same direction, we could distinguish the words and cadence of the song. It was the swan-song of Eva.

> Release thou, release thou
> The prisoner of hope.

We entered the room. Nina was seated at her harp, robed in white, and crowned with flowers. Her attendants stood at a distance, gazing upon her mutely, as if transfixed with astonishment at her strange demeanour. Her brilliant eyes, her burning cheeks, and the unnatural fervour of her voice betokened a state of the greatest excitement. The salon, her ancient music room, was arranged as if for the reception of guests—the coverings were withdrawn from the brocaded chairs, and the branches were filled with wax lights. Nina did not at first seem aware of our presence, when her strain was at an end, however, she arose, came towards us and welcomed us with a smile of childish delight.

"What is the meaning of all this, my poor Nina," cried Bda, with visible discomposure.

"It is my fête," answered Nina, with a childish waywardness of expression. "Because it has not been kept in many years, shall it never more be celebrated? because none of you have brought me any flowers, shall I have no roses and jasmines? It was too ungracious in you all to neglect poor Nina thus, but Nina forgives you, for she is happiest of all, tonight."

"And why are you so happy, Nina?"

"Because I am a bride, and the bridegroom is coming tonight. I know it, I am assured of it."

"You know it, Nina? have you then tidings of Gaetano?"

"All is right, never fear," said she with a smile, pressing her hands upon her bosom. "I know it, I feel it, we shall meet tonight.

See!" she said, pointing to a small table which stood in an alcove, covered with fruits and wines. "See, I have arranged a supper also, supper for him, for me, for all of you—but it shall not be tasted until he come. Shall I sing for you meanwhile?"

She seated herself again at the harp,

The Hermaphrodite

In the Legacies of Nineteenth-Century American Women Writers series

The Hermaphrodite
By Julia Ward Howe
Edited and with an introduction by Gary Williams

In the "Stranger People's" Country
By Mary Noilles Murfree
Edited and with an introduction by Marjorie Pryse

Two Men
By Elizabeth Stoddard
Edited and with an introduction by Jennifer Putzi

To order or obtain more information on these or other University of Nebraska Press titles, visit www.nebraskapress.unl.edu

CPSIA information can be obtained
at www.ICGtesting.com
Printed in the USA
LVHW03s0008220818
587727LV00002B/308/P